D0195097

HALF INTEREST
IN A SILVER DOLLAR

The Saga of Charles E. Conrad

James E. Murphy

MOUNTAIN PRESS PUBLISHING COMPANY
Missoula, 1983

Copyright © 1983
James E. Murphy

Library of Congress Cataloging in Publication Data
Murphy, James E. (James Emmett), 1910-
    Half interest in a silver dollar.

    Bibliography: p.
    Includes index.
    1. Conrad, Charles E.   2. Merchants—montana—Fort
Benton—Biography.   3. Fort Benton (Mont.)—History.
I. Title.
HF3023.C64M87   1983   381'.092'4 [B]   83-17256
ISBN0-87842-166-1

TABLE OF CONTENTS

1	Introduction to the Conrads	1
2	The Conrads of Virginia	5
3	Spanning the Continent by Steamboat	9
4	Building and Naming Fort Benton	13
5	The Conrads Meet I. G. Baker	20
6	Expansion of the Trade Area	24
7	Gold Trade at Fort Benton	29
8	Saving the Mounties	33
9	A Test of Courage	39
10	White Men, Indian Women	43
11	Treaty No. 7	45
12	Fortune Making on the Missouri	49
13	Red Cloud, Queen of the River	57
14	Fort Benton's First Newspaper	64
15	The Early Cattle Business	69
16	The Stanfords	73
17	Frontier Styles and Fashions	80
18	Fort Benton in 1881	86
19	Courtship and Marriage	92
20	Frontier Parlors	97
21	The Profits and Perils of Freighting	100
22	The Indian Trade	104
23	Approaching the Peak	107
24	Fort Benton's Busiest Year	111
25	1883, The Beginning of the End	115
26	Great Falls Rises as Fort Benton Falls	118
27	The Manitoba Comes to Fort Benton	121
28	The Years of Transition	125
29	An Empire Dismantled	128
30	Search for a New Frontier	134
31	Not Even a Dog Fight Relieved the Monotony	137
32	Farewell Fort Benton	139

33	The Flathead Valley		141
34	A Town Is Born		146
35	The New Home		152
36	Solving the Servant Problem		160
37	The Stables		163
38	Christmas at the Conrad Mansion		170
39	The Christmas Pudding		174
40	Life at the Conrad Mansion		179
41	The Grandmothers		184
42	The Conrad Buffalo Herd		194
43	Charles E. Conrad — Empire Builder		201
	I.	The New Beginning	201
	II.	The Continuing Quest	208
	III.	Detour Into Politics	215
	IV.	The Quest Ends	222
44	Lettie Conrad's Memorial to Her Husband		229
45	Christmas for Captain Winter's Children		233
46	Lettie Conrad		239
47	Halloween at the Conrad Mansion		246
48	Charles Edward Conrad, Jr.		253
49	Charles Davenport Conrad		262
	I.	The Early Years	262
	II.	Marriage and Later Life	270
50	Catherine Conrad		280
51	The Family Fortune		288
52	The Death of Lettie Conrad		292
53	The End of the Family Fortune		295
54	Alicia Conrad Campbell		300
	I.	Early Life and First Marriage	300
	II.	Dream Accomplished	310

ACKNOWLEDGEMENTS

Many people helped on this book; some worked almost as much as the author. This will acknowledge my appreciation and thanks to at least some of them.

I spent many hours with Alicia Conrad and we became fast friends. Much of the book is based upon what Alicia told me in these conversations. Some of the things stretched my imagination, but those capable of verification proved to be true. The story of what happened to the poppy blossoms when her mother died seems hard to believe. But, to Alicia, it was true and I cannot entire disbelieve it. I loved Alicia and believed her. I hope the reader will also.

Sylvia and Mary Pat, my wife and daughter, helped in many ways. They tried to teach me syntax and similar things but with little success.

Joel Overholser, Editor Emeritus of the Fort Benton River Press, always willing to draw on his extensive files and fact-filled mind, came up with information I could not find elsewhere.

Jack Lepley, Fort Benton historian, opened his picture files and provided hard-to-find photos.

Dale Johnson, archivist at the University of Montana, led me to dusty cartons and helped me to paw through them in search of an elusive document or fact, which we usually found.

The staff at the Flathead County Library, particularly Rita Krause and Michael Ober, were always willing to help. So was Dave Walter and the staff at the Montana Historical Library.

John Van, County Clerk and Recorder of Flathead County, helped me search out files which produced valuable information.

I am very grateful to Dave Walter for editing my manuscript. He is a fine editor and can make verbs do far more things than I can.

And to Mary Ann Mular, who typed many things many times, and yet retained her composure, good humor and sanity.

All of the letters from Charles E. Conrad to his wife, Lettie, are used with the permission and courtesy of the Montana Historical Society; the correspondence between the Conrad brothers, William G. and Charles E. and from Charles E. Conrad, Jr. to Lettie Conrad are by the courtesy and permission of the University of Montana as was the information regarding the construction and cost of the Conrad Mansion.

Charles E. Conrad, circa 1892 Courtesy Conrad Mansion Directors

CHAPTER 1
Introduction to the Conrads

No peas in a pod were the Conrad brothers, William G. and Charles E. They shared interests in frontier merchandising, the fur trade, transportation, mining, banking, and cattle, each of which they pursued relentlessly in search of profits. During the period from 1868 to 1891, the Conrads furnished all of the needs and desires of any level of government, of any Indian tribe or reservation, of any miner, or any settler in Montana Territory and Western Canada. They purchased these items wherever they could be found throughout the world, then delivered them to anyone at any place in that vast territory, whether by boat, ox team, horseback, or afoot — always at a substantial profit.

Apart from making money, the brothers shared almost no interests. After coming to Fort Benton, Montana Territory, in 1868, each found his niche in their money-making pursuits. Charles was tall and athletic. He loved the out-of-doors and seemed completely without fear. He took charge of building and operating the remote fur-trading posts, supplying them, and dealing and trading with the Indians. In these activities Charles E. Conrad had no peer. William tended toward corpulence, was far more comfortable at a desk than in a saddle, and left all exploits requiring bravery and hardship to Charles. William's field was the organization of the various enterprises and the acquisition and shipment of merchandise and supplies. In these activities there was no more able man on the frontier than William G. Conrad.

Charles shunned public office, avoided publicity, and had no desire to be in the eyes of the public. William loved office-holding — the higher, the better. He thrived on publicity and sought to be in the forefront of all his activities. He was the first mayor of Fort Benton and a county commissioner of Choteau County. He served with distinction in any public office he held, and ambition prodded him to ever higher levels.

William G. Conrad's political career reached its height at the Democratic National Convention of 1908. This apex and the road leading to it

1

are described in an article headlined "Hon. Wm. G. Conrad of Montana Rose to Fame," which appeared in the Spokane *Spokesman Review* of October 18, 1908. The writer, M. G. Scheitlin, described Conrad's less than meteoric rise in these words:

> Precisely at 10 minutes to 4 o'clock on the afternoon of Friday, July 10, J. Hoge Tyler of Virginia arose in the democratic national convention and almost placed in nomination for the vice-presidency of the United States William G. Conrad of Montana.
>
> Mr. Tyler had taken 10 minutes, all the rules allowed, eloquently to proclaim the peculiar and compelling qualifications of his candidate, as yet unnamed. Then, pausing, solemnly, he said:
>
> "When I began to speak I expected to place in nomination for the high office of vice president William G. Conrad to whom all the things I have said apply. However, on behalf of the grand old state of Virginia, I now second the nomination of John W. Kern of Indiana."
>
> Precisely at 10 minutes to 4 o'clock on the afternoon of Friday, July 10, therefore, by virtue of having almost been placed in nomination before a thousand sleeping delegates, William G. Conrad became a national character. His hairbreadth escape from being a near nominee left him among the also-mentioned and free to pursue his political ambitions untrammeled by defeat.
>
> Mr. Conrad comes from the West. He is the firmest believer on record in the beauties of the doctrine that the way to get a thing is to ask for it. He began by asking for the presidency or the vice presidency — small things, but good enough for the man from Montana. So far as political history in the United States goes, Mr. Conrad is the first man who ever made such a request. The men who know they cannot get either of these positions never ask for them, the men who believe they can, pretend not to want them. Nobody speaks right up like Mr. Conrad and asks for them. Thereby has Mr. Conrad made himself famous.

Scheitlin's article has a tendency to belittle William G. Conrad as a national figure, but he was aware of Conrad's stature in the State of Montana. He wrote:

> He went to the State Senate whenever he wanted to but it got irksome. When his party wanted him to run for governor, a position he probably could have obtained, he declined. For years, however, the affairs of the state were administered from Mr. Conrad's magnificent private offices over one of his banks, because the quarters provided by Montana for its governors at that time were a disgrace to the state. The name of Conrad is written all over the business of the state. There are Conrad banks, Conrad mines, Conrad cattle ranches, Conrad town sites, and Conrad irrigating plants and land redemption projects. At Great Falls, Mont. he has a splendid residence, while in Helena he has the most magnificent residence in the State. These and his Virginia home he keeps open at all times and seasons, maintaining a corps of servants in each. He can appear unexpectedly at any of his three homes and find breakfast ready just as if he had been living in that particular home for a year.

W. G. Conrad
Courtesy University of
Montana Library

The man who would be president and doesn't care who knows it is 60 years old. He is taller than the average and heavier but not as stout as Mr. Taft or Mr. Bryan, but of imposing presidential or vice presidential dimensions. His hair was black once, but now is gray, and his moustache, which completely covers his mouth, is almost as gray as his hair. The distinctive feature of his face is the eye and eyebrow. The former is small, black and set deep; the latter is shaggy, bristling and black. He is a Mason, an Elk and an Eagle; something of a 'jiner' in a small way, besides being a vestreyman in the Episcopal church.

And now, well, Mr. Conrad has almost been placed in nomination for the vice presidency.

Perhaps the man who starts to nominate him four years from now will not change his mind before he finishes his speech.

The 1908 Democratic National Convention took place 40 years after the Conrad brothers stepped off a Missouri River steamer at Fort Benton

3

to seek their fortunes in a frontier environment entirely new to them. Scheitlin had his tongue firmly implanted in his cheek as he wrote, but even then the ability and resourcefulness of William G. Conrad shines through. Charles was probably the more able and stable of the brothers. Their very considerable fortunes had already been acquired by the time Charles died in 1902. Before this, William's interest in politics was more in the nature of a hobby and satisfied his desire to be in the public eye. The try for the vice-presidency indicates a desire for a measure of immortality that probably would not have been attempted had Charles then been living.

The 40 years from 1868 to 1908 were interesting and important years, especially in the development of the West. In this development no one played more important roles than William G. and Charles E. Conrad.

CHAPTER 2
The Conrads of Virginia

The life of Charles E. Conrad and the history of Fort Benton, Montana Territory, are so intertwined that the story of one cannot be told independently of the other. At the time Conrad came to Fort Benton, the tiny settlement was in its infancy, and there was little indication that it would become the supply point for the entire Territory of Montana and Western Canada. Nor was there any evidence that Conrad and his brother, William G., would become the largest merchants and would build the most extensive system for the transportation of goods and supplies in all of the West.

In the fall of 1868, the Conrad brothers walked down the gangplank of the river steamer that had brought them from St. Louis, Missouri, to Fort Benton, Montana Territory. Neither brother mentioned the name of the boat. The Centennial edition of the Fort Benton *River Press* lists the *Success* and *Andrew Ackley* as having landed in August of 1869 and no arrivals thereafter. It was probably on one of these boats that the brothers made their journey up the Missouri River. Charles had turned 18 on May 20 of that year, and his brother was just two years older. No party or gathering of friends greeted them at their arrival, but both sensed the opportunity offered by the vast land which was to be their new home.

Lured west by stories of fortunes being made by gold seekers and those who supplied them, the brothers had left their war-ravaged plantation home in Virginia and the genteel life they had known for the rigors of the Western frontier.

Though they were young, the Conrad brothers had closed the first chapter of their lives. The second chapter, commencing with their landing at Fort Benton, the head of navigation on the Missouri River, would be so different that they could not possibly conceive of the manner in which this chapter would unfold.

Charles was the third eldest of 13 children born to James W. Conrad and Maria Ashby Conrad. Both the Conrads and Ashbys had been distinguished families in Virginia almost since its first settlement. All 13 of the children were born at Wapping Plantation near Front Royal in the Shenandoah Valley. The plantation had been developed by Joseph Conrad, the father of James, and consisted of rolling acres of fertile land crowned by a two-story, porticoed, white mansion, typical of the Southern architecture of that day.

Life at the plantation was pleasant and gracious. Charles became steeped in the easy lifestyle and warm hospitality typical of the pre-war South. He grew up in the best horse-and-hound tradition and was well on his way to becoming a Southern gentleman when the Civil War erupted and destroyed the way of life for which he had been groomed.

James W. Conrad was a colonel in the Virginia State Militia, which had been called into service soon after the men of the South realized that the hated Yankees could not be dispatched with the ease that had first been anticipated. The general belief in the South was that a rebel yell and a couple of shots from a squirrel gun would send the Yanks scurrying back to the rocky hills of New England and the mire of the Eastern cities.

Despite their youth, Charles and William rode off to war with their father, leaving the care of the plantation to Maria Conrad and the slaves. They expected a quick end to the war and an early return to the peaceful life they had always known.

Youth did not deter Charles from active and vigorous participation in the Civil War. He soon became noted for his cool-headed bravery in battle. For two years he was a member of Mosby's Partisan Raiders, an intrepid group that ranged over all of the battle fronts, wreaking extensive damage on Northern supply depots, troop installations, and communications. The daring activities of this group, especially in supposedly safe areas behind the enemy's lines, made it feared and detested by the Union forces. The most famous exploit of the group was the penetration of federal lines to seize General Sloughton from the protection of his troops at Fairfax Courthouse and carry him ignominiously back to the headquarters of General Robert E. Lee for interrogation. Although never gaining officer status, probably due to his youth, Conrad was said to be one of the bravest men in Mosby's command and could be depended upon to devise strategy or change it in the midst of battle.

The father and both sons escaped serious injury and, at the end of the war, returned to Wapping. They had seen the devastation war had wrought to the plantations in their fields of battle but hoped that Wapping had come through the war unscathed. James Conrad was confident that the courage of his diminutive wife was equal to any situation that might have arisen.

Maria Conrad was barely five feet tall but made up in energy what she lacked in size. The first years of her marriage were happy ones. Slavery was still the economic backbone of the South. Even the bearing of 13 children did not interrupt the gentle flow of plantation life. No matter how many children came, there were always plenty of mammies to care for them. The gentle upbringing and life of Maria created a veneer that hid a savage instinct for survival. During the long war, Maria Conrad held together not only her own large family, but also the black children who were deserted by their parents. These former slaves roamed the

Fort Benton in 1868 Courtesy John G. Lepley

South searching for freedom, wealth, and domination over their former masters that had been promised them by the men of the Northern armies.

It was she who kept the plantation together as war flowed through the South. General William Tecumseh Sherman was among the first to recognize that to win a war the noncombatant enemy must also be defeated and demoralized. His march to the sea not only accomplished this aim but also destroyed the economic base of the Old South.

The hopes of the returning father and sons were dashed when the plantation came into view. The destructive war and enforced neglect had ruined the beautiful buildings and productive land. Gone were the slaves who had tilled the large plantation and cared for the lovely mansion. Four unproductive years, together with the depredations of Union soldiers and foraging slaves, had wiped out the wealth of the Conrads. The policies of Reconstruction, forced upon the South by a vengeful Congress, gave little hope that the plantation would provide even a livelihood for the large Conrad family, much less the luxury they had known before the war.

The family was desperate. Young Charles started to work as a clerk in a general store at Sterling Valley, Cayuga County, Virginia. The experience gained from this job would prove of more value to him later than the immediate, meager salary did to the family. It soon became evident that as Southerners, trading and bartering among themselves, they could never make enough to keep the family together. A council of the family determined that Charles and William should strike out on their own to find some place that offered greater opportunity.

Their first destination was New York and the home of their aunt, Mary Hunter. This trip they made on foot, the only transportation they could afford. The Hunters were engaged in the manufacture of arms and china, and Mary Hunter found employment for both boys. They worked in New York, sending back to the family all of the money they earned above their bare living expenses.

The boys soon realized that the care of the family would be their responsibility. They knew that working in a family business at jobs provided by a sympathetic uncle would not be enough. In New York they heard stories of the opening of the West and of the fortunes being made by those engaged in the search for gold and by those who supplied the gold seekers. They had seen an older part of the nation destroyed by war, and the stories of the West intensified their longing to take part in the opening and development of this new land. After about a year in New York, Conrad wrote to the family of their decision to go West, a decision that required that they save a portion of the money that they had been sending to the family.

Eagerness caused them to start for the West when they had accumulated barely enough money for the long trip from New York to Fort Benton, Montana Territory, most of which would be accomplished by river steamboat. Both boys were intelligent, resourceful, honest, ambitious, and accustomed to danger. After they had paid for their passage, these qualities and robust health were about all they had to take with them.

CHAPTER 3
Spanning the Continent by Steamboat

In the summer of 1868 the two brothers boarded a steamboat at St. Louis that would take them 3,175 miles up the Missouri River to Fort Benton, Montana Territory, the head of river transportation to the West. The boat carried cargo for the I. G. Baker Company, a name that soon became familiar to them. The trip up the Missouri was exciting and awe-inspiring. Bands of Indians, herds of buffalo and other wild game, and a land mass even more immense than the stories had prepared them for combined to keep them enthralled.

W. G. Conrad later told of the experience in an article which appeared in the December 16, 1906, issue of the *Great Falls Tribune*. He wrote that:

> I came to Fort Benton in the fall of 1868, travelling from St. Louis to Fort Benton, a distance of 3175 miles by steamboat. The voyage took us just 66 days and was in itself a great experience. A good part of the distance, the Missouri River flowed through a wild and unsettled country without a sign of civilization for days at a time, and inhabited by roving bands of Indians.

Conrad's sketchy account of that journey does not impart the sense of the long trip that is given by Lou Stocking Stewart, daughter of an early Fort Benton resident. Her remembrance of the trip was reprinted in *Our Fort Benton*, a delightful collection of stories of early-day Fort Benton published by Nora E. Harber, a long and respected resident of that city. Of her trip, Stewart wrote:

> May 27, 1880 is a date to be especially remembered by a number of Montana pioneers, myself among them, for it marked the arrival of the steamer *Red Cloud* at the Fort Benton levee after a continuous voyage of 77 days coming up the river from St. Louis. And I, personally, shall remember the day for still another reason, because this was my last trip on one of the early-day steamboats.
>
> The *Red Cloud*, of the I. G. Baker line, was one of the largest boats on the river and one of the most palatial. A stern-wheeler, it measured 225 feet in length with a 34-foot beam. Upon this trip the boat was very heavily loaded with freight and carried some 200 passengers, the most of them bound for the port of Fort Benton. The long journey was partly due to this excess weight as the boat drew over four and one-half feet of water and was consequently hard to manage in the narrows and when negotiating rapids. Without its load aboard, the boat had a draught of just over twenty inches.

Steamboat *Red Cloud*, circa 1877
Courtesy John G. Lepley

As for the cargo, I might compare this trip of the *Red Cloud* to that of Noah's ark. We had aboard almost everything one could enumerate in the way of livestock — cattle, horses, mules, pigs, chickens, ducks and turkeys. Over my stateroom was chained a big Newfoundland dog that kept me awake nights by dragging his chain about. Then there was the usual tonnage of foodstuff, mainly salt pork, bacon and flour which was to be distributed at the different towns along the river.

The passengers were a fine class of people, many of them on their first trip up the river and determined to make a success of western life. They were not adventurers, but homeseekers who later located throughout northern Montana. The more affluent occupied the upper deck cabins, while those who had yet to make a stake had more modest quarters in the lower or main deck. The two groups, while friendly, kept mostly to their own parts of the boat and each provided its own social diversions.

Captain James McGarry was in charge of the *Red Cloud* and he and his officers were fine to everyone. We had three good meals each day, well cooked. The menu included bacon, beans, salt pork and all kinds of dried fruits, the latter a great luxury. Several times we had deer, antelope and buffalo meat, for a change. The meals and service were just as regular as on an ocean liner.

As I have said, we travelled slowly on account of being so heavily loaded, then there were many stops to take on wood for the boilers. Almost every ten or fifteen miles along the upper river there were wood yards where cord wood was ricked up awaiting the boats. The steamers would put in to shore and the wood would be carried aboard and corded up on the lower deck. In those days wood cutting was a paying business. The men would cut the wood and have it dried and ready for the spring time, charging four or five dollars a cord. There was seldom a shortage, as timber of all kinds was plentiful along the Missouri river bottoms.

During the days when the weather was nice it was interesting to be out on the deck for there was always something fascinating about watching the changing shore line, and who could ever forget the beauty of the moonlight on the river! It was exciting to get the "feel" of the boat as it fought its way ahead in swift water with the paddle wheel churning a foamy ribbon in our wake, and to watch for the first glimpse of the unknown country around the bend just ahead. Then I liked to watch the deck hands as they sparred over a bar and the mate, stationed at the bow, continually sounding the channel for depth. In the lower reaches of the river we had little trouble, for the water was very high that year and had overflowed the lowlands. At St. Joe and Omaha it was nearly twenty miles wide.

Bottoms along the Missouri abounded with small game which we could often see plainly from the boat. We were many times in shooting distance of buffalo which we usually sighted on the higher hills. However, one day a band of some 200 started to cross the river in front of the steamboat and we were compelled to lay up until they had passed across. The men tried to kill one, but the fur and hide were too thick for the shot to take effect. This was quite a novelty for the tenderfoot.

After leaving Sioux City, we saw Indians every day until we arrived at Fort Benton. They were trading skins, buffalo robes and other pelts at the different trading posts, Fort Randall, Fort Peck and Fort Berthold. When the boat landed, or tied up for the night, they would come aboard and take in the sights, and before leaving they would smoke their pipe of peace and then go. The old-time river captains had very little trouble with the Indians as they were in the habit of being rather stern in their dealings and the braves knew that the privilege of coming aboard depended upon their good behavior. Their clothes were made of buckskin and they always wore gaudy blankets, with little colored beads, and shells in their hair. Faces were highly painted.

The finest lot of Indians we encountered was at Standing Rock, members of the Sioux tribe. I could not help but contrast this peaceable meeting with our stop at Standing Rock in June, 1876, when news of the Custer tragedy was brought in and twenty-four women, waiting there for news, learned that their husbands had been killed in the battle of the Little Big Horn.

One of the sights I saw at Fort Berthold on this trip was an Indian cemetery. They buried their dead up on poles, wrapped each brave in robes, with what he possessed such as guns, bows and arrows.

Two or three hundred miles before coming to Fort Benton the steamboats came through a rough country. The river was full of rapids and sandbars. The banks were high. Here we encountered many more delays due to the narrow channel and shallows. However, there were some striking rock formations along this part of the route. At Cannon Ball the rocks were shaped like a ball. At another point was a large rock, almost the size of a steamboat, which looked as though it had been carved out by some person, but in reality was nature's own work.

We rounded the butte and made fast at the Fort Benton levee on May 27th. Freight was unloaded, a new cargo put aboard and a few days later the Red Cloud was again headed down stream. She was wrecked two years later on Wight Point, above Fort Peck, in what has ever since been known as Red Cloud Bend.

I shall never forget that eleven weeks on the Missouri with its pleasant associations. There was dancing in the main cabin at night, with violins and guitars for the music (there was no piano aboard), square dances for the most part with the waltz another favorite. Then card games such as Pedro which was so popular at that time. I recall as if it were yesterday, the crew standing on the lower deck and singing as we came into port, old southern favorites such as "Suwanee River." There was the customary salute fired from the cannon on the levee and the Red Cloud's whistle in reply. And all along the shore the people of the town came to bid the stranger welcome.

I feel the same way about it today as I did when I stepped ashore at Fort Benton fifty-seven years ago. My trip back from the states on the Red Cloud was the most pleasant of any journey I have ever made on a Missouri river steamboat.

In the same book, May Flanagan, who as a girl lived at the old garrison fort at Fort Benton and whose aunt was married to entrepreneur T. C. Power, gives her recollection of the thrill felt by the Fort Benton people at the arrival of a steamboat:

The arrival and unloading of steamboats became an absorbing interest. Captain McGarry of the Block P line always invited me to breakfast when his boat arrived. We always had corn grits for breakfast and I thought I was enjoying a great delicacy. We imagined that we could distinguish the whistles of the different boats. The Bachelor had a plaintive, wailing whistle, which made us sad as the boat gave a last toot on disappearing around the bend of the river, and when the old Bachelor sank, we grieved that we would never hear its weird old whistle again. A steamboat coming around the bend and swinging up the channel was a beautiful sight, and if it came in the dusk of a summer evening with the glow of the furnaces showing thru open doors, the headlight throwing its broad beam ahead, and the negro crew singing a river chant, it gave a thrill that not all the years can make one forget.

Summer boats often meant new furniture, new striped stockings or perhaps a new-style hat, oranges and maybe grapes. So convinced were we that apples were dried or came in cans that when we discovered fresh apples we designated them as "skin apples," and corn on the cob was "stick corn." It was fascinating to watch the unloading of a boat and wonder what would come off next; there were stoves, barrels of flour, barrels of whiskey, buggies, chickens and hair-footed Clyde horses. Then the streets would be filled with ox and mule freight trains as the goods from warehouses was loaded onto the prairie schooner and started on the long haul to Helena, Deer Lodge or Canada.

CHAPTER 4
Building and Naming Fort Benton

Fort Benton was named in 1850, the year Charles E. Conrad was born. Prior to that year it had been called Fort Lewis, to honor Captain Meriwether Lewis of the Lewis and Clark Expedition. On his return trip in 1806, Lewis killed a Blackfeet warrior in the area, which created a bitter hatred among the Blackfeet for all white men. It is said that in the early 1800s more scalps than furs were collected in the Blackfeet country. In 1843 the American Fur Company sent Alexander Culbertson to make peace with the Blackfeet.

Culbertson was liked and respected by the Indians. He established a peace that lasted about 30 years. When more and more whites began to come into the area, the Blackfeet became alarmed and started to make sporadic attacks on the whites. In the June 9, 1976 issue of the Fort Benton River Press, the editor Joel Overholser said that in April, 1865, some Blood Indians "stole around 40 horses at Fort Benton which was something akin to a basketball championship in Indian minds."

To give some protection to the settlers, the U.S. Army established forts and sent detachments of soldiers to guard wagon trains and settlements. Many of the soldiers were Southern prisoners-of-war who were given the choice of staying in Union prison camps or serving with the U.S. Army in the West. Conditions in the camps were so miserable that by comparison fighting Indians seemed a most desirable life. In the West these Southern soldiers were called "Galvanized Yanks" because they acquired enough of a galvanization or veneer of Yankeeism to distinguish them from the uncaptured Southern soldiers who came West following the Civil War.

Indian attacks and skirmishes continued until 1869, when 56 whites were killed and 1,600 horses stolen. Later in that year came the devastating smallpox epidemic. So many of the Blackfeet died from this disease that they never again posed a major threat to the settlement of their lands by the ever-encroaching whites.

In 1846 Culbertson established a trading post upriver and on the opposite side of the Missouri from the current site of Fort Benton. Because Culbertson was held in such esteem by the Indians, the little post endured despite its location in the territory occupied by the fearsome Blackfeet, Piegan, and Blood tribes that roamed from the Yellowstone River to the Rocky Mountains.

13

Front street of Fort Benton in 1878 — Note steamboat on the right. Courtesy John G. Lepley

Located on the south side of the river, it was difficult for the Indians to cross when the river was jammed with floating ice in the late fall and spring. At the request of the tribes, Culbertson in 1847 dismantled the 150-foot-square log fort and floated it down the river. It was reassembled a few miles downstream and on the opposite side of the Missouri River, where it continued as a trading post in the rich fur trading area that surrounded it.

On Christmas night in 1850, at a ceremony more alcoholic than religious, the tiny settlement was renamed Fort Benton to honor Senator Thomas Hart Benton of Missouri. This was the christening of the embryo town which would become the head of Missouri River navigation. The event was described in the January 1, 1883 issue of the *Fort Benton Record*:

> There was one occasion, however, in the history of the Old Fort, from which the participants undoubtedly derived a fair amount of enjoyment, the following account of which is from the pen of the late Lieut. James H. Bradley, 7th Infantry, and appeared in the *Record* of 1875, but is well worth reproduction at this time.
>
> In the year of our Lord 1850, a joyous party assembled on Christmas evening, in a recently constructed adobe building at the trading post of the American Fur Company, on the upper Missouri River, known as Fort Lewis. In the gathering there was a two-fold object: to celebrate the advent of Christmas by suitable rejoicings, and to dedicate to its ultimate uses the first adobe building erected within the present limits of the Territory of Montana. Major Culbertson — then in the prime of life — was there as chief of the establishment, and gathered around him were sixty or seventy white

subordinates, who constituted the garrison of the fort, with their wives and children, and the reader needs only to be told that the great majority of the former were Canadian and Louisiana French, of the class called voyageurs, to know that merriment and jollity reigned supreme. Several violins were in active operation, and to the flow of sweet sounds, scores of nimble feet tripped merrily, and joyous voices mingled in the bursts of jovial song.

At last, in the midst of this rousing carnival, the tall form of Major Culbertson was seen to rise and signal silence. When the uproar had subsided sufficiently to permit his voice to be heard, he addressed the assembly in a little speech in which he recounted the noble qualities of one of America's distinguished sons; dwelt particularly upon his services a few years before in behalf of the American Fur Company, when he rescued it from a ruinous litigation that threatened its complete overthrow; and proposed that in his honor the post, then in process of construction in adobe, should from that time forward be known as Fort Benton. With loud cheers, his audience signified their approbation, the violins struck up a lively air, the dancing was renewed with increased vigor, and, passing from lip to lip of the hilarious assembly, the name of Fort Benton went forth to the world, and is now recorded in millions of maps from one end of civilization to the other.

The assembled frontiersmen thought the Senator deserved the honor in recognition of his interest in and efforts toward the moving of the frontier ever westward. The Senator had indeed rendered meritorious services to the American Fur Company, of which Culbertson was part owner. The Company sought to dominate the fur trade and was ruthless in its trade practices. Liquor was a potent trade item with the tribes. Its sale to the Indians had been prohibited because of the devastating effect it had upon them. Drink-crazed Indians would trade all of their furs, their arms, their clothes, and even their squaws to get more liquor. The federal government was strict in enforcing the ban on liquor, and penalties for violation were stiff. The fur trade brought such enormous profits, and the welfare of the Indians was of so little concern to the traders, that liquor remained an important trade item despite the ban. The American Fur Company ignored the law to get the furs. Its manager at Fort Union, Kenneth McKenzie, smuggled in a still that made a poor quality of whiskey, but even the worst liquor brought in a large quantity of furs. His own liquor loosened McKenzie's tongue and he bragged of his success to a person who reported him to the government. Retribution was swift and the fur company was about to lose its license to engage in the fur trade which was making it rich.

The Company called for the help of Thomas Hart Benton, United States Senator from Missouri. The influence of the Senator was sufficient to overcome the most conscientious efforts of the government agents to enforce the law. Senator Benton, in Culbertson's words, quoted in the January 1, 1883 issue of the Fort Benton Record, rescued the company "from a ruinous litigation that threatened its complete overthrow." Such favors could not be ignored and might be needed again for, to the Company, liquor was an almost indispensable item in the fur trade.

There seemed to be little interest in any further honor for Captain Lewis. He had made the discovery, but his work was done. Westward expansion was the present need, and honor would go to the man best able to assist in the effort. Whatever other pay the Senator received for preserving the Company's license, his name would be honored, if bestowing it upon a brawling frontier post could be called an honor.

In 1850 the nation had no more powerful advocate for development of the West than Senator Benton. He was nicknamed "Old Bullion" for his "hard money" philosophy. Benton favored any measure that would assist the growth of the West. His hard-currency proposals were designed to end land speculation and encourage actual settlement. He believed that this result could be accomplished by reducing the price of land and that cheap land would enable the Eastern workingman to migrate to the West. Soft money and speculation had driven the price of land beyond the reach of prospective settlers and had impeded the growth that Benton believed must come to the West.

The Senator's interest in this new land was whetted by personal connections. His daughter, Jessie, was married to John C. Frémont, whose explorations in the western United States had brought him national prominence. Both Benton and Frémont hoped that continued exploration and expansion might provide the springboard that would catapult Frémont into the presidency of the United States.

Culbertson had chosen the fur trading site with care. It was a gathering place convenient to both the mountains and the prairies. Upstream, the Jefferson, Madison, and Gallatin Rivers come together at the Three Forks, to form the Missouri River. All mountain rivers accommodate themselves to the lowering of the terrain through which they flow by rapids, the roughness of which depends upon the degree of elevation change. After leaving the Three Forks, the river flows in the Rocky Mountain region until it reaches the Gates of the Mountains, below Helena. The river is peaceful until it then negotiates a final descent to the plains. Here the change in elevation is so abrupt and extreme that the river cannot adjust itself with rapids, but tumbles over a series of cascades and falls, some estimated by Meriwether Lewis to have a fall of 50 feet.

Captain Lewis, writing in his diary for June 14, 1805, noted:

.... hearing a tremendous roaring above me I continued my route across the point of a hill a few hundred yards further and was again presented by one of the most beautiful objects in nature, a cascade of about fifty feet perpendicular stretching at right angles across the river from side to side to the distance of at least quarter of a mile. ... I now thought that if a skillful painter had been asked to make a beautiful cascade that he would most probably have presented the precise image of this one; nor could I for some time determine on which of these two great cataracts to bestowe the palm, on this or that which I had discovered yesterday; at length I determined between these two great rivals for glory that this was pleasingly beautiful, while the other was sublimely grand.

The river's final descent was near the current site of Great Falls, Montana. Here lay a ten-mile stretch of cataracts and falls so powerful and treacherous that navigation over them was impossible. The roar of these descending waters could be heard for miles. Approaching this sound must have been an awesome and sobering experience to one making his way upstream, not knowing what he would encounter. Lewis and Clark displayed some timorousness as they fought their way toward the Missouri's headwaters. Less hardy men might have turned back from the fearsome noise, not proceeding until the source of the sound had been identified.

When the river had found its way through this ten-mile stretch, it appears spent and becomes staid and demure. As the Missouri approaches Fort Benton, it swings around a bend to the right and then flows in an almost straight line for about a mile. It then curves to the left and passes from sight on its less spectacular way to join the Mississippi near St. Louis.

It is along this straight stretch of the river that Fort Benton was located. Growth was slow when it supplied only the fur traders. Their needs were not great, for with a little flour, powder, and shot they could live off the land. The pelts they took could be carried on their backs or on horses if they were fortunate enough to have them, to the trading post and then downriver in boats manned by one or two men. A 1864 requisition for I. G. Baker's store in Fort Benton reveals the nature of the supplies brought in:

> Dried cherries, apples, raspberries, peaches by barrel or sack, 50 barrels hard bread, 20 kegs S & H sugar, 20 half barrels each golden and S & H syrup, 100 kegs rifle powder, 72 sacks trade balls, 200 gallons coal oil, 1 barrel candles, blankets of all description, bright calico and shirting, beads, Chinese Vermillion case, 200 pounds American Vermillion, Chinese yellow, other paints.
>
> Clothing, boots, shoes, hats, thread, cloth, oil cloth, towels for white trade, saddles, spurs, bridles, bits, collars, wagon timber, spokes, axles, couplings, hardware, tools, nails, drugs, David Pain Killer, mustard, liniment, epsom salts, seidletz powder and alum.

Fort Benton did not progress from trading post status until 1862, when John Smith found gold in Grasshopper Creek, 200 miles southwest of Fort Benton. This was the first major discovery of gold in Montana and was the signal that brought thousands of gold seekers to what would become Montana Territory. An estimated 10,000 miners arrived at Fort

Fort Benton in 1878 with steamboat at levee Courtesy John G. Lepley

Benton between 1866 and 1869, all headed for the gold fields. Other strikes were made in Alder Gulch, Last Chance Gulch, and many smaller sites. Most of the stampeding gold seekers brought only the equipment and provisions they could carry themselves or load on pack horses, for there were no roads or viable transportation routes into Montana.

The best artery for the transportation of goods and supplies from the east was the Missouri River. The first steamboat reached Fort Benton in 1860 and proved that it was feasible to use the river to transport supplies and heavy equipment manufactured in the East up the Missouri from St. Louis to Fort Benton. There was no fear that the preeminence of Fort Benton as the head of river traffic would be contested. Competition from any upstream site was effectively blocked by the thunderous cascades of water tumbling over the high rocky escarpment known as the Great Falls of the Missouri.

Joel Overholser, editor emeritus of the *River Press* in Fort Benton, searched the files of his newspaper for figures showing the tonnage of river traffic. He estimates that from 1831 to 1858 there were 530 tons brought upriver and 5,471 tons and 418,500 buffalo robes hauled down. The upriver tonnage consisted of staples, supplies, and whiskey, the whiskey having precedence over anything else. Overholser's research shows that there were shortages of flour, salt, tobacco, and even coal oil, but never whiskey. It was the magic elixir that eased the pain of tooth extractions, limb amputations, and numbing cold. It broke barriers of loneliness and blotted out images of loved ones perhaps never again to be seen. Other supplies might be left at the dock, but cargo space was always found for whiskey.

After the discovery of gold in 1862, the upriver tonnage rose spectacularly, while the downstream tonnage remained the same. Upriver tonnage in 1862 was 1,000 tons compared to 530 tons for the years 1831 to 1858. These figures increased to the peak year of 1881, when 14,000 tons came upriver to Fort Benton for unloading and distribution. From 1858 to 1890 151,629 tons were hauled upriver and 23,554 tons and 680,540 buffalo robes down.

Thomas C. Power, who was to become one of Montana's leading merchants and distinguished citizens, arrived at Fort Benton in 1867. Power said, "There were just two store buildings and a few huts and cabins." One of the stores was owned by I. G. Baker, who loaned Power a large tent to protect his merchandise until a more permanent structure could be provided. When Power arrived there was nothing but room. No real-estate agent met him and no one tried to sell him land. He, like the others before him, chose a likely spot, "squatted" on it and opened his business. As Fort Benton grew, the land along the river became crowded and valuable. First-comers started to think about titles to prove ownership. Late-comers thought of how to squeeze a favorable site out of what was left and perhaps use some of their neighbor's land as well. Problems soon arose as to who had a right to what.

The problem was solved by the development of the doctrine of "squatter's rights," which decreed that he who first squatted on the land and used and developed it could obtain title from the government. On September 28, 1877, the United States issued to Choteau County Judge John W. Tatten a U. S. patent, "in trust for the several use and benefit of the occupants of the Townsite of Fort Benton." Thereafter Judge Tatten started to grant deeds to the occupants of the lots on which they had squatted. For the first time they became secure in the ownership of their land. No right was superior to a squatter's right. It could be confirmed by a deed from the Probate Court upon proof of the squatting and payment of a fee of $10.

CHAPTER 5
The Conrads Meet I. G. Baker

The Fort Benton that the Conrad brothers saw as they came from the boat landing on that fall morning of 1868 had plenty of bustle and activity. Cargo was being unloaded from the river steamers and piled on the docks. From the docks it was loaded in wagons for delivery to then-settled parts of the Northwest, as far away as Walla Walla, in Washington Territory, served by the Mullan Road.

When the upriver cargo was unloaded from the boats, the loading process started. Upstream came the supplies for the men who were mining gold, trapping beaver and other fur-bearing animals, and shooting the buffalo. Downstream went the hides and peltries, the gold, silver, and copper ore for smelting and refining, some to as far as Wales in Great Britain. The boats did not dally at the terminals. Winter and the vagaries of the river made the freight-hauling season short, and boats kept moving while they could. Rest came with fall and winter, when low water and ice stopped all traffic. By then the boats had returned to St. Louis, where they were repaired and loaded to be ready to start upstream at the first sign of spring.

The Conrad boys found a wagon train going to Helena and decided one of them should accompany the train to see if Helena offered greater opportunities than Fort Benton. They had one silver dollar between them and decided to let it determine who would go. Heads would go to Helena, tails would stay in Fort Benton. William flipped the dollar and called heads. The coin landed on the dock heads up, so William headed for Helena with the wagon train, taking with him the silver dollar. Charles stayed in Fort Benton for a more leisurely examination of its opportunities.

Charles wandered around the town. The activities centered around the stores and the docks. He was surprised at the wide range of goods offered. There were oranges and other fruits that had come in by boat. There were cabbages — which was not surprising, for cabbage is a good keeper. Eggs, at least advertised as fresh, were plentiful. Dried fruit, flour, salt, beans, and cured meat were the staples. Fresh meat was not shipped, since it would spoil on the long boat voyage and also because fresh meat roamed the land, swam in the streams, and flew through the air in great abundance.

The I. G. Baker Company store in 1877 Courtesy John G. Lepley

The greatest activity occurred at the docks. Here during the navigation season river boats arrived frequently, to be stripped of the upriver cargo and loaded with the downriver shipments. The highest prices sometimes went to the owner of the wagon train that arrived first. So, "get 'em loaded and get 'em out," was the cry. The wagons were pulled by teams of oxen, horses, and mules. Most common were the ox trains, called bull trains, even though pulled by steers, which were favored over the more fractious bulls. The bull whackers did not whack the bulls nor did the mule skinners skin the mules. Both used a rawhide whip about 20 feet long with a plaited lash at the end. This instrument of persuasion was wielded with far more accuracy than mercy to keep the wagons rolling. The oxen moved only about half as fast as horses, but because they were more placid, easier to feed, keep, and handle, they were favored over the horses by about four to one.

The wagons were placed in groups of three, one behind the other. The first wagon was called the "lead wagon," the next the "swing," and the last the "trail." The lead wagon usually carried 8,000 pounds, depending upon the type of freight; the swing about 5,500 pounds and the trail 3,500 pounds. The three wagons were hitched together and pulled by either 18 oxen or 14 horses or mules.

Fort Benton is situated on the banks of the river with a high bluff to climb before reaching the surrounding plains. This was a stiff pull which tried man and beast and came soon after the wagons were loaded and moving out. The nature of the strain is preserved in Charlie Russell's

21

painting, "The Wagon Boss." The man in the painting is sitting on his horse as he watches the progress of the wagons up the grade. Art critics believe the man pictured is Ed Trainer, wagon boss of the Baker Company.

As Charles Conrad watched the scene at the docks, he must have been thinking about where he would fit into the picture. The skinners and whackers were a mean and ornery looking lot. There was no temptation to join their fraternity. He headed for the dock and, in the clothes in which he had arrived, started carrying freight. He hoped his enterprise and willingness to work would be noticed. His mode of dress was a startling contrast to that of his fellow workers. He soon caught the eye of I. G. Baker, owner of the largest mercantile establishment at Fort Benton. In addition, Baker owned boats used in the river trade and a freighting outfit that carried goods to surrounding towns and outposts on both sides of the international boundary.

Baker approached Conrad and asked for whom he was working. Conrad answered that he was not working for anyone, he was just working, that he did not have a job and needed one. Bright, energetic, honest young men were not plentiful in Fort Benton at that time. Baker told him to go to his store where there was not only plenty of work but opportunity as well, as his business was growing rapidly and he needed help in overseeing and managing it.

This was the opportunity Conrad was looking for, and he started to work for the I. G. Baker Company as a clerk in the store. Baker was a kind, honest, and generous man. He was pleased with the manner in which Conrad accepted and discharged responsibility. When brother William returned from Helena two weeks later, Charles had gained the esteem and admiration of Baker. William was enthusiastic about the opportunities in Helena, but both boys had a long talk with Baker about where their best opportunities might lie. Baker told them his business enterprises were all making money, but that he needed to expand and build posts in the outlying reaches. He said he needed dependable people to help him and explained that his wife was getting tired of the pioneer life in the West and would like to return to their former home in St. Louis. He added that, if they would go to work for him and proved capable of managing the expanding frontier empire, he would sell them an interest in the company and make it possible for them to pay for their interest with their earnings and gradual acceptance of responsibility. In discussing the prospects of the partnership, he suggested that in the future he would return to St. Louis and oversee the procurement of supplies and would turn the management of the business over to them. In time he would sell them his remaining interest.

The opportunity offered them by Baker was far more than the boys had anticipated. William promptly forgot about Helena, and they both started to work for the I. G. Baker Company.

The difference in nature and temperament of the brothers gradually defined the areas of responsibility and management they would assume. William, the older, was heavyset and short of stature. He was aggressive and shrewd in business and had a deepseated desire for public office and recognition. That he was a formidable candidate — or that Fort Benton was solidly Democratic — was proved in 1878. On September 13, William announced his candidacy for County Commissioner of Choteau County. The November 8, 1878 issue of the *Fort Benton Record* announced the results of the election: Conrad 231, Orr 2. William had a natural talent for management and direction both in business and community life, so he fell easily into the management of the company operations at Fort Benton.

Charles was six-foot three-inches in height, handsome, slender, and erect. His black beard and penetrating eyes added to his commanding presence. He held no desire to be in the public eye, nor had any taste for public office. He was kinder, more generous and understanding than William and commanded respect where William demanded it. Both were capable, honest, dependable, and ambitious; both had the latent, but as yet unrealized, thirst for empire building.

CHAPTER 6
Expansion of the Trade Area

In the spring of 1870, Charles E. Conrad moved to Canada, where he would remain most of the time for the next decade. I. G. Baker had wanted to expand the lucrative fur-trading activities of his business. As sole proprietor, he could not tend the Fort Benton operation and still have time to establish fur-trading posts in the vast territory of the Northwest, hundreds of miles into the wilderness. The Conrad brothers had been with Baker for more than a year. During that time the aptitudes of the brothers had become clearly defined. William had a genius for business planning and organization. A computer-like mind enabled him to maintain an inventory control that assured an adequate stock of the right supplies at all times. He plotted the routes of the freight outfits and kept accurate track of their progress. It was his intention never to have an empty wagon going to or coming from anywhere.

A letter from William to Charles, dated March 24, 1883, gives an example of William's planning:

> Dear Brother: I am in receipt of your two messages. All of our freight will go by the C. P. (Canadian Pacific) Railroad from (Fort) Macleod. (Fort) Davis will only ship enough to Maple Creek to load 8 ox trains, the balance of the shipment will be held back until the road reaches Medicine Hat. Will not ship the flour and balance of the Indian supplies until road reaches Medicine Hat. We will lay down Indian flour at Medicine Hat for $2.50 per sack. Flour at Winnipeg, freight, $45.00. On bonded goods from Montreal via the lakes to Medicine Hat I expect to get $1.50. I am sure it will not exceed the $1.75, so it looks as if there will be nothing for two of the trains to do north until July 1st. These are the ones that go to Maple Creek to haul the flour to Fort Walsh. After it is through can load Davis merchandise and go to Macleod. I hope we get the hauling of the Calico (Ranch) supplies from Walsh to Maple Creek. If so, it can be done by the same train that hauled the flour. I have offered to do it for $75.00. I think I would ship what flour is at Benton to Macleod as soon as possible for we can sell it at a better price there.

In May of 1873 the Northwest Mounted Police wrote I. G. Baker and Company asking for a quotation of freight rates. On May 9 William responded, quoting rates for Canadian hauls from various points on the Canadian Pacific Railway: "Maple Creek to Fort Macleod 3¾¢ lb.; Maple Creek to Calgary 5¢ lb.; Medicine Hat to Ft. Macleod 2¾¢ lb.; Medicine Hat to Fort Calgary 4¢ per lb.; opposite Blackfoot Crossing to Ft. Macleod 2¢ lb.; opposite Blackfoot Crossing to Ft. Calgary 3¢ lb."

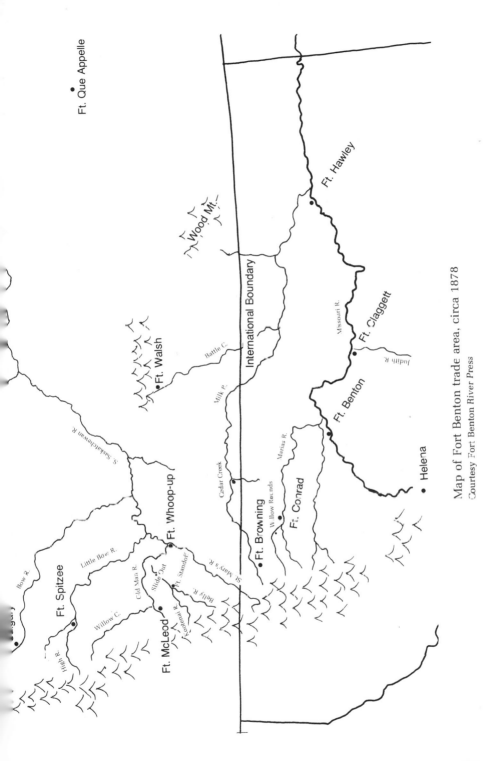

Map of Fort Benton trade area, circa 1878
Courtesy Fort Benton River Press

In its December 16, 1906 issue — two decades after the railroads had destroyed the importance of Fort Benton as a transportation hub — the *Great Falls Tribune* carried an article by William G. Conrad entitled "Business of Early Days at Fort Benton." In the article Conrad described the city's trade and trade area:

> Not many persons outside of the few surviving pioneers of those times realize that a few miles from Great Falls, at historic Fort Benton, was located between 30 and 40 years ago a business metropolis that had, as a radius for its active business activities, nearly a whole continent, that purchased goods from New Orleans on the south and the Great Slave Lakes on the north, almost within the Arctic Circle, and sold goods all over the world, in St. Louis and New York, in London and St. Petersburg, a business running up into many millions of dollars in value annually, and which supplied articles of necessity and luxury to savage tribes in North America, who had scarcely seen a white man or knew the ABC of civilization, to cultivated and wealthy merchants and citizens of the United States and to the aristocrats and royal families of Europe. Yet such was the fact. And this was in the days when there were neither railroads or wagon roads in most of the western country, when it took 60 days by the shortest route to travel between Fort Benton and St. Louis, and many months over trackless prairie and unbridged streams with slow ox teams to transport the goods to distant posts far beyond the frontiers of civilization to barter them for rare and valuable furs that later might perchance add to the beauty of some court lady in London or St. Petersburg. No such commercial dominion exists today in Montana despite our superior advantages. The coming of the railroads annihilated time and distance in the great western country and brought us many advantages, but it at the same time wiped out our independent trade dominion and annexed the country to the commercial territory of the great eastern merchant princes.

This huge trade area was built up largely by the Conrad brothers after they took over I. G. Baker and Company in 1874. But the original impetus was provided when Charles headed north into Canada to establish trading posts.

Charles knew that success in the fur trade depended upon maintaining good relations with the Indians and establishing trading posts at convenient places. William stated in the same *Great Falls Tribune* article that, to maintain the trade, the firm had

> ... as many as eight trading posts located in some instances far from civilization and consisting of a strong fort surrounded by a stockade. These places we kept supplied with goods to barter to the Indians. We pushed these trading operations very far north into the Hudson Bay country at the time and purchased furs from the Indians around the Great Slave Lake and within the Arctic Circle where it is daylight half the year and darkness the other half.

These were the posts that Charles built and kept supplied. William said that the fur trade was conducted mainly in the winter and the acumulated furs were hauled by ox train to Fort Benton when travel became possible in the spring.

The location of the posts and the distances involved gives some indication of the enormity of the work of keeping the posts supplied and the furs disposed of. In 1870 Conrad built a post 100 miles east of Fort Browning. It was abandoned the following year and a new post was built on the Marias River, 100 miles from Fort Benton. In 1871-1872, a new post was built at the mouth of Cedar Creek, 90 miles from Fort Benton, and one in Canada on the Belly River, 200 miles from Fort Benton. In 1872-1873 two new posts were established, one at the Spitchie River, a tributary of the Bow, 300 miles from Fort Benton, and another at Badger Creek which was 150 miles from the Company's headquarters.

In 1871 the *Fort Benton Record* reported that the Conrad outpost in Canada at the junction of the Little Bow and Oldman Rivers and the post at the junction of the Belly and Oldman Rivers, respectively known as Robbers Roost and Slough Bottom, were both sacked by the Indians. Charles rebuilt both.

Conrad also built stores at Calgary, Macleod, and Fort Walsh, which were supplied from Fort Benton. Again William's article in the *Great Falls Tribune* is helpful in understanding the size of the operation. He is quoted as saying that in one year the firm handled as much as 30,000 pounds of freight by bull train. To do this they employed at one time about 500 yoke of oxen and several hundred head of mules.

A good deal of our freighting business was for the Canadian government and the United States government. We had a contract at one time to supply the mounted police of Canada with all the supplies they needed, including the cash to pay them off, and similar contracts with the United States government. These contracts included all sorts of supplies, from grain and forage for the horses to canned goods and dry goods. Speaking of canned goods, nearly all we ate in those days outside of meat and flour came out of cans. I have seen at one time as many as seven steamers unloading on the Fort Benton levee, with canned goods and other mountains of freight, till it looked like a long tier of buildings. If anyone thinks those were days of small beginnings in business affairs, I could show old books of the company which carried figures mounting up in their annual totals to many millions of dollars, and our firm was only one of a number doing business in Fort Benton. I recollect once opening a letter which contained an order for $160,000 worth of provisions at one delivery. The part of our business that consisted of trade and barter with the Indians for furs was immensely profitable, but it did not last long. We dealt largely in buffalo and wolf hides with the Indians in the section, while further north we secured the more valuable furs, such as mink, marten, otter, beaver, silver fox and other fine furs. We maintained offices in Toronto, a store in Montreal, and business offices in Helena, St. Louis and other cities, while operations were conducted from Fort Benton as headquarters.

The Conrad brothers were 18 and 20 years old when they came to Fort Benton. Their only experience was in plantation living and war. In 20 years these two young men built up and managed the largest and most successful trading empire in the West. When they liquidated this establishment, in 1890, and moved on to other interests, Charles and William were just 40 and 42 years old. Already they had played an active and important role in one of the most dangerous and exciting times in Montana history.

CHAPTER 7
Gold Trade at Fort Benton

In 1869 I. G. Baker returned to St. Louis with his family. The manner of his departure was an indication of his ability to turn a profit from almost any situation. Frances Baker Pollock, the daughter of Baker by his second wife, wrote of their departure:

> After the last steamboat had left Fort Benton in the late fall of 1868, a number of miners came to town hoping to find transportation to the states. They were greatly disappointed in finding no boat nor any prospects of one. It was then that my father built a mackinaw 100 feet long. Rooms were divided by canvas or calico curtains. There was one long dining table, a wood burning cook stove and a negro cook. When water was wanted, deck hands dropped a bucket with a rope attached over the side of the boat and drew up a supply of Missouri River water. The miners were glad to pay $100 in gold to float down the river on the mackinaw. My mother was one of the passengers and I was with her, a baby in arms, also the black nurse, Ann, and her daughter. They had been taken up the river from St. Louis to Benton. There was only one other woman passenger, an English woman. After two months floating down the river my mother and her party left the boat at Omaha. Captain McCloud said, "This boat can go anywhere a mule can go."

The mackinaw boats were usually used in the fall when the water level of the river was too low for the steamers. They could compete with a mule, but only so long as the mule stayed in the river. M. A. Leeson's *History of Montana* quotes Lieutenant James Bradley's description of a "mackinaw." Bradley, an officer in the U.S. Army, was stationed at Fort Benton in the 1860s. He wrote:

> The boats were usually broad, flat-bottomed crafts, with square sterns and roughly built, to be sold for lumber or abandoned at the end of the voyage. They were supplied with oars and sometimes with sails, but the rapid current of the river was relied upon for the main progress. Under favorable circumstances a hundred miles a day was accomplished by these vessels. Frequent running aground, danger from Indians and occasional shipwreck were among the incidents of the voyage and the party was fortunate that got through without any mishaps.

Baker would thereafter stay in St. Louis to manage the financing, the procurement of supplies, and the loading and movement of the cargo

The mackinaw *Last Chance* leaving Fort Benton for Carroll,
circa 1878 Courtesy Montana Historical Society

westward. In the spring of 1869 Baker sent his brother, George, to Fort
Benton to become manager of the business, and the name was changed to
I. G. Baker and Brother. George was much like his brother. He, too, was
kind and generous and an active member of the Methodist Church.
George continued his brother's practice of selling no liquor and closing
the store on Sundays. The Conrads also followed this practice after they
became owners of the entire business. The Sabbath became a day when
Baker, the Conrads, and other employees gathered at the closed store to
visit and relax. There was then little Christian activity in Fort Benton,
and the store on Sunday became a haven for those who wanted an escape
from the frontier life carried on at the saloons and sporting houses.

The Conrad brothers became increasingly active in the management of
the business, which was taking a new turn. The placer gold that had
provided the initial impetus for the settling of Montana Territory and the
growth of Fort Benton began to dwindle toward the end of the 1860s. The
Union Pacific Railroad was completed in 1869, but the overland haul
from Corinne, Utah Territory, the nearest railroad point for Montana,
was too long to offer effective competition to the water traffic on the
Missouri.

Fort Benton had grown and thrived on the gold trade. Here the

30

thousands of miners landed and from here they were supplied. The gold the miners produced was brought to Fort Benton to be shipped down-river. Fort Benton benefited from the landing of the miners, from their stay, and from their departure, rich or broke. Gold production in Montana from 1862 to 1950 was estimated by the Montana Bureau of Mines to be over 18 million ounces. "Gold is indestructible and everlasting and no doubt all of the 18 million ounces produced in Montana is still in existence," said the *Montana Magazine's* September-October, 1980 issue. 1866 was probably the peak year for profits in the Montana gold trade. In that year the steamboat *Luella* left Fort Benton with 2½ tons of gold dust worth $1,250,000. This was the largest shipment of the year but not the only one. Other boats were hauling both gold as cargo and passengers who carried their gold with them. During the years from 1866 to 1869, gold was an important medium of exchange in Montana. This use required only limited quantities, and a huge amount of gold was shipped downriver to the Eastern markets. The steamships were well-fitted for the trade but could be depended upon for only about four months of the year, generally May, June, July and August. The miners worked their diggings during all of the favorable weather. Many miners arrived at Fort Benton in the late fall loaded down with gold, only to find the last steamer gone. By this time only mackinaws could make the trip. These were built, outfitted, and started down the river in great numbers, filled with miners and their gold.

The gold was placed in strong boxes, to which was attached a buoy with a long rope. If the vessel sank, which was not uncommon, the floating buoy would indicate the location of the box for easier retrieval. George Baker, of I. G. Baker and Company, said that such care was taken, and so well guarded were the mackinaws, that no gold was ever reported irretrievably lost. After 1869 the production of gold, which had been the economic base of Montana Territory, began to dwindle and then to fade into insignificance.

The Fort Benton merchants probably profited more from the gold trade than did the miners, since their profits were more certain and secure. The Baker Company was an important depository of gold awaiting shipment. Gold in all forms would be brought in for safekeeping. A chute was provided to receive the gold during the hours when the store was closed. The miners were so confident of the honesty of the Baker people they would place their sacked gold in the chute, then wait to hear the reassuring thud as it dropped to the floor inside. With their gold safe, the miners could be off for a night on the town without the fear that it might be stolen as they frolicked in the bars and sporting houses. No matter how drunk they got or how many times they were rolled, their gold would be waiting for them at the Baker store when they sobered up. A news story in the June 1, 1875 issue of the *Fort Benton Record* stated: "The new Hall's patent burglar and fire proof safe lately purchased by

31

the I. G. Baker Company cost $1,000 and weighs 4000 pounds." The safe must have instilled even more confidence in the owners of gold looking for a place of safekeeping.

Bags with no names would be identified by marks, weight, or composition. George Baker recalled one bag in particular which was so heavy that it dented the floor when it landed. There was no name on the bag, but identification was easy, as they felt sure of the owner when he came three days later to claim his gold and described the size of the bag deposited.

Business at Fort Benton declined as the mines depleted the gold supply. There were rumblings of the Northern Pacific Railroad coming into Montana, but that competition would not materialize until 1883. The future of Fort Benton did not seem too bright in 1869 to those who thought it was dependent on gold.

The year 1870 was ominous. Forty-two steamboats arrived in Fort Benton in 1869, but only eight docked in 1870. The freighting business dropped alarmingly. There was an out-migration of people that decreased the population of the town to about 150. The Conrads were among the few whose vision told them that the demise of Fort Benton had not yet come. They perceived that the trickle of cattle coming into Montana presaged a new and thriving industry. They knew that they must expand their operations in Canada, where they were now preeminent. Their wagon trains would be able to supply western Canada less expensively and more quickly than any other mode of transportation. This advantage would continue until the completion of the Canadian Pacific Railway in 1884. The Conrads did not see 1870 as a time for gloom and retrenchment. It was a time to expand and make ready for the halcyon days they believed lay ahead for Fort Benton.

CHAPTER 8
Saving the Mounties

In 1873 the Canadian government organized the North West Mounted Police. Prior to 1869, the Hudson's Bay Company owned much of the land which now comprises western Canada. Because of its ownership, the Company could exclude all but its own agents and licensees. There was little trouble with the Indians, for the white men had not overrun the country and destroyed the forests, ranges, and animals on which the Indians depended.

The Hudson's Bay Company was chartered in 1670 by King Charles II of England to trade in and settle the area of Canada draining into Hudson Bay. In 1690, prompted by Prince Rupert, a cousin of the King, a charter was granted to the Company, giving it almost sovereign powers over an expanse of land the actual size and area of which would not be known for another century. So heavily did the Company rely on the antiquity of its grant of right to the territory that American fur traders, excluded from the Company's domain, contemptuously referred to the initials of the Company, HBC, as "Here Before Christ."

By 1821 the Company had strangled out all competitors in the vast region and exercised monopolistic economic and governmental powers. Huge fortunes were made for the proprietors, but the operations were kept so secret that the full extent of the profits was never known. The Company's practices were challenged by those wishing to open up the area for settlement. By 1869 the opposition became so powerful that, on December 1, the Company transferred to the Canadian government its vast Hudson's Bay land holdings for 300,000 pounds.

Following the transfer, the Canadian government had no way of supervising the huge area either in government structure, law enforcement, or police protection. Traders from the United States crossed the border in great numbers to tap the rich fur trade and furnish liquor to the Canadian Indians. Selling liquor to Indians had by then been outlawed in the United States, so the liquor traders simply moved across the border and started the degradation of the Canadian Indians.

The only law then in western Canada was that exercised by each individual. The Indians were demoralized by whiskey and slaughtered by the white men. Atrocity stories finally stirred the Canadian government to action. Sir John MacDonald, Prime Minister of Canada, after some period of waxing and waning enthusiasm with the idea, was finally forced by the Cypress Hills Massacre to form the North West Mounted Police, a name later changed to the Royal Northwest Mounted Police.

That incident, known as the Cypress Hills Massacre, when disassociated from the emotions aroused at the time, was in reality an almost ordinary skirmish between whites and Indians. Had it happened south of the border, it would have attracted little publicity. Occurring when and where it did, it became an international incident, partly because T. C. Power employees saw it as opportunity to discredit the I. G. Baker Company and to drive it from the Canadian trade.

The Northwest Mounted Police Courtesy University of Montana Library

It started when a party of wolfers, returning to Fort Benton in May of 1873, made their last camp about five miles short of their destination. Nearness to the town caused them to relax their vigilance. During the night a group of marauding Indians stole all of their horses, leaving them in the ignominious and unaccustomed position of having no means of locomotion except their own feet. The wolfers struggled into Fort Benton, where derision and ridicule added to their discomfort.

The party did not stop to enjoy the long-anticipated delights of frontier civilization. They soon reequipped themselves and started out to regain their stolen property and to restore their pride. They came upon a band of North Assiniboine camped in the Cypress Hills, a short distance across the international border, northeast of Fort Benton. They believed that the Indians knew where the horses were hidden, and whiskey and hatred combined to destroy reason in both the Indians and the whites. Who fired the first shot is disputed, but that shot started a battle in which the Indians were almost wiped out.

Canadian newspapers described the incident as a wanton massacre of defenseless Indians by a group of depraved and lawless madmen. Papers in the western United States hailed it as a victory for the stalwart pioneers in their continuing efforts to subdue the bloodthirsty Indians. Later investigations indicated that Abe Farwell, a T. C. Power and Brother representative who had a small trading post near the battleground, deliberately and falsely magnified the incident to make it appear that employees of I. G. Baker and Company had incited the incident. The Power interests hoped by this ruse to secure the arrest and convictions of the Baker representatives. If discredit could be cast upon the Baker Company, it could be eliminated from the Canadian trade, leaving Power with a monopoly.

The suspected duplicity of the Power interests became sufficiently known or suspected that it failed in its purpose, but the Cypress Hills Massacre had the effect of hastening the formation and dispatch of the Mounted Police to the Canadian West.

In 1873 the Canadian Parliament finally created the Mounted Police. A force of 300 was authorized initially. Recruitment and training were started and, on July 8, 1874, Lieutenant Colonel George Arthur French led the first detachment out of Dufferin, a small outpost 60 miles south of Winnipeg.

The beginning of the march was auspicious and colorful. All of the reports received by Prime Minister MacDonald advised that the coats of the troops be red. The Indians associated red with friendship and authority. Red symbolized to the Indians the blood of the Queen's enemies. They looked upon the Queen as a friend and protector, and reserved their animosity and hatred for the provincial officials who were close to them. With the red coats, the newly created Mounties wore blue or gray cloaks lined with red, long dark boots, dark pants with a yellow stripe and pith helmets — not particularly suited to the rigors of the prairies, but typically English. The first 275 men started out, divided into six companies of hastily trained recruits. Their officers were untried men thoroughly uninformed as to survival on the harsh prairies, where the sun blistered in the summer and the cold numbed in the winter.

The proud formation of the columns did not last long. Soon the men were plodding across the untracked prairies of Manitoba and Saskatchewan, short of food, short of water, and lost a good share of the time.

Veterans of Northwest Mounted Police Courtesy University of Montana Library

By the time they reached eastern Alberta, the grass was sparse and dry, the prairie treeless, the water mostly alkaline, the food short, and winter coming. About the middle of September, the party halted in the Sweet Grass Hills, northeast of Fort Benton. They were lost, starving, and fearful of the Indians by whom they thought themselves surrounded.

Colonel French knew that without help the expedition would perish. He also knew the general direction of Fort Benton. French and Major Macleod slipped through the Indian lines at night and set out to get supplies for the starving men and animals. They reached Fort Benton without incident and went first to I. G. Baker and Company, where they met C. E. Conrad and told him of their plight. Conrad responded by giving them dinner and telling them that I. G. Baker and Company would furnish all the supplies they needed on credit, with payment to be made on such terms as French could arrange with the Canadian government.

The Conrad brothers loaded wagons with supplies for men and animals. Charles Conrad went ahead with one wagonload of emergency supplies drawn by fast horses, which arrived well ahead of the slower oxen. He found the troops starving, but gallantly clad in their bright red tunics. Their food was gone except for part of a wagonload of tea. The quartermaster must have decided that, whatever their fate, they would meet it with a cup of hot tea as befitted a well-bred Englishman. The horses were also starving. They had been herded close to camp to keep the Indians from running them off and had soon exhausted the limited natural forage, leaving little but dust on which to nibble.

The company was surrounded by Indians. Conrad saw that they were of the Blackfeet tribe, whose language he spoke. He learned that the Indians were not hostile but had been attracted by the flamboyant uniforms of the Mounted Police. They were not on the warpath and had no intention of attacking, but the inquisitive nature of the Indians held them to the spot until they discovered what those brightly dressed outlanders were going to do.

After Conrad explained the situation to both the soldiers and the Indians, a hunting party was sent out and soon there was a supply of fresh buffalo meat. The horses were allowed to range and started to get back their strength. The slower wagons arrived and the demoralized troops regained their confidence and composure. Colonel French was somewhat embarrassed to learn that he had encamped just a few miles east of the Whoop-Up Trail, the main road between Fort Benton and Canada. Had he moved on westward for a short distance, he would have crossed that trail and more than likely seen wagon trains going both north and south.

When the troops and animals were sufficiently recovered to travel, Conrad guided them to Fort Whoop-Up, a notorious whiskey trading post that the police were dedicated to reform or close. Word had preceded them, and by the time they arrived the traders had pulled out, taking their whiskey. Macleod and French were impressed with the size and strength of the Fort and offered to buy it for $10,000. The proprietors asked $25,000, and Conrad advised them to refuse. Jerry Potts, a noted guide, was employed by Macleod at the suggestion of Conrad. He led the party to a site on the Old Man River, where a fort was constructed. At the insistence of the men it was named Fort Macleod. This was the first headquarters of the Royal Canadian Mounted Police. From here, a small force of redcoated men would bring law and order to a lawless land and become legendary in the annals of law enforcement.

The act of kindness rendered by Conrad to the starving Mounties was the beginning of a relationship between the officers of the Mounted Police and the I. G. Baker Company that lasted as long as the Company was in business. It was reported to the officials of the Canadian government, who thereafter favored the Conrads in contracts for supplying beef, hay, and other supplies to the reservation Indians and government posts, as well as to the police. The Conrads even took over supplying money for the Canadian payrolls and Indian allotments, handled mail deliveries, and furnished freighting services between Fort Benton and the Canadian outposts.

I. G. Baker store at Fort Macleod, Alberta, circa 1874
Courtesy University of Montana Library

Even before the fort was finished, C. E. Conrad built a store near Fort Macleod and followed the police to Calgary, Fort Walsh, and all of the main Canadian settlements. In addition, Conrad established trading posts all over the Northwest and kept them supplied with trade goods and provisions. The furs and buffalo hides were hauled to Fort Benton for shipment to St. Louis. Conrad also opened an outlet in Montreal, which became a very profitable venture.

The Hudson's Bay Company was challenged everywhere, with the Baker Company winning most of the trade battles. Before 1869 the Hudson's Bay Company had owned the lands of western Canada and could exclude trappers and traders from the United States. After they sold these lands to the new nation of Canada, Hudson's Bay became just another trading company, and the Americans moved into the territory in large numbers to share in the lucrative trade.

CHAPTER 9
A Test of Courage

Charles Conrad spent much time with the different Indian tribes. He had a flair for learning their languages and became able to converse fluently in most of the dialects. This ability to communicate served Conrad well not only in the fur trade but also in establishing lasting friendships with the various tribes and their chiefs. Conrad gained the respect of the Indians, who found he was fair and could be trusted. His courage on the frontier was tested early and was of a quality that no man wanted to test twice.

'The *Anaconda Standard*, which carried his obituary, quoted an old-timer as saying:

> It reminds me that he was one of the coolest men in the face of danger and one of the best Indian traders this country ever saw. He had a certain power over the red man that seemed to compel him to do as he wished. I remember one time when he and a number of us were up on the Blackfoot reserve when the Indians had become peaceable, but they were not to be trusted at all when they thought they had the advantage of the white man. Nothing but the cool-headed bravery of Mr. Conrad saved us from annihilation. We had a warrant for an Indian boy who was charged with killing a calf that belonged to the Conrad Company and we wanted to arrest him.

> There were at least 5000 warriors camped in that place and they were packed in very closely. Johnnie Healy was then sheriff and he was and is, as everyone knows, so brave that he is simply reckless, and he held the warrant that was to enable us to take the boy into custody. We had no interpreter along as Conrad was an expert and we located the boy by information from the same Indian that had told us about his killing the calf and we were sure we had the right boy. In fact they — that is, the boy and his parents — did not attempt to deny it. We had explained the arrest and I was assisting in putting the boy on a horse and tying him to the saddle when the father slowly pulled out his rifle and leveling it at my head said something to me in Indian that I knew meant 'stop that.'

> I hardly knew what to do, and I suppose did not realize my danger when Johnnie Healy whipped out his revolver and was about to shoot the Indian.

> At the same instant another Indian gave a war whoop and in the time it takes to tell it we were surrounded by 1000 warriors and most of them were armed. Things looked pretty serious for us and if Healy had shot we would

have been wiped from the face of the earth, but luckily for us, Mr. Conrad grabbed Healy's gun and forced him to put it up. Then Mr. Conrad told the Indians that we did not want to hurt the boy, that we would take him to Benton and have him tried before the court for killing the calf. "He will come back to you safe and sound whether he is guilty or not," said Mr. Conrad. "And even if you kill all of us, the soldiers will come and kill you. You cannot escape. Make the father of the boy put down his rifle and we promise you that we will not hurt the boy."

The Indians then took the rifle away from the angry father, who under the circumstances was not to be blamed very much. He stood around in a sullen attitude as if uncertain what to do. Mr. Conrad asked them to make an opening for us so we could go home but they seemed determined not to do so. Mr. Conrad, after parleying with them for quite a while told us to draw our guns but not to shoot 'til we had to. Then he told the Indians that the first one who touched the horse's reins he would kill instantly and if they gave him any trouble, we would kill the boy, even if all the white men were killed. After a moment's hesitation they began to give way as we advanced. When we were clear of them we put up our guns and drew a sigh of thankfulness that the good management and courage of Mr. Conrad had relieved us of a very serious embarrassment.

To finish the story, we took the boy to Fort Benton where we placed him in jail until the next term of court. His mother followed us on foot all the way, slept on the jail floor until her boy left for the penitentiary when she returned to her home. The sentence in the state prison for two years was a good thing for the young man, whom the Indians called White Calf on account of his misdemeanor for it taught him a trade and he is now a respected Indian carpenter up on the reservation.

It is difficult to believe that the description of her father by Conrad's youngest daughter, Alicia, and that in the *Anaconda Standard* address the same man. Alicia said of her father,

He was a gentle man. Like all the Conrad men, he was absolutely devoted to children. He had much concern about them and took such tender and watchful care over them. Father always called me "Little Miss Lady" and loved to carry me on his shoulders. I loved it too, for he was so tall and handsome and from that height I could look down and have a feeling of strength and security.

I remember that, well before Christmas, Father would select something he thought Mother would especially like as a gift. He would bring it home (the Conrad Mansion in Kalispell) and we would hide it under the pineapple bed in the Grey Room which is now called the Gold Room. The bed had a skirt that hung to the floor and was made from the same material as the drapes. Each night when Father was home he would tuck me in my little youth bed in the master bedroom on Father's side of the bed. After hearing my prayers he would shoo Mother out of the room and say in a conspiratorial whisper, "Let's go down and see if Mother's present is all right." I would get out of bed and, in my nightie with Father holding my hand, we would steal out of the room and very stealthily we'd go down the hall to the

Grey Room and peek under the bed, and yes, there it would be — nothing had happened to it. We might look at it two or three times a day when he was home and always before going to sleep.

At Foy's Lake I learned to swim before I could walk very well and always loved the water because Father taught me not to fear it. He would put me on his back and swim high in the water so I could get the feel of how it was to swim. With his safeguarding me that way, I learned to swim easily and without fear, and it was a great joy to me.

Father loved fairies and loved the Kipling poem about Puck. Anything about Puck. He was partial to the ancient fairy lore, especially of England, Scotland, and Ireland. He would read me those poems and I grew to love them as he did. The tenderness and delicacy of his fanciful imagination for children was a lovely thing.

Father never would have anyone else break a horse. He did it himself and only with love and gentleness, no other way. His horse, Champ, was a very beautiful Morgan saddle horse with an Arab head, which was very unusual. He was a dark chestnut and the most beautiful horse I ever saw. My opinion was shared by all the people who handled him and took care of him. For pleasure riding Father liked to use a small, flat English saddle and a soft rubber bit. He understood neck reining and stock saddles and could do it well, but never with a hard hand or a metal bit. Father would never have anything in harness or under saddle that could not be handled with a soft rubber bit, and there was never a metal bit, riding crop, or whip in our stables.

Father could be firm, too. His brothers, W. G. Conrad and Howard were at the dinner table one night when they were staying as house guests. W. G. was two years older than father and Uncle Howard two years younger, and they (W. G. and Howard) never liked each other. W. G. was a rather pompous figure who liked to put his thumbs under his vest and make Olympian pronouncements. I was always frightened of him, and it pleased me when someone referred to him as "W. Jesus." Father always insisted that the dinner table be a place for pleasant conversation, laughter, and conviviality. But this night there were words between W. G. and Uncle Howard that brought a discordant atmosphere to the table. In a quiet voice Father said to the brothers, "Boys, go to your rooms and when you can behave you may return to the table." Both these grown men stood up and said to Mother, "Letty, excuse us please," and went to their rooms. After some time had passed they came down and rejoined the group and the rest of the evening was harmonious. Father would not quarrel with anyone nor would he allow a quarrel in his home.

Joel Overholser, editor emeritus of the Fort Benton River Press, who for years has studied the history of Fort Benton, wrote in a letter dated January 6, 1978:

More and more I'm coming to the belief that this (Fort Benton) may have been one of the toughest towns in the old West in the 1860s and '70s, that badmen would have disappeared without a gurgle. Charles Conrad in particular seemed to stand out for personal courage in a time when acceptance of danger was a very common characteristic, at least among survivors.

Alicia was never able to reconcile the gentle and loving father she knew with the hard-driving, fearless, and sometimes ruthless empire-builder, the stories of whose exploits of daring and cool business genius came to her from many souces. Her belief in fairies was a great comfort to her in this. She almost believed that the good fairy who could change the ugly toad into a prince charming could work the same magic with her father.

CHAPTER 10
White Men, Indian Women

Sometime prior to 1876, Charles E. Conrad was married to an Indian girl. By the folklore of the Conrad family, the Indian maiden was a princess, the daughter of a Blackfeet chief, and very beautiful. It is fairly certain that Conrad and the Indian girl were married by a Catholic priest and that both considered it a solemn marriage, blessed by the Church, and intended to last.

The passage of time since the frontier days has largely obliterated any of the relationships between white men and Indian women except that of the so-called "squaw man." These men, throughout the times and places of their wanderings, had casual relations with Indian women to satisfy a physical need, with no thought of marriage or of permanency in the relationship. When a white man of high caliber took an Indian wife, it was usually a true marriage consummated by a priest. If the marriage were terminated, many times it was because the Indian wife refused to go east and live in the world of the white man.

The marriage of Alexander Culbertson, the founder of Fort Benton and one of the most influential men in the settlement of the West, is an example. In 1840, by an Indian wedding ceremony, he married Natawista, daughter of the Blood Indian chief, Father-of-all-Children. She was 15 at the time of her marriage, and thereafter they were seldom parted. She accompanied him on all his trips, whether in his capacity as a peace emissary to the various Indian tribes or on business trips to St. Louis. She grew to love the luxurious Planters Hotel in St. Louis and became equally at home there as she was in the tepees of the Plains Indians which she visited with her husband.

After Culbertson retired from the American Fur Company, the couple lived in Peoria, Illinois, for about 10 years. Here their marriage was again solemnized by a Catholic priest. They made frequent trips back to Fort Benton, where both were respected and welcomed as guests in all the homes. In 1869 they returned to Fort Benton, after their children were raised, educated in the East, and prospering. The following year they parted for the first time in 30 years.

Natawista had been invaluable to her husband in his successful career of negotiating with the Indians. She spoke the languages of all of the tribes and acted as interpreter. When he retired, and she could no longer help the Indians in the same manner, she grew restless and yearned for the old life. In 1870 she returned to her people, who were then in Canada. She never adjusted fully to the old life, continuing to be called Madame Culbertson and maintaining some contact with whites as friends. Natawista stayed with her people until her death in 1893. She had a Catholic funeral and was buried in a Catholic cemetery near Standoff, in Alberta, Canada.

The solemn relationship between Conrad and his Indian wife is indicated by the fact that their son, who was born in 1876, was named Charles Edward Conrad, Jr.

As the white man gained greater dominance over the traditional homelands of the Indians and the buffalo became more scarce, the Indian tribes moved away in search of new lands, hoping to maintain their traditional way of life. Thus it was that in 1878 Conrad's wife's father decided to move his tribe to the unsettled lands of central Canada. This decision caused the young Indian mother much anguish. Before her marriage she had been converted to Catholicism and thought her son would have more opportunity under the guidance of his white father than as a mixed-blood with the tribe. Her deep need to stay with her people proved stronger than the marriage vow. Conrad promised that their son would be raised a Catholic and be given a good education. The wife left with the tribe and never returned to Fort Benton. The young boy was left in Fort Benton with his father.

How long the boy remained in Fort Benton is not known. He was not there when Alicia Stanford, Conrad's future wife, arrived in June of 1879. Sometime after his mother left, the two-year-old child was placed in a Catholic school in Montreal, Canada.

There was no place in Fort Benton to provide care for a motherless child. Conrad was then overseeing the distant business operations of the Baker Company in Canada. He was away from Fort Benton much of the time, which made it difficult to care for a small child. It would have been easy for Conrad to desert his son, but he did not do so. He acknowledged the boy as his son, provided him with a good education, and helped him in his subsequent business ventures. None of these ventures was successful. They were kept going by loans advanced by father to son, none of which was repaid. These loans grew to a total of almost $50,000, a princely sum in those early days.

During his lifetime, Charles E. Conrad kept in contact with his son and visited him — sometimes accompanied by his second wife — in Montreal when in the East on business trips. In his will Conrad made the same provisions for the Indian son as were made for the other three children. The son died before he received his share of the father's estate, but while he lived, Charles E. Conrad was always true to the promises made to his Indian wife in 1876.

CHAPTER 11
Treaty No. 7

Charles Conrad greatly extended the Baker Company's trading area. He had trappers bringing in furs from as far as the Great Slave Lake in northern Canada, and he became an expert in fur quality. Particularly fine furs were singled out for special treatment and care. Some prices were negotiated on a single-pelt basis in the capitals of the world, especially London and St. Petersburg, Russia.

The business of the Company flourished through the efforts of the Conrads. By 1873 their share of the profits had enabled them to purchase a one-fourth interest in the Company from I. G. Baker. The next year they purchased the entire interest of George Baker, who returned to St. Louis. The Conrads were now in full control and continued to expand.

Charles E. Conrad respected and liked the Plains Indians. The Indians quickly sensed this and returned to him an even deeper respect, based largely on the knowledge that Conrad was always fair and honest in his dealings with them. They also knew that Conrad was absolutely fearless and capable of swift and certain retribution for any breach of their relationship. As a result, the Indians probably had more trust and confidence in Conrad than in any man on the frontier since Alexander Culbertson.

As the bond deepened, the Indians began to consult with Conrad in all important matters affecting the tribes, especially their dealings with the white man and his government. This relationship lasted until Conrad's death. Even after he moved from the area, the chiefs of the Plains Indians came to Kalispell to consult with Conrad and to get his advice on matters they thought too important to decide alone.

This was true also of the Canadian tribes, made up largely of the Blackfeet, Piegans, Bloods, Sarcees, and Stoneys. By the year 1877, whites were moving into southern Alberta with cattle. The area's buffalo were almost extinguished, so the only meat available to the starving Indians was the cattle of the whites. The stealing of cattle brought cruel retribution, a cow being considered of more importance than an Indian. Red Crow, chief of the Bloods, was then the most respected leader of the Indians of southern Alberta. He saw that peace must be made between

One Spot
Pipe bearer of
Crowfoot
Blood Blackfeet

Red Crow
of
Blood Blackfeet
Chiefs

North Axe
of
Piegan Blackfeet

Chief Red Crow (center) at the signing of Treaty No. 7
Courtesy Montana Historical Society

the two races, for the traditional life of the Indian was doomed.

While there remained any hope, the tribes resisted. But this resistance was broken by the terrible winter of 1886-1887. First came heavy rains, which froze. Heavy snow followed, along with record-breaking cold and blizzards. The cattle herds were devastated. With the buffalo gone, there was no food for the Indians.

There was widespread starvation among the tribesmen. Chief Red Crow led not only his people, but the chiefs of the other four tribes, into negotiations. When the final terms of the treaty were determined, Red Crow would not sign until he had conferred with his white brother. Conrad studied the proposed treaty, and both he and Red Crow decided that it treated the Indians fairly, protected their rights, and was as good as they would get.

The signing ceremony was at Blackfoot Crossing on the Bow River, about 60 miles southeast of Calgary, on September 22, 1877. First to sign was the lieutenant governor, on behalf of Queen Victoria. Chief Red Crow then signed by touching the pen as a sign that he agreed to the treaty, and an "x" was placed by his name. The same procedure was used by each of the other four chiefs. At the insistence of Chief Red Crow, Charles E. Conrad signed the treaty as a representative of all the tribes.

This became Treaty No. 7. By its terms, the five tribes ceded to the Queen all of their land in southern Alberta, except their reservations. In return, the government "would guarantee hunting rights in the area ceded (with some exceptions), reserves of one square mile for a family of five, annual treaty payments, annual ammunition allotments, tri-annual clothing for the chiefs, payment of teachers, provisions of tools and cattle and farming equipment." Following the signing, the Royal Canadian Mounted Police played "The Maple Leaf Forever," and the tribes stayed on for a celebration.

After the passage of 100 years, the Indians decided to commemorate the event to show how they had fared. A delegation was sent to London to invite Charles, Prince of Wales, to a reenactment of the ceremony. He accepted the invitation. On July 6, 1977, Prince Charles, Ralph Steinbauer, Lieutenant-governor of Alberta, Chief Leo Pretty Young Man of the Blackfeet Tribe, Chief Nelson Small Legs, Sr., of the Peigan Tribe, Chief Jim Shot Both Sides of the Blood Tribe, Chief Clifford Big Plume of the Sarcee Tribe, and Chiefs John Snow, Alvin Two Young Men, and William McLean of the Stoney Tribe all met to reenact the signing. Charles E. Conrad was there by representative in the person of his grandson, Charles Conrad Campbell.

Following the Lieutenant-governor, each chief signed by touching the pen as had his predecessor. Charles Conrad Campbell signed for his grandfather. The band of the R.C.M.P. again played "The Maple Leaf

Forever." Then each chief stepped forward to tell of the progress of the Indians under the treaty. Each chief spoke of betrayal and failure to live up to the terms of the treaty. Typical was the speech of William McLean, Chief of the Stoney Tribe. He said, "We love our Queen and are happy to have her son here today. In him and in the Crown we place our future." He spoke of the lack of education among his people. He said, "We are like a raft floating down the river that does not know where to land. We know that the past 100 years have only been one step on the pathway our tribe must take in trying to achieve its goals, but I do not want it to take another 100 before we take our rightful place with our fellow citizens of Canada."

Charles Campbell recalls that the Indians spoke with reverence and love for the Queen and her son. They remembered the respect in which their people had held his grandfather. Their feeling of betrayal was directed toward the provincial government and the people who had occupied the provincial offices during the years of the treaty. For Charles E. Conrad, they had only memories of admiration and respect.

One thing differed at the reenactment. A lady broke through the Mounted Police line, kissed Prince Charles, and then ran quickly to the protection of her husband. Both the Prince and the husband showed frustration, but the lady, Exilda McKevett, age 70, was calm and serene, having accomplished something she felt compelled to do. From the safety of her husband's arm she said, "I did what a million girls would like to do. It was completely impromptu — just one of those things."

CHAPTER 12
Fortune Making on the Missouri

For some years the Conrads and T. C. Power had watched the steam-boat traffic on the Missouri River, both in regard to the profits being made and the delays they experienced in moving their freight up and down the river. The profits could be enormous — as much as $125,000 for a single upriver trip. Steamboat captains were notorious profit seek-ers. If a higher paying cargo appeared, they did not hesitate to leave a less lucrative shipment in St. Louis and bring upriver goods that gave them a larger profit.

In the fur-trading days of the early 1860s, cargo brought up the Mis-souri could be roughly calculated to be worth one dollar per pound as trading stock. In many cases, the value was higher. A bottle of trade whiskey, usually cut and treated, or a cup of inexpensive beads could be traded for a buffalo robe. Trade whiskey was a vile concoction com-pounded to satisfy the supposed taste of the Indians for a potent, burning liquor. The belief was that the hotter, the more fiery the taste, the better the Indians liked it. They gave it the name "firewater," which was an apt description of the brew furnished to the Indians by the white fur traders. On the wall of the museum at Fort Benton hangs a recipe for Indian whiskey:

To muddy Missouri River water add:
1 quart alcohol
1 pound black chewing tobacco
1 handful red peppers
1 bottle Jamaica ginger
1 quart black molasses
Mix well and boil until strength is drawn from tobacco and peppers. Drain and trade it to the Indians for furs, hides, robes, etc.

The cost of transportation was so great that markups for retail trade ran from 50 percent up. One dollar per pound seemed to be the minimum for anything, whether it was flour, sugar, salt, coffee, or feathers. In 1867, 11,872 tons of cargo was brought to Fort Benton by steamboat during the approximate four-month riverboat season. This would translate into a

Steamboat *Josephine* enroute to Fort Benton
Courtesy John G. Lepley

value of $24,000,000 worth of freight brought to the Fort Benton merchants in that year alone. At 12½ cents per pound, the boat owners would have divided almost $3,000,000 for the four-month season, without including the downriver cargo.

Steamboat captains could become rich in one trip from St. Louis to Fort Benton. In 1866 the captain of the *Peter Balen*, a rather thrown-together boat built hurriedly for the river trade, brought up 400 tons of cargo, charged 12½ cents per pound, and pocketed $100,000. For the return trip he loaded on furs, hides, and pelts on which he received an undisclosed sum to augment the considerable fortune made on the upriver trip. Such one-trip fortunes were common until there were sufficient boats in the river trade to make it competitive, whereupon transportation costs went down and stabilized.

The June 9, 1976 issue of the *River Press* includes an article indicating that such profits made for an easy-come-easy-go philosophy among the river captains:

> Bill Massie, one of the greatest steamboat pilots on the Upper Missouri, in 1866 piloted Joe Kinney's *Cora* to Fort Benton. Those were the days of the hostile Sioux, their young men sniping at the passing steamboats, following them for days hoping to gobble up a wooding party or catch a boat stranded on a bar. In spite of the perils, the *Cora* had a great trip earning $50,000 for her owner. At the St. Louis levee Kinney paid off his captain $7,500, including a bonus for one of the best trips ever made to the mountains.

Bill Massie paused outside a St. Louis gambling house, then entered. Hours later he walked out, dead broke or almost. Digging deep he found a lone dime, flipped it to determine whether to buy a cup of coffee and a sandwich or a cheer-up drink — both badly needed. It came up neither heads nor tails, instead rolled into a sidewalk grill. "And that dime looked as a $50 slug," said Massie walking away to hunt up another job.

The profits earned by the boat owners and captains were not distributed downward with any liberality. The boat crews, who strained to get the heavily laden craft over the shoals and shallow water and keep up the steam of the boilers, did not receive any substantial share of the profit pie. Nor did the men who chopped and piled the wood along the shoreline, to be loaded on the steamers as they passed up and down the river. An advertisement in the *Fort Benton Record* for August 24, 1877, notes the need for workers. It reads: "Woodchoppers wanted. Ten to chop and ten to put into the river. $1.50 per cord for choppers and $50 a month for assistants."

The lives of those men who supplied wood for the steamboats were lonely, hard, and dangerous. Their small camps were located at distant points along the river. Smoke from their fires and the sound of their axes betrayed them to marauding Indians, to whose depredations many lost their lives. During the years from 1867 to 1869 more than one-third of the woodchoppers were killed by Indians. The smallpox epidemic of 1869 devasted the Plains Indians, and thereafter the life of a woodchopper was not so dangerous.

The supply of wood was not endless. The cottonwoods grew along the Missouri, but beyond its banks were treeless prairies. When steamboating died on the Missouri, its banks were almost denuded from Fort Benton to Bismarck. The cottonwood was rapidly consumed by the fireboxes, for it burned very quickly. By the time the railroads came, the timber along the river was almost gone. Without another source of fuel, the river steamers soon would have gone out of business, even without the railroads.

Freight rates for cargo brought upriver in 1865 varied from 10 cents to 18 cents per pound. In 1866, with more boats, the rates averaged about 11 cents per pound. In 1871 a United States government contract was let at $3.36 per hundred pounds from St. Louis to Benton. This was somewhat lower than the rates for private individuals and business concerns. These rates remained about the same until the coming of the railroads.

The extension of the Northern Pacific Railroad into Bismarck, Dakota Territory in 1873 brought great changes in the transportation system serving the West. Bismarck replaced St. Louis as the rail terminal. Prior to the coming of the railroad, the town had been named Edwinton. The early town fathers thought that, by adopting the name of Germany's Iron Chancellor, they might attract the thrifty German settlers they needed so badly. The river boats plied between Bismarck and Fort Benton during the shipping season. In the fall they would return to St. Louis to avoid being frozen in for the winter. In the winter months, the boats were completely repaired and refurbished. During the short freighting season, each boat tried to make as many trips as possible. Only repairs necessary to keep them afloat and moving were made during the season. Anything that could wait was delayed until the boats returned to St. Louis in the fall for their idle period of some seven to eight months.

On April 28, 1878, the steamer *Big Horn* arrived at Fort Benton with a cargo taken on at St. Louis for its first trip of the year. This was the earliest arrival of record. The *Nellie Peck* came to Fort Benton on May 27, 1875, the latest spring arrival in 10 years. The *Helena* arrived at Fort Benton on September 6, 1878, which was the latest autumn arrival of record.

The water levels of the river established the shipping season. In years of high water, the big boats could reach Fort Benton early and make several trips before the water level fell in the fall and ice began to form in the winter. In years of low flow, the boats might reach Fort Benton on their initial trip in the spring. After the first trip to Fort Benton, if they had made it, the boats then would operate between Bismarck and Cow Island. There was usually enough water to accommodate the shallow-draft river boats between these two points, but in the driest years even this trip was risky and dangerous.

Cow Island was an important link in the transportation system that served Fort Benton. It was situated downstream from that town about 120 miles, and the river between the two points was too shallow for the river steamers to traverse, except during the period of high waters in the spring of the year. Most of the time the larger boats could make their first trip of the year all the way to Fort Benton to unload. As the level of the river dropped, half of the cargo might be unloaded at Cow Island to increase the buoyancy of the boat and allow it to make the trip to Fort Benton. Once unloaded, the boat might return to Cow Island and bring up the other half of the cargo.

When the river reached low level, all the cargo was unloaded at Cow Island and transported overland by wagon train. This route ran up Cow Creek Canyon, 32 miles of narrow, precipitous cliffs through which the trail wound and climbed up to the open prairie. It then turned across the prairie to the ford over the Marias River known as Big Sandy and then southward into Fort Benton.

The steamers could haul freight in to Cow Island faster than the wagon trains could haul it out. During the busy season, freight piled up at the unloading docks at Cow Island, sometimes in monumental mounds. It was reported that, in 1886, a cargo of beer froze while stored at Cow

52

Steamboat *Helena* at Cow Island on the Missouri River,
October 5, 1877 Courtesy Montana Historical Society

Island, and for a time beer was sold by the square foot as a solid mea-
surement rather than liquid. The Indians soon learned of this treasure
trove of food and merchandise, which they felt was theirs to steal. To
thwart the Indians and protect the cargo, Cow Island was fortified with
rifle pits, which during the shipping season were manned by soldiers
who guarded the government supplies and by the mountain men who
protected those of the private firms.

Michael Foley, who was one of these early guards and later a justice of
the peace at Belt, Montana, recalled (Montana Newspaper Association
Inserts, IV, 20) that Cow Island contained several hundred acres of land
and was covered with "as pretty a growth of cottonwoods as I ever saw."
Foley said that, in the early nineteenth century, some traders found a
lone cow on the island, hundreds of miles from any others of its kind. It
was supposed that she had been stolen from some white settlers in the
Middle West by Indians who drove it to the island, where it was left.
Whatever the source of the cow, her presence so impressed the traders
that the unnamed tract of land in the Missouri River was christened Cow
Island and so remains to this day.

Little of the history of Cow Island has been preserved. LeRoy Anderson and his late wife, Rena, of Chinook, Montana, have spent years
trying to uncover the Island's past and will one day publish what they
have learned. At the present most of what is known is gleaned from

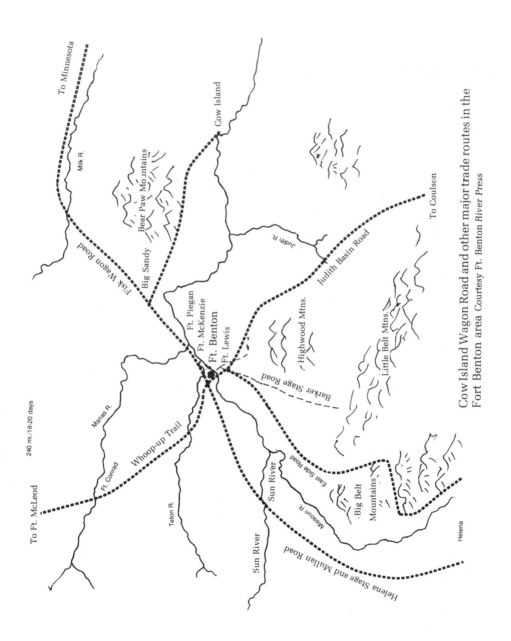

Cow Island Wagon Road and other major trade routes in the
Fort Benton area *Courtesy Ft. Benton River Press*

54

newspaper accounts of the battles fought with the Indians for the protection of the cargo stored on the Island, awaiting the arrival of the bull trains.

One of the most famous battles was fought between a small detachment of 12 soldiers, supplemented by four private guards, and the remnants of the Nez Perce as they retreated from the Battle of the Big Hole, trying to reach Canada.

Michael Foley was stationed at Cow Island as a clerk to oversee the shipment of freight to points all over Montana. On September 20, 1877, the U.S. government moved to Cow Island the commissary that had supplied the engineers working on Dauphin Rapids — in all 30 tons. Twelve soldiers were left to guard it. In addition, there were approximately 20 tons of privately owned cargo guarded by Foley and three others. The soldiers pitched a large tent on the mainland, on the east bank of the river. To guard against inclement weather, a 2½-foot trench was dug around the entire tent, with the excavated dirt mounded up on the outside of the trench.

At about three o'clock in the afternoon on September 23, a party of Indians appeared on the west bank of the river and crossed over, landing at a point upstream from the army camp. Chiefs Joseph and Looking Glass approached the camp, and Foley went to meet them. Joseph asked for whiskey and ammunition. He was told there was no whiskey and no ammunition to spare. He then asked for food, and Foley told him to take what he wanted from the pile. The squaws were called, and they diminished the pile considerably, taking it over the brow of the hill and out of sight.

The Indians then left. Foley scouted their camp and saw the warriors, almost 300 in number, preparing for an attack. He returned to camp and warned that an attack could be expected about sundown and that their only fortification was the tent-trench dug by the soldiers. The little group of 16 hauled water, food, and ammunition into the trenches and sat back, ill-fortified and hopelessly outnumbered.

The attack came at sundown and was repulsed. Joseph urged his braves on again and again, but the fire from the ditch threw them back each time. Then Joseph sent the squaws to carry off more of the supplies, awaiting complete darkness for another attack. When the Indians had pilfered the pile of all they could carry, the rest was set afire. There were 250 sacks of bacon in the freight pile, and when the bacon began to burn, the flames leaped high in the air, illuminating the surrounding area. The light revealed any maneuvers the Indians sought to make.

The fight lasted until 10 o'clock the following morning. Then the Indians buried their dead and withdrew. Chief Joseph said later that this was the toughest fight of his life and that he could not understand how only 16 men could withstand all of the warriors of his tribe. The defenders suffered one casualty, a soldier shot in the shoulder.

Later that morning, a detachment of soldiers and citizens from Fort Benton arrived. Their commander was Major Guido Ilges. He wanted the group of defenders to join him in the chase after the Indians. Foley advised him not to cross the river and not to follow the Nez Perces. With only 75 men, they could not hope seriously to challenge the 300 fighting men of Chief Joseph. According to Foley, Ilges ignored his advice and followed the Indians. They were saved only by the fact that Joseph thought they were the advance guard of General O. O. Howard's command. Foley said, "As it was, one man got killed and the volunteers came back to Cow Island pell-mell and went home."

No one will ever know the number of tons of freight that passed through Cow Island on its way to stock the merchants of Fort Benton, who sent it thence to supply the pioneers of Montana and Canada. The Indians gave the Island its name and, had it not been for the newspaper accounts of their depredations, we would have no recorded history of the time when it played an important role in the settlement of the West.

CHAPTER 13
Red Cloud, Queen of the River

All of the Missouri River boats serving Fort Benton were of shallow-draft design, which evolved from the experience of the boat captains. Improvements conceived by these men during the summer were, as far as possible, incorporated into the old boats during their winter stay in St. Louis and always were used in the design and building of new boats. Many of these designs were attributed to Captain William Massie, who was widely recognized as the most competent master on the river.

The shipping season on the Missouri was about four months. If a merchant did not receive his goods during that period, he had nothing to sell during the late fall, winter, and early spring. Attracted by both the potential profits and a dependable supply of merchandise, the Conrads and T. C. Power entered the transportation business on the Missouri River with the same enthusiasm and vigor that characterized all of their business activities.

In 1875 the two firms purchased the steamboat *Benton* and put it into service on the Missouri. It was the most comfortable and the fastest boat on the river. It was also the most dependable. The *Benton* made 59 trips to Fort Benton between 1875 and 1887, a record never equalled by any other boat. In 1876 the *Benton* left St. Louis on March 28 and arrived at Fort Benton on May 15. This trip of 49 days was faster than the other boats on the river, which made the *Benton* the most popular passenger boat then in service. She was essentially a cargo ship capable of carrying more freight than any of her competitors. In June of 1884, she took on 250 tons of wool, bullion, grain, and merchandise, which was the largest cargo ever loaded out of Fort Benton.

The Conrads bought the *Red Cloud* in 1876 for $25,000 cash. Built in 1873 at Jeffersonville, Indiana, for the Tennessee River fleet, it was extensively remodeled during that winter. The length was extended 50 feet, making her 228 feet long, with powerful engines and a moderately shallow draft. She was to become a fierce competitor and supplanted the *Benton* as the most popular boat on the river.

In the spring of 1877, the *Red Cloud*, with Captain Smith at the helm, left St. Louis ahead of the *Benton*. On her first trip she was passed by the *Benton*, commanded by Captain William Massie, which arrived at Fort Benton on May 8. The *Benton* returned to Bismarck and on her second, upriver trip under Massie set a record of 11 days and one hour to Fort Benton. After this trip, Massie took over the *Red Cloud* and returned her to Bismarck to load. On the first trip back from Bismarck to Benton, Captain Massie and the crew laid the cottonwood to her and made the trip in 9 days and 23 hours, arriving at Fort Benton on July 11. This was 18 hours and 45 minutes faster than any boat had ever made the run. On her next trip from Bismarck, the *Red Cloud* did even better, arriving at Fort Benton on July 18, only 8 days and 17 hours out of Bismarck, for a record that was never bettered.

The *Fort Benton Record* (Date) told of this record-making run and printed the log of the journey:

> Left Bismarck on the morning of the first at 9 o'clock. Tied up first night at Big Knife River; second, below the slide; third, above Tobacco Gardens; fourth, above the mouth of the Yellowstone; fifth, two bends below Poplar Creek; sixth, at Porcupine Creek; seventh, first bend below Ponchett's grave; eighth, ran all night without stopping; ninth, laid up at Fort Benton at 15 minutes before nine on the morning of the 11th, drawing three feet eight inches of water.

On this trip she carried 175 tons of freight and 15 passengers.

The *Red Cloud* was an outstanding boat when there was plenty of water in the river during spring, but her size and draft prevented profitable operation during low-water years and in the fall. This left the Baker Company without dependable river transportation in these seasons. The volume of its Canadian trade at this time made it imperative that it be able to obtain supplies well into the fall. So the Conrad brothers designed and had built the *Colonel Macleod*, a steamer that solved the troublesome problem of low water and that extended their season almost until ice formed on the river.

In 1878 the Conrads put the *Colonel Macleod* into service between Bismarck and Fort Benton. She was named for Colonel James F. Macleod, who commanded and helped to shape the future of the Royal Canadian Mounted Police. Because of his friendship with C. E. Conrad, most of the police supplies were bought from the I. G. Baker Company, so the honor was well-deserved. With this new ship, they hoped to extend the season of river traffic. The larger and older boats were usually forced to unload at Cow Island in the late summer because of the low flow. The long overland haul from Cow Island to Fort Benton was expensive, slow, and dangerous. An extension of the season could save thousands of dollars for the I. G. Baker Company.

The *Colonel Macleod* was new in design and construction. It was built in Cincinnati, Ohio, of white-oak logs — 80 to 100 feet in length, and

Advertisement for I. G. Baker Freight Line Courtesy John G. Lepley

reputed to be tough as whalebone — to withstand submerged snags which were an ever-present danger in the treacherous river. All of her machinery was extremely powerful and lighter than the conventional design. The *Colonel Macleod* was one of the first boats in which steel was substituted for iron. She was successful in extending the season. Her last trip in 1878 ended on November 23, creating almost a two-month extension of the usual steamboat traffic.

The *Colonel Macleod* made 13 trips to Fort Benton in 1888 and 1889, mostly in low-water months. Her sturdy construction withstood the vagaries of the river, but she fell prey to carelessness. On November 18, 1879, while docked at Bismarck, the steamer *Butte* toppled from her stays, struck the *Colonel Macleod*, and sank her in 8 feet of water. The damage was too extensive to repair. Her career ended under the waters that she had skimmed so lightly.

The *Red Cloud* remained the queen of the river, but she, too, was ill-fated. Following the loss of the *Colonel Macleod*, the *Red Cloud* became the workhorse as well as the flagship of the I. G. Baker Company, averaging over 300 tons per upriver trip and as many as 300 passengers. In 1882, after wintering in St. Louis, she brought to Fort Benton a full load of cargo and 330 passengers, 205 of whom were Mounted Police.

On July 12, 1882, the *Red Cloud* was headed upriver from Bismarck to Fort Benton, fully loaded. A short distance from Fort Peck, she hit a submerged snag which tore out one of her sides, and she sank in three minutes. No lives were lost, and she remained intact long enough to salvage part of the cargo, but not the 3,000 sacks of flour she was carrying. Salvaged was a large copper bell. The bell was donated to the Episcopal Church at Bismarck, where it was placed in the steeple to call church meetings, rather than to announce to Fort Benton that the *Red Cloud* would soon be rounding the bend of the river bringing new supplies and new people for the settlement of the West. The splendid ship lay derelict until it finally broke up in a spring flood, and her remains were scattered far down the Missouri River.

The *Red Cloud* was not replaced by the Conrads. The year 1882 was the beginning of the decline in Missouri River traffic that ended completely with the coming of the railroads. Thereafter, the I. G. Baker Company leased boats or contracted with other transportation firms, until it closed its vast merchandising and transportation operations in 1891.

On June 12, 1890, water transportation to Fort Benton was finished forever. On that day the *F. Y. Batchelor* brought in the last commercial cargo and whistled the last departure. Perhaps it was fitting that the *Batchelor's* whistle was the last heard. May G. Flanagan recalled that "the *Batchelor* had a plaintive, wailing whistle, which made us sad as the boat gave a last toot on disappearing around the bend of the river."

The whistle sound certainly matched the mood of the Fort Benton people, who realized that the preeminence of their town as a hub of transportation had ended.

The I. G. Baker Company had one other boat on the river. On August 17, 1907, the little steamer, OK, docked at Fort Benton. She was a small excursion boat, brought in more for nostalgia than for utility. The Baker bad luck with boats plagued her too. She caught fire on June 30, 1908, and not even nostalgia saved her from destruction.

Water traffic on the Missouri was an enormous business. From a small beginning of 10 tons in 1831, traffic increased to the high of 14,000 tons in 1881. Joel Overholser has estimated that from 1831 to 1890, 152,159 tons came upriver and 28,554 went down. During the early years, down-river tonnage far exceeded upriver tonnage. From 1831 to 1858, an annual average of 20 tons went upriver and 200 downriver. During these years the area was occupied primarily by trappers who needed few supplies but who dispatched large quantities of furs and buffalo hides — 418,500 of the latter from 1831 to 1858.

The year 1862 saw a reversal of this traffic pattern. In that year 1,000 tons came upriver and 200 tons went downriver. This was the year that gold was discovered, and gold seekers and those who supplied them started to pour into the region. This reversal continued to be ever more disparate. From 1862 to 1890, there was an annual average of about 5,000 tons carried upstream and about 900 tons shipped downriver. Over-holser estimates that the I. G. Baker Company handled about one-third of the total, which explains in some measure the size of its operations.

During the steamboat years, there were 102 different boats competing for a share of the river traffic. Their names ranged from Nymph to St. Peter. Fifty-four were named for women, the name "Kate" being the most popular. The St. Peter belied its name when it brought in smallpox and precipitated an epidemic that devastated the Plains Indians and almost destroyed the Blackfeet.

In addition to the steamship Benton, the Conrads and T. C. Power shared ownership of the Benton Transportation Company, which owned and operated the Thwang House Hotel and the Choutcau House in Fort Benton. They worked harmoniously in the businesses they owned to-gether. In the operation of their separate businesses, they were fierce competitors, not disdaining a little deception. In an undated letter, William wrote Charles about the bidding on freight hauls in Central Montana. On one haul, the proceeds of which was to be split between the Conrads with Power, William cautioned, "Don't say how much we get out of Broadwater for Power thinks it is only $1,000.00."

In the spring of 1876, the United States was nearing its centennial and plans for the commemoration of this event were being made all over the

The *Rosebud* Courtesy John G. Lepley

nation. Fort Benton had reason to celebrate. The gloom of 1870 was past and forgotten. Business was booming; the Canadian trade was increasing each year, and cattle were coming into Montana Territory in increasing numbers.

The Chouteau County livestock industry had begun earlier in the 1870s, when a freight outfit had to winter in Fort Benton with no hay available for the livestock. The wagon master turned the bull teams loose in the shelter of the Highwood Mountains to rustle for themselves, never thinking that the animals would survive the severe Montana winter. In the spring a half-hearted search was made to find the oxen. To the surprise of everyone, they were found not far from the place they had been turned loose in the late fall — fat, healthy and ready for work. The grass that sustained the buffalo remained nourishing throughout the winter, and the oxen thrived on it. The existence of wide-open spaces and nutritious grass became more widely known, and soon cattle by the droves were coming in from Texas, Oregon, and from wherever they could be found and driven. In addition to the space and grass, more profit could be made by raising a steer in Montana than in Texas, because of the former's more nutritious grass and better markets.

Charles Goodnight, a Texas cattleman, made a comparison of the Montana and Texas costs, which was reprinted in the *Fort Benton Record* in January 1882.

62

THE TEXAS ESTIMATE

Interest on value of one cow at $12.50 for one year at 10%...........$ 1.25
Cost of sirage (services of graded bull) 1.50
Holding cow and calf on range one year and branding......................1.50
Holding steer two years and six months..2.50
Taxes for three years at 5 cents per year.. .15
Driving to Kansas Market (Caldwell or Humbolt) .... .50
Proportion of animal loss on herd...1.35
$ 8.75
Value of steer 3½ years old in Kansas market.................................23.00

Net profit $14.25

MONTANA ESTIMATE

Interest on value of one cow at $20.00 for one year at 15%...........$ 3.00
Cost of sirage...2.50
Holding cow and calf one year and branding 1.50
Holding steer two and one-half years...2.50
Taxes for three years at 21 cents per year... .63
Driving to local market (Western Territory).. .50
Proportion of animal loss estimated on herd......................................2.00
$12.63
Value of 3½-year-old steer in Montana market 28.00

Net profit $15.27

CHAPTER 14
Fort Benton's First Newspaper

In 1875 Fort Benton acquired its first newspaper, the *Fort Benton Record*, with W. H. Buck as editor. The first issue came out on February 1, 1875. In his announcement and statement of policy, Editor Buck wrote:

> It is with feelings of deepest pleasure and a full sense of responsibility that we present to the public of Montana the first number of *The Fort Benton Record*, a journal to be devoted to the interests of Benton, Sun River and adjacent country. It was intended to be a journal wholly devoted to the advance of temperance but recent inquiries have assured us that such an enterprise cannot as yet be sustained. Friends of the cause may rest assured, however, that our interest in the good work is not in the least abated and while we cannot in this Journal give expression to sentiments that might prove distasteful to this community to which we look for support, we shall never oppose those principles which we know to be just and right and which are too firmly implanted in our nature to be eradicated by the motive of self-interest.

Editor Buck would have needed few inquiries to find that a temperance journal in Fort Benton would be short-lived. Fort Benton and whiskey grew and prospered together. Whiskey was indispensable, both as a trade item and as a palliative to ease the hardships and dangers of frontier life. It was a preferred item of cargo. Food, fuel, and other necessities might be left at the docks in St. Louis or Bismarck, but never whiskey. Having lost this battle, Editor Buck was later able to convince himself that revenues from whiskey ads did not compromise his firmly implanted principles or indicate any motive of self-interest.

In June of 1875, the *Fort Benton Record* reported:

> The recent activity in our streets has suggested the balmy days of '67 and '68. Our town has been flat on its back for several years but at last good times have come again and all feel sanguine that a new era of prosperity has begun. In this connection we will express the hope that our citizens will not forget there is nothing like a newspaper to advance the town in distant regions and thus bring additions to our population and wealth.

Benton is all business. The river is hid by a wall of freight, the streets are almost impassable with teams, while clerks, roustabouts, dogs and pigs make up a scene at once amusing and interesting.

The steamboats hauled freight in faster than the bull trains could haul it out. On June 24, 1876, the *Fort Benton Record* noted that there were 700 tons piled on the levee waiting to be loaded out and that there were 106 undelivered letters. I. G. Baker and Company made a dent in the pile when, in June, their mule trains pulled out with 30,000 pounds for Fort Macleod. William must have liked mules, for the July 14, 1876, issue of the *Record* reported:

By a late transaction between Messrs. John Powers and W. G. Conrad, the latter gentleman became the proud owner of a fine pair of carriage mules.

On July 4, 1876, Fort Benton and the nation celebrated their Centennial. Benton had no Liberty Bell to ring, no Bunker Hill to climb, no Delaware River to cross, nor did it have the many politicians of the East Coast to make ringing speeches. However, it celebrated the event with a gusto characteristic of Western frontier towns. The ladies, too, had prepared. On June 12, the *Fort Benton Record* commented:

Style in dress exhibited by the ladies of Fort Benton is not inferior to that of the great cities of the country. Our merchants are to be commended for introducing into this market all of the latest fashion of Parisian or any other known originals. Besides, we have a style of dress particularly our own.

The Centennial celebration started early and lasted late. Whiskey, patriotism, and optimism provided the fuel that stoked the activities. Jacob A. Kanouse, one of the town's attorneys, was chosen to give the Fourth of July oration. In a burst of optimism — probably laced with whiskey and the prescience of a typical lawyer — Kanouse predicted that Fort Benton would develop into a great hub of commerce and one day would become the "Chicago of the Plains." Optimism was endemic on the early frontier and a necessary ingredient to life. Posterity was a far-off thing associated with peoples and areas where roots were planted deep. On the frontier, a man's fortunes were in his own hands and could be short-lived. Time was a contemporary and personal thing that might end tomorrow, which was to many the far horizon.

Editor Buck may have avoided a temperance fight, but in other things the size of the adversary did not cow him. He had little sympathy for the Indians or those who did. He felt that President Ulysses S. Grant's Indian policy amounted to molly coddling. When T. C. Power gave support to Grant's policy, Buck started to oppose Power in almost everything he did. In the September 10, 1877 issue of the *Record* Buck said, "General mismanagement is the officer who seems to be in charge of Indian affairs in the United States."

I. G. Baker and Company had a small cannon at its store on Front Street. When a steamer appeared around the bent east of town, the

THE BENTON RECORD.

VOX POPULI, VOX DEI.

VOL. I. Benton, M. T., February 1, 1875. NO. 1.

Masthead of the first edition of *The Benton Record*
Courtesy Montana Historical Society

cannon was fired. Buck liked this custom, as the sound carried into his office. On June 1, 1875, he wrote:

At 15 minutes past 5, May 27, 1875, the small cannon at I. G. Baker and Co. was fired to announce the arrival of the first steamboat of the season, the *Nellie Peck*. The *Benton* came in at 10. This was the first arrival of the *Benton* and the latest arrival in 10 years.

The late arrival presaged a good year. On December 11, 1881, the following item appeared in the *Record*:

December is perhaps the dullest month in Fort Benton yet our merchants have all the business they can well attend to and there is work for all who want it.

That Editor Buck had a sense of humor, of sorts, and a flair for frontier journalism is attested by the following random quotes from his paper:

Since the swine law came into force, all the hogs have disappeared from Front Street. Nothing personal in this item.

Can ladies with enameled faces be said to belong to a polished society?

No Chinese bank has failed for 500 years. When the last failure took place, the officers' heads were cut off and flung into a corner with the other assets. A good thing to bear in mind.

The first original poem of the season was received yesterday. We regret that a great press of business prevented its publication, but it did very nicely for the office boy to wrap around his mince pie.

66

Buck also was a supporter of women's rights:

> Store girls all over the country are taking a firm stand on the sit down question. They have the support of the general public.

And not one to waste his money, he mourned that the *Record* had paid $7.50 to Wells Fargo to ship a $3.50 subscription book. Had it been shipped on the steamer *Benton*, it would have arrived three days earlier at a cost of about 12 cents.

On March 30, 1877, the *Fort Benton Record*, in screaming headlines, announced a new "gold discovery." Memories still lingered in the minds of those who had experienced the gold rush days and the fortunes they produced. There was always hope of new discoveries and new rushes, so it was not difficult to arouse the interests of editors and gold seekers. The *Record* stated that engineers believed that untold millions in gold lay in the bed of the Missouri River below the Great Falls. To get this treasure, the Missouri River Falls Exploring Company had been formed, with one million dollars in capital. The company was headquartered at 14 Wall Street in New York. It was "positively known" that Cornelius Vanderbilt was only prevented by long illness and death from being the head of the new company. In 1874 he had sent men to Fort Benton to explore the possibilities. They posed as hunters and fishermen and spent several weeks investigating the project.

The plan was to turn the river into a new channel five miles above the falls and obtain access to the old bed, thus laying bare "the untold millions of gold now lying under the foaming waters." The *Record* predicted "that in a few weeks Benton will be swarming with busy strangers and reaping the benefits to which its location entitles it."

The project must have died aborning, for all mention of it soon disappeared from the *Record*. Not even the magic name of Cornelius Vanderbilt could keep it afloat. The craze for gold caused men to believe it was worthwhile to tame and turn a mighty river on the hope that gold might be found in its old bed. Not all the people in Fort Benton believed. The successful merchants knew that their gold would continue to be found in trade. But even they were willing to chart new courses, if there were a reasonable chance for profits.

The editor of the *Record* could condone a major assault upon the river 30 miles upstream, but was a jealous guardian of its banks at Fort Benton. In the April 27, 1877 issue, the town's residents were scolded for taking gravel from the levee and causing damage to the river banks. If anyone needed gravel, it should be taken from the hills back of town, not from the banks of the Missouri River.

From its start in 1875 until it went broke and was sold at sheriff's sale in 1885, the *Record* faithfully recorded the history of Fort Benton as it unfolded before the eyes of Editor Buck. In 1879, Buck promised the largest newspaper in Montana. He did it, with nine columns in width and 28 inches long. After he went broke, Editor Buck went to New York. He returned to Fort Benton the next year and tried to get reestablished in the newspaper business, both in Fort Benton and Choteau, but failed in both. On October 25, 1883, the *Fort Benton River Press* reported that W. H. Buck was a clerk in the Superior Court in New York at a salary of $2,000.00 a year. Probably more than he ever made from the *Record* at Fort Benton.

CHAPTER 15
The Early Cattle Business

In 1878 the Conrads plunged into the cattle business with an initial investment of more than $500,000. Soon they owned thousands of cattle divided among the different cattle companies that they organized. By this time their parents, brothers, and sisters had come to Fort Benton. Brothers and brothers-in-law were absorbed by their various enterprises. At one time, in conjunction with family members, they owned the Conrad-Price Cattle Company, managed by Charles Price, husband of the Conrads' sister, Mollie. They operated also the Million Dollar Cattle Company, the Conrad-Harris Cattle Company, the Conrad-Stanford Cattle Company, and the Conrad Circle Cattle Company — in all of which relatives shared ownership and management.

The Conrad Circle Cattle Company became one of the largest and best-known cattle outfits on the Western plains. On December 16, 1906, the *Great Falls Tribune* told of the formation, in 1882, of the Benton and St. Louis Cattle Company by the Conrad brothers. It was capitalized at $500,000 and, within two years, had the largest herd in Montana Territory. This company was later renamed the Conrad Circle Cattle Company. When the corporation was finally dissolved, in 1911, it had paid out $1,600,000 in dividends, most of the dividends being paid before the turn of the century.

As trade in Fort Benton dwindled, the Conrads increasingly centered their interests in cattle. They worked assiduously to cultivate good relations with the Canadian officials responsible for letting contracts for supplying beef to the Mounted Police and the reservation Indians. They were especially friendly with Colonel Macleod, Commissioner of the Mounted Police, and Lieutenant Governor Edgar Dewdney. Both men were given interests in some of the many businesses operated by the Conrads. In addition, the brothers contributed liberally to candidates for Canadian public office whom they thought might help them obtain beef contracts. In April, 1891, William Conrad, then in White Post, Virginia, wrote to his brother, Charles:

> I am glad you contributed $500 towards John's election. It will be money well spent. I wrote him a letter congratulating him. I got three letters from

Mr. Dewdney wanting us to help out Davis. I telegraphed Curry and told him to instruct Macleod to carry out Mr. Dewdney's wishes. I also got a letter yesterday saying Parliament would meet the 29th and that tenders would be out soon and a copy would be sent to us. I think we ought to get the beef contract and turn every cow into beef but I will write you as soon as I get the tenders more fully and want your ideas about it.

The terms of the Canadian contracts were favorable to the Conrads. The vast quantities of beef required tended to eliminate all but the largest cattle outfits. The contracts usually called for steers "double wintered in Montana." This was not a gimmick to sell Montana beef but a recognition of its higher quality. The cattle sold by these contracts was mostly grass-fed. The buffalo grass of Montana was so nutritious that it produced better beef than competing areas. A three-year-old critter "double wintered in Montana" meant that it had been eating Montana grass for at least two years and would make beef of a better quality. In 1880 the Conrads furnished over 5,500,000 pounds of beef under these contracts. Their favors to Canadian officials might allow them to fudge a little, as is indicated by a letter from William to Charles, dated April 14, 1891:

The Indian contracts are to be let on May 9. I would like your ideas what we had better bid. I do not care about the price but would like to know if you don't think, as I do, that we should get these contracts and work off our cattle. I think too we can collect some accounts by having the contract and take cattle and turn them into beef. I am sure we can use over 10% cows and this would be a sale of 2000 head of cattle. If cattle get high, all we have to do is sell our best steers and put others in our contracts.

On April 18, 1891, William wrote to Charles:

I enclose one set of blanks for bidding on Indian supplies. ... I noticed they take 25% cows at 20% discount and prefer double wintered cattle and an affidavit should be furnished that they are raised in Montana and double wintered in Montana. ... Looks like beef will be high this year, but we could work off rough cattle and some cows on this.

That a few problems arose is shown in an undated letter, written by Charles to His Honor, Commissioner of Indian Affairs, Ottawa, Canada:

Referring to the previous correspondence relative to the "offal" of cattle billed to the Indian Reserve under the contract, we would respectfully ask that early and favorable consideration may be given to our claim. The contract states, that the hides and offal of all animals killed on the reserve shall be the property of the Indian Department. The Indian agents in the Northwest have insisted upon our delivering to them as offal and without payment, the tongues, liver and tallow. We submit that these parts should not be considered as offal. And, inasmuch as they are issued to the Indians as beef, we should be allowed their weight as beef. We submit that what is offal to the Indians may be offal to us and what is issued to the Indians as beef may be allowed to us as beef. The average weight of the parts for which we ask payment is 40 pounds per animal. Although beef has steadily increased in price, we have spared the offal to carry out our contracts to the letter.

As the open range in the United States dwindled because of settlement, the large cattle companies started moving into Canada. They were welcomed at first, but with the coming of the railroads, agitation started for settlement of the prairies of Alberta. In 1886 it was announced that John Conrad, a brother, had leased 900,000 acres and would run 10,000 head of cattle. The Conrads had two brands in Canada, one in the name of W. G. Conrad and the other in the name of the I. G. Baker and Company. One range was on the south slope of the Cypress Hills and the other on the Little Bow River.

In November of 1886, the *Macleod Gazette* stated that: "2,098,670 acres in Alberta were under lease for grazing to 58 cattle companies who paid $2,008.42 in rentals, being but half penny per acre." This paper strongly opposed the leasing policies of the Canadian government and favored opening the lands for settlement. Cattle operators did not advertise in the papers. Settlers and those who served them might. The leases were for long periods, usually 20 years, one head of cattle per acre. Because of the size of the lease, the cattlemen could not keep sufficient cattle on the range to meet this requirement. The cattlemen had enough political influence to have this minimum raised to one head per 20 acres but could not meet even this requirement.

As the railroads brought in more people wanting to settle, the agitation for lease cancellation grew stronger. Almost every issue of all Canadian papers demanded cancellation of the leases and opening the land for settlement.

The hard winter of 1886-1887 took a terrible toll of the range cattle. The *Macleod Gazette* reported in its January 18, 1887 issue that the summer of 1886 had been long and hot, which dried up the grass. There were heavy rains in the fall which froze. On top of this ice came snows which hardened into crusts the cattle could not break through. Then came cold winds and long blizzard conditions, which killed the cattle by the hundreds of thousands, both in the United States and Canada. In response, to an inquiry as to how the cattle survived, Charles Russell replied with the now-famous post card on which he drew a single, thin, starving cow and the message, "Waiting for a Chinook," a title later changed to "The Last of the 5000."

There was no way for the rancher to restock in a hurry. In 1888, Edgar Dewdney, then Canadian Minister of the Interior, started to cancel leases for noncompliance, applying the provisions of one animal per 20 acres. There followed a wholesale cancellation of leases. The *Macleod Gazette* announced, on September 12, 1888, that leases on 660,000 acres had been cancelled by Dewdney for noncompliance. The power of the press outweighed with Dewdney the past favors he had received from the Conrads.

This hard winter proved how important the famous Chinook winds were to the cattlemen. On March 1, 1887, the *Macleod Gazette* reported that:

> The long looked for Chinook came in earnest on Sunday night. It blew with terrific force all day Sunday and Monday. Sunday morning the snow was nearly all gone but the drifts, and by night only the larger drifts remained. Nearly all the windows of the I. G. Baker and Co. were blown out doing considerable damage to the goods. The winter started people thinking about smaller herds with more owners and is a strong argument against the leasing laws.

Had the Chinook come in January, the herds would have survived, and the history of Canada might have been different.

The Conrads built up their herds, bringing in new cattle from Texas and Oregon. In 1891 they were again supplying thousands of cattle to the Canadian government on contracts to supply beef to the Indians and the Mounted Police. But when Charles died, in 1902, William's interest in the cattle business died with him.

CHAPTER 16
The Stanfords

The year 1879 was important in the personal life of Charles E. Conrad. His long-time friend, James Stanford, was an officer of the Mounted Police, stationed at Fort Macleod, south of present-day Calgary. He had dealt with Charles Conrad in the procurement of supplies and the two had become friends. In June of 1879, an Indian runner came to Fort Benton with a message from Stanford to Conrad. Stanford's mother, sister, and younger brother were to arrive in Fort Benton on the steamboat *Red Cloud*. Stanford had intended to meet them and get them established, but due to an Indian uprising, he was unable to leave. He asked Conrad to meet his family and get them settled in their new home in Fort Benton.

Stanford's mother was born Catherine Elizabeth Alicia Coggin in Derby, England, in 1830. She spent the early part of her life in the beautiful apple country of Kent County and always retained a love of this part of England. She was the thirteenth in line having the name Alicia, but always went by the name Catherine. The first Alicia lived in London in the latter part of the year 1600. She married a man named Tyson. Both were of Saxon origin and in that language the original spelling of the name meant "princess of foreign birth."

At an early age, she and her older brother lost both of their parents. Her brother was apprenticed to a cartoonist and engraver in London. The engraver's name was Cruckshank and he was famous for the cartoons which were used to illustrate the works of Charles Dickens. The brother died of the plague, leaving Catherine completely alone. She then went to live with an uncle in London. Her life with this old bachelor was a rather lonely one. Kindly and well-meaning though he was, the uncle was totally unequipped to give the love and understanding that was needed by a refined English girl-child.

The uncle supervised her education. At that time all well-bred English girls were schooled in manners and marriage. They also had to learn French and become accomplished in music. Manners the uncle could teach and did, but his course on marriage was somewhat deficient, for in

Catherine Stanford
Courtesy University of Montana Library

this he was an inexperienced tutor. Catherine became very accomplished in both French and music. She spoke French fluently and became a concert-level pianist.

Catherine lived a life of refinement and ease in England. She was a superb horsewoman and loved the hunt, where gaily dressed hunters rode after the hounds as they chased foxes over the English countryside.

Along with a venturesome spirit, she had that longing for family ties that so often exists in those people who grow up alone and lonely. Most of her family had migrated to America, searching for religious freedom. One family member, William Penn, had founded Pennsylvania, and there were cousins scattered along the Eastern seaboard. This longing created in her a burning desire to go to America to be with her cousins, an idea that seemed totally barbaric to her uncle. Catherine's craving for America could not be stayed, so the uncle, with grave misgivings, finally gave his consent, but absolutely forbade her to travel alone.

Chaperones to America were hard to come by in London in that day.

James Stanford
Courtesy University of Montana

Refined people thought of the new country as vulgar and common, peopled by the dregs of English society. Catherine was almost in despair until she met Guglielmo Marconi. The young Italian was in London, where he was perfecting and propagandizing his idea for the wireless. He was going to America in connection with this same business and offered to be Catherine's chaperone on the boat trip across the Atlantic. This doubled her uncle's trauma, for not only was Catherine's chosen chaperone a man, but surely a dangerous idiot if he believed messages could be sent through the air over long distances. Catherine's hard determination soon eroded the uncle's opposition, so she set sail for America with Marconi as her chaperone.

It is not known if Catherine ever contacted her Quaker relatives in Philadelphia, but she did find adventure, marriage, and happiness. The ship docked at Lynn, Massachusetts, where almost immediately she met a young musician named James Stanford, who was to give a violin concert at Lynn. As though preordained for Catherine's benefit, Stanford's accompanist became too ill to perform, so the young violinist

75

asked her to substitute for him. This she did, evidently with much skill, for he asked her to go with him on the rest of his tour as his accompanist. The venturesome spirit that had brought her to America prompted her to accept.

The mutual love of music shared by Stanford and Catherine was a bond that ripened quickly into love even though he was older by 26 years. They were married and made their home in Halifax, Nova Scotia. Stanford then decided that the concert tour was not the life he wished to live as a family man.

Family he did have. At the time that Stanford and Catherine were married, he had seven daughters, all older than their new stepmother, and all beautiful and talented. Despite the differences in age, Catherine and her stepdaughters got along well. None of the seven ever married and all held responsible positions. The daughters never saw Catherine after she moved to Fort Benton, but, after her daughter, Alicia, married C. E. Conrad, the Conrads visited in Halifax several times, always seeing the seven sisters. There was always a strong bond between Alicia Conrad and her seven stepsisters, and the bond was extended to Charles Conrad after their marriage. James and Catherine had four children, all born in Halifax, Alicia in 1853, James in 1856, George in 1858 and Harry in 1868.

Halifax was an important shipping center. The business of the city revolved around ships that brought in and carried out cargo that originated and was destined for ports all over the world. James Stanford saw that there were fortunes to be made, so he went into shipping with the same gusto that he had bestowed upon his violin. In time he had vessels in all of the important waterways of the world.

Hides were an important cargo. The hides were sent to the cities of Europe to be made into shoes, which were then shipped back for sale in the United States and Canada. Stanford became interested in the leather-making process and spent some time in Russia to learn the art of making Cordovan leather. He established a tannery in Halifax, which became famous for this product. He eventually had six large sailing ships carrying his leather to all parts of the world. On the return trips, the ships would carry the supplies and products to fill the insatiable appetite of the ever-expanding new world.

Hard times came and he was struggling to save his ventures at the time of his death, which was sudden and unexpected. One evening while reading Dickens to his family, he suffered a fatal heart attack. With no background in business, Catherine was unable to save the various enterprises he had started. The businesses went into bankruptcy, one by one, leaving the little family in genteel poverty.

Catherine's older sons had gone west. James Stanford was in Alberta, where he was helping to create the Royal Canadian Mounted Police.

George had gone to Australia in search of adventure and would remain there for 17 years before rejoining his family in Montana. The only daughter, the fourteenth Alicia, went to live with relatives in Chester, a town far from Halifax. Catherine Stanford and 11-year-old Harry, or Hal, stayed in Halifax, very poor and discouraged. Somehow the decision was made that the family would move west and join James, who at that time was the only settled, stable member of the family. More important, he was the only one with any money. The arrangements were difficult and lengthy. Catherine Stanford, so distraught that she was unable to arrive at any decisions, left the planning to her son, James, and daughter, Alicia.

In 1878 James tried to move the family to Fort Benton. This attempt failed, probably for a lack of money. Young Alicia was greatly disappointed. She was miserable where she was and longed to start a new life away from the scene of her father's bankruptcy and the unhappy aftermath. On January 14, 1879, James wrote to Alicia:

> Dear Sis: I can guess pretty well what you have to put up with but never mind, Sis, your troubles are nearly over and you can rest assured I won't fool you as I did last spring. The only thing that bothers me much is bringing you out to this country. There are some very nice ladylike women here who will treat you ver kindly, but the men, Good Lord, the men. Diogenes might hunt here with his lantern forever.

> I am glad you tried to spend Christmas as well as you could and to keep up the old Christmas tree custom. We had a public Christmas tree here. I was one of the Committee. My presents consisted of a mitten and a carrot.

This time the plans would work out. On February 10, 1879, James again wrote his sister:

> Dear Letty: The balls and parties have at last given you time to write, have they? I mailed to you on the 7th a letter of instructions regarding your coming out to me. I also sent a duplicate letter to Mother on the 9th in case one gets lost. Tell Mother I will enclose to her today 3 post office orders for $50.00 each, making a total of $150.00. Tell her also that tomorrow I will send her two P.O. orders of $50.00, making a total for her two days of $250.00. Tell her the reason I do not send a letter with the orders is because it is against the Post Office's rules to send a money order with a letter. Tell her to acknowledge receipt of the money orders as soon as they arrive so as to set my mind at ease. Tell her that all she will have to pay will be your passage and freight from Rochester to Pittsburg. I have arranged about the fare and freight on steamboat. The surplus money is to make you presentable. Dress yourself as well as you can with what you have to spare but be sure to leave enough to pay all expenses to Pittsburg and for washing on the river. Now thank God, I feel pretty much at rest and anxiously wait until I get a letter from you saying that you are all safe on board steamboat. Don't come out here prepared to work for a living as I guess it will take both of you all your time to keep house for me. Very curious about Benton? Well, it is better than Chester anyway and is growing rapidly every day.

Stanford Tannery in Halifax, Nova Scotia Courtesy University of Montana Library

Did Hal get his dressing case? And is he pleased with it? Love to Mother and Hal and I hope you're all happy at the proposal of seeing your affectionate brother and son.

Everything worked as planned. After getting to Pittsburg, the little Stanford family traveled by boat across the United States to Fort Benton on three rivers — the Ohio from Pittsburg to Cairo, Illinois, then upriver on the Mississippi to St. Louis, then up the Missouri to Fort Benton. On such a long trip it is understandable that James would caution his sister to save enough money for washing on the river.

The boat on which James Stanford had arranged passage from St. Louis was the *Montana*, queen of the river. In June of 1879, the *Montana* docked at Fort Benton, and the Stanfords got their first glimpse of their future home. It was not reassuring. They had expected to be met by their brother and son, but there was no familiar face on the dock.

To the eyes of Catherine Stanford and her 18-year-old daughter, Alicia, the people who stood at the boatside were a rowdy-looking lot of frontiersmen and Indians with eager, curious, and questing eyes. Quick glances at the crude buildings and tents brought no reassurance. Catherine said later that she had fleeting thoughts of getting back on the boat with her brood and returning to civilization, when a tall, courtly, handsome young man came to greet them. He introduced himself as Charles E. Conrad. He explained that Jim Stanford had been detained at Fort Macleod and had asked him to meet them and to see that they were safely settled. The evident good breeding and kindly manner of young Conrad brought a surge of confidence to the little family. The crowd no longer seemed sinister. They became a friendly people, interested in all newcomers, especially white women, and were anxious to help them become a part of the new community.

Conrad escorted them to a horse-drawn conveyance, which carried them to the new home that Stanford had built for himself and the girl he hoped to marry as soon as the affairs of the Mounted Police became more stable. A wagon drawn by two span of oxen hauled the furniture and treasured pieces that had made the long trip with them.

The ride along Front Street, the principal thoroughfare of the town, revealed a pandemonium of activity. Merchandise, supplies, and hay were piled in every available place. Men were unloading the steamers and stacking the cargo in a manner that seemed haphazard to the Stanfords. Others were loading the piled goods into wagons, to which were hitched from three to eight spans of oxen. As they watched, a little more order became apparent. The stacks of merchandise were marked by signs bearing names totally unknown to them: Fort Macleod, Whoop-up, Fort Walsh, Calgary, Walla Walla, and unpronounceable names they assumed were of Indian derivation. Wagon trains were pulling out loaded and returning empty in numbers that left little room for the carriages and buggies. Clouds of dust rose from the hoofs of the oxen as they plodded and stomped. The dust settled on the new arrivals and was to become a part of their lives, except during the rains when the streets became a sea of mud. During the cold winters the mud formed into ruts that would not become smooth until they became mud again in the spring.

The Stanfords were barely settled into their new home when callers came to welcome them. They brought food and offers of friendship and assistance. The wives of Fort Benton were hungry for news from the outside. There were so few of them that any addition was welcome, especially those who brought culture and refinement. The ladies all had similar backgrounds and were the wives of the merchants of Fort Benton who had established homes. They appreciated the talents of Catherine Stanford and Alicia and welcomed them warmly.

CHAPTER 17
Frontier Styles and Fashions

Alicia Stanford's arrival at Fort Benton alleviated the shortage of marriageable women by one. On February 15, 1878, the *Fort Benton Record* noted this shortage: "Benton is well supplied with launderesses. Only a community largely composed of bachelors (there are no old maids in Benton) could give employment to so many." And the *Record*, on November 9, 1881, reported,

> In Benton girls command thirty or forty dollars a month and cannot be had at those figures. The able-bodied and stout-lunged bull whacker or the hired man of a ranch does not command in most instances higher wages. The girls who get $40 a month for their services in Montana have no more arduous duties to perform than those who work for five or six dollars in the States and hence the truth of the proposition that this territory is something in the nature of a paradise for hired girls.

The *River Press*, on April 6, 1881, stated: "Yesterday's coach from Assinaboine contained 5 passengers, all destined for Benton. Two of the party were ladies. We like to welcome that class of people in our midst as they materially aid in making beautiful homes out of what might otherwise prove to be but a barren wilderness."

Not all of the arriving females were so welcomed by the press. In its June 20, 1879 issue, the *Fort Benton Record* noted a rumor "that one of the leading saloon keepers was importing a number of Hurdy Gurdys. We are not sure that this will be a detriment. They will be several shades better than the negro prostitutes and might have the effect of driving them out." Black ladies of pleasure were not uncommon on the Western frontier. Following the Civil War, many of the newly freed and rootless black males were taken into the U.S. Army and sent West to guard the wagon trains and supply trains. Where the black men went, black women followed, and in many cases prostitution was their sole means of livelihood. So strong was the tradition of protecting women in the West that the 1880 federal census listed prostitutes as "Variety Performers."

Summer bonnets and hats of the period
Courtesy Dover Pictorial Archive Series, from *Harper's Bazar*

Rude as Fort Benton seemed to the newly arrived Alicia Stanford, it had improved greatly during the preceding few years. In the January 26, 1877 edition of the *Fort Benton Record*, Editor W. H. Buck wrote that the older residents, who had personal experience of the lawless years immediately following the town's rise, found it difficult to believe the late remarkable improvement in morals, order, and refining influences. He then went on to say:

> It was once the fashion to deride our town, to regard it and speak of it as a sort of pandemonium where the powers of darkness sat in never ceasing council devising measures for some deed of outrage, violence and crime. It was doubtful whether we ever deserved the unenviable reputation but it cannot be denied that there was too much foundation for the ill repute. But that time is happily past.

The most gratifying feature of our present is the large number of families now resident in our midst. We are no longer a community of bachelors, but number our families by the dozens. It is not now a novelty to see a baby carriage upon our streets.

We are as yet unfortunately destitute of both church building and resident ministers but our school is well attended by promising, respectably clad, well mannered boys and girls, and pleasant parlor assemblages, graced with all the amenities of the higher social life are of common occurrence.

That we are almost wholly indebted to our lady residents for the improvements we have witnessed none will deny. Better homes have been built for them with many appliances of comfort and luxury. Open evil and self-satisfied rudeness have found themselves no longer tolerated and have fled.

Some of our residents have thought that the zeal displayed by our county officers has now and then been too great. But where drunk and lawless men are abroad women will not wish to live. If we would have them continue to live among us, no abatement can properly be made from the recent thorough law enforcement. If we return once more to the state of looseness and indifference in the enforcement of our none too stringent laws, we will run the risk of driving from our midst the genteel element that is so powerful for good but so quick to take alarm.

Alicia Stanford said in later years that nowhere had she found men more mannerly and courteous than in Fort Benton. When meeting a man on the street, he would invariably lift his hat to her and lower his eyes to the ground in deference and respect. She related also that the gambling halls would scatter the used playing cards over the sidewalks to cover the dust and provide a cushion for the ladies to walk on. There were plenty of used cards, for a new deck was used for each deal to insure against the marking of the cards by the cardsharps.

Their first glimpse did not prepare Alicia Stanford and her mother for the style of women's dress in Fort Benton. Expecting dresses of calico, muslin, and even hides, they were surprised to see the latest style in all articles of women's clothing. The general styles pleased the editor of the Record, but he did not care much for the hats. In the July 6, 1877 issue of his paper, the editor was of the opinion that, "The diminutive straw hats now worn by the female population of Fort Benton make a lovely lady look as though someone had slapped her on the head with a plate of fried eggs."

In the January 11, 1878 issue of the Record, Editor Buck described the styles without comment, which must have meant he approved, since he had no qualms about expressing an adverse opinion:

Shaggy beaver hats are most liked in the Gainsborough style.

Marble paper and envelopes are the latest novelty in stationery.

Embossed velvets are greatly used in combination with silk or satin.

Autumn and Winter Fashions
Courtesy Dover Pictorial Archive Series, from *Harper's Bazar*, 1882

Evening bonnets are all white with a border of white ostrich feathers.

Point lace vests with Louis XIII cuffs are the new extravagance for full dress.

Veils of black tulle are something new covered with small gold flies or Brazilian bugs.

The new bows of ribbon worn on the left side of the waist are called Chatelaine bows.

The latest and most expensive traveling bags are made of Japanese stamped leather.

Bustles, corsets and caps
Courtesy of Dover Pictorial Archive Series, from *Harper's Bazar*

Favorite scarf pins are made of two snakes twined together and having bright enameled scales.

Bustles are no longer worn. Three flounces on the back breadth of underskirts take their place.

Habit arabesques shaped like gentlemen's frock coats are among the fresh importations for ladies wear.

The fashion of Paris for young men to send bonbons to their lady friends has subsided here in these dear times.

Lace mittens are worn for evening wear matching the dress in color.

A new way of fastening on ladies hats is to bore the tops of their ears, put in gold loops and have the hat strings tied through these.

LaCredela is the most stylish breakfast cap worn. This is made of a gay striped silk handkerchief and trimmed with lace.

Richelieu ribbed hosiery is new.

Mourning stockings are embroidered with jet beads.

Spring bonnets were a little heap of artificial flowers.

House and Traveling Dress
Courtesy Dover Pictorial Archive Series, from *Harper's Bazar*

More fashions were described in the *River Press* in its November 17, 1880 issue

All black for handsome dinner dresses.

Gay stripes in silks and woolens.

New glove is the Sarah Bernhardt which fastens at the wrist, worn wrinkled on the arm like a stocking.

Black lace scarfs are worn around the throat.

The merchants of Fort Benton tried hard to stock the latest styles in women's fashions. That they were successful is indicated by the praise of Editor Buck and by the surprise of Catherine Stanford and Alicia at the good grooming and dress of the ladies of Fort Benton.

85

CHAPTER 18
Fort Benton in 1881

Alicia Stanford was 18 years old when she came to Fort Benton. The death and bankruptcy of her father, when she was 16, changed her life completely. She had lived in luxury with a family long accustomed to intellectual and cultural pursuits. Her stepsisters had been educated before the family fortunes dissolved. All seven had started careers in music and teaching and were self-sufficient. Alicia was sent to live with an elderly aunt in Chester, a small town too far from Halifax to maintain much contact with her family. Here she was thoroughly unhappy and alone. It was from this situation that she came to live in Fort Benton.

There was little culture to be found in Montana Territory, especially in Fort Benton, which was devoted almost entirely to commerce. In the October 5, 1881 issue of the *River Press*, Editor Jeremiah Collins said that Benton was far behind other towns of the Territory in opportunities for social intercourse and mental and moral improvement. Benton's population at the time was 1,618, but the editor believed that Bozeman, with a population of 894, and Deer Lodge at 940, offered a great deal more sociability, culture, and true refinement, while Virginia City, with a population of only 624, had earned the title of the social center of the Territory.

The editor of the *Record* was distressed with the physical deficiencies as well as with the social. On May 18, 1878, he wrote: "Benton is having more than its usual share of mud this year, and its usual share is enough to keep a web foot from becoming homesick." By 1881 the editor had sensed a new need. In the May 4 issue he wrote: "What Benton needs just now more than anything else is a boulevard where happy couples can kill time and linger lovingly on Sabbath evenings." The editor's mind made the transition from mud to boulevard much faster than the action of the city officials. The condition of the sidewalks and streets was not solely the fault of the city fathers and merchants. Lumber was scarce and expensive. The only timber near Fort Benton was the cottonwood which grew along the banks of the river and creeks. Within hauling distance of the town the stream banks were denuded of trees which had been cut for fuel for the steamboats and for homes in Fort Benton. The wood merchants, called fiends by the editor of the River Press, charged 12 and 13 dollars for a cord of inferior wood, which lasted only five days.

The only lumber suitable for buildings and sidewalks was that brought up the river, which was a laborious and expensive process. A brickyard had not been established, and the use of adobe was not satisfactory because of the nature of the soil and the harsh climate. Housing was scarce and many families arriving in Fort Benton were faced with camping out until housing was found or they moved on to other areas, which they did in large numbers.

Any need suggests the possibility of a profit in its fulfillment. And any possibility of a profit attracts an entrepreneur eager to seek that profit. The lumber shortage at Fort Benton fired the imagination of one local citizen who devised a scheme to make his fortune. Timber suitable for lumber was plentiful in the Highwood Mountains, 30 to 40 miles upstream from the city. Though the timber was abundant in the mountains, getting it overland to Fort Benton was almost impossible.

The scheme was to cut the timber in the winter, put it in the river in the spring, and let the high water float it to Fort Benton, where it would be removed from the river, processed into lumber, and sold at prices high enough to bring instant riches. To stop the logs at Fort Benton, a boom was built across the river. Enlisting a crew was no problem, for in the winter the bull drivers, whackers, and roustabouts were idle. Such an unlikely crew was assembled in the mountains, where they toiled all winter felling trees, cutting them into logs, and snaking them to the river's edge to await the spring rising of the river.

Everything went according to schedule and, when the ice left the river and spring run-off brought it to high water, the logs were dragged and pushed into the river. When the last log was in, the crews mounted horses and raced to the boom to be ready to retrieve the logs when they reached their destination, cut them into lumber, and reap the fortune that is due to the man of enterprise and daring.

All eyes were trained upstream for a first glimpse of the approaching logs. At last they were sighted on their bobbing course down the river and a shout of satisfaction burst forth from the watchers. The first logs arrived at the boom and were stopped. On and on they came, each new log hitting its brother, halted at the boom. Jubilation at the success of the scheme was great but not long-lasting. Long before the last log was in sight, the boom reached its capacity and parted, broken in the middle. Downstream went the logs, creating navigational hazards all the way to New Orleans. Gone was a dream of riches, but on the frontier such dreams came and went, the light of the dying dream illuminating the birth of the one that followed.

By 1878 Fort Benton had a grade school but no high school. There was great agitation for a high school by the mothers who wanted their children to be educated — something that had not concerned the fur traders and merchants when the town was devoid of white women and children. An article in the January 11, 1878 issue of the *Record* indicated the difficulty of financing a new school. It reported that the "Christmas Ball for the benefit of the school was a great social success but sorry to say the expenses exceeded the receipts."

When the school was finally built, there were still problems. In January, 1882, four white families of Fort Benton withdrew their children from the school because two black children were admitted. The editor of the *River Press* allowed the white families this privilege, but noted that the school was going on just the same. On January 19, 1882, an article in the *River Press* reported:

> The school Trustees met on Tuesday to consider the question of admitting Negro children to the school. The opinion of State Superintendent of Public Instruction R. H. Howey, concurred in by T. J. Lowery, Attorney General of Montana, said that Fort Benton must provide separate schools.

Nevertheless, in the face of this decision, the School Board, by unanimous vote, resolved that black children could go to the public schools if they wanted to. The *River Press* editor agreed with this decision and said: "One child is as good as another, no matter what color, so long as he behaves himself." By this action the Fort Benton School Board provided an early common-sense solution to the problem that plagued the nation. It defied the Superintendent of Public Instruction, the Montana Attorney General, and ignored the separate-but-equal doctrine laid down by the United States Supreme Court. The defiance went unpunished and set a precedent that was followed in Montana in the relations of blacks and whites.

However disappointed the editors were in the social life and amenities offered at Fort Benton, they were well-pleased with the commerce and business. The *Fort Benton Record* noted, on April 27, 1877, that lots on Front Street were selling at enormous prices.

> A lot not very eligibly situated was sold this week by Judge Sanborn at the rate of ten dollars per *foot* and $1800.00 was recently refused for an old log house situated near the levees. Light taxes and the brilliant future now dawning on Fort Benton are beginning to have a most desirable effect upon real estate.

On December 28, 1881, three years after the arrival of Alicia Stanford, the *River Press* listed the business houses of Fort Benton, which would be a little changed from the scene that Catherine Stanford and her family saw on their first drive down Front Street, the main business street.

Front Street of Fort Benton in 1872 Courtesy John G. Lepley

General Merchandise
I. G. Baker & Co.; T. C. Power and Bro.; W. S. Wetzel; Murphy, Neel & Co.;
Kleinschmidt & Bro.

Clothes
Hershberg & Nathan; Gans & Klein

Hardware
W. J. Wackerlin & Co.

Dry Goods
Baker and Delorimer

Banks
Bank of Northern Montana; First National

Retail Grocery
W. H. Burgess

Druggist
Dr. W. E. Turner; M. A. Flanagan; W. J. Minar

Furniture
F. C. Roosevelt & Co.

Saddle and Harness
I. H. Rosencrans; Davidson and Moffitt; Sullivan and Goss;
August Beckman

News and Novelty
Crane & Green; Fred W. Buckson; Max Kabaker; Swartz and Kelly

Wholesale Liquors
T. J. Todd & Co.

Hotels
Choteau; Overland; The New Hotel; Montana House Centennial;
Eataphone Rest, Board $6.00 a week

Livery Stables
Harris and Strong; Jas. McDevitt & Co.
Meat Market
J. J. Kennedy
Jewelry
C. M. Lanning
Photographer
Justus Fey
Attorneys
Donnelly; Buck & Hunt; J. A. Kanouse
John W. Tattan; Max Waterman; W. B. Settle
Physicians
F. A. Atkisson; J. W. Wheelock; W. E. Turner
Newspapers
River Press; Record
Saloons
Choteau; Exchange; Dick Brennan; Chas. Bourassa; Talbot & Co.;
Occidental; Al Lester; John Evans; George Farmer; W. G. Allen;
John Fisher; Eagle Bird; B. B. Tierney; Overland; Frank Hughes;
Marshall and Wilson; Wm. Foster; J. C. Ward
Churches
Catholic, Father Camp, Pastor; Episcopal, J. C. Blackiston, Pastor;
Congregational, W. A. James, Pastor
Undertakers
Peter Smith, general undertaker, coffin maker
Brick Yards
Jas. DeWolf; J. R. Wilton
Secret Societies
Benton Lodge No. 25, A.F.&A.M.; Choteau Lodge No. 11, IOOF
Restaurants
Grand Central; G. W. Bullet & Co.; Bob Mills; Mrs. Murray
Stage Lines
Helena and Benton; Benton and Assiniboin; Benton and Martinsdale
Blacksmith
Moe Bros.; Rufus & Payne; Frank Lepper
Barbers
Sam Spaulding; Charley Bryer
Carpenters
W. G. Jones; J. K. Wilton; Gus. Senieur; Peter Smith
Wash Houses
A. J. Sing, Benton Wash House
Baker
John H. Gamble
Wanted
A milliner, a flouring mill, a lumber dealer, a planing mill,
a machine shop, a railroad.

This list of businesses described Fort Benton at its peak. More freight came up the Missouri River in 1881 than during any other year.

With a population of only about 1,500, it is somewhat surprising that

Fort Benton had three doctors. Not only is this a rather high doctor-patient ratio, but Grace's Celebrated Salve also was available. The September 6, 1878 issue of the *River Press* carried an advertisement for this wondrous healer which announced that:

Grace's Celebrated Salve cures flesh wounds, frozen limbs, salt rheum, chillblains, sore breasts, sore lips, erysipelas, ringworms, calluses, chapped hands, burns, scalds, wounds, festers, piles, bunions, warts, pimples, cancers, stings, sores, wens, abcess, sprains, cuts, blisters, corns, felons, ulcers, shingles, sties, freckles, boils, whitlows, scurvey, itch, ingrown toenails, nettle rash, mosquito bites, fly bites, spider stings and all cutaneous diseases and eruptions generally. Invented in the 17 century by Dr. Wm. Grace, Surgeon in King James' Army. Through its agency he cured thousands of the most serious sores and wounds that baffled the skill of the most eminent physicians of the day and was regarded by all who knew him as a public benefactor. Sold by all druggists, grocers, and at all country stores throughout the U.S. and British Possessions at 25 cents per box, 30 cents by mail.

No claim was made that babies could be delivered by this miracle medicine, but so few were born that this phase of medicine could not have provided a livelihood for three doctors.

1881 was a good year for Fort Benton, but 1882 would be even better.

CHAPTER 19
Courtship and Marriage

The November 7, 1879 issue of the *River Press* announced that C. E. Conrad had returned from Fort Walsh in Canada to spend the winter in Fort Benton. Alicia Stanford was then leading an active life in Fort Benton. An advertisement in the *Fort Benton Record* announced that Miss K. B. Tonge and Miss A. D. Stanford had opened a Select School for Young Ladies and Children. They offered careful instruction in Ancient and Modern History, Geography, Penmanship, Physiology, Astronomy, Natural Philosophy, Mythology, Chemistry, and Calisthenics. These were the subjects for the elementary branches. The higher branches included French and Drawing, and Instrumental and Vocal Music were offered as extras.

Such a curriculum would indicate that the two ladies had received a broad, general, cultural, and classical education that went far beyond the needs of life in Fort Benton. But the people of the rough, rowdy, and crassly commercial community had a deep-seated desire for these things, if not for themselves at least for their children. The little school was well-attended, and the ladies Tonge and Stanford were able to fill a longing for culture that existed in the frontier town among all classes of people, by offering a curriculum as broad in the field of education as did Grace's Celebrated Salve in the field of medicine.

During the fall and winter, social activities at Fort Benton were quite lively. Typical was a broadside announcing a benefit performance for the Episcopal Church. Held at Stocking's and Masonic Halls, the planned entertainment included:

> a dramatic performance, singing, select readings, etc., by local talent. In Masonic Hall, supper will be served and dancing indulged in: Admission to Stocking's Hall 50 cents. Supper, including one dozen oysters in any style, $1.00, Dancing, 50 cents.

Concerts were regularly offered, the music furnished by the bands of the Army units stationed at the Fort. Representative of this type of entertainment was one offered by the Third Infantry String Band.

The programme: March — Mein Oestreich — Budic. Potpouri — Duguenots — Meyerbeer. Waltz — Die Fantasen — Ziboff. Quadrille — The Merry Maiden — Schlepegrell. Galop — The Jolly Brothers — Faust. Charles Luppy, Bandmaster.

The January 4, 1882 *River Press* told of the Calico Ball held at the Choteau House Hotel. The ladies wore calico gowns and brought a necktie of the same material for their escorts. The paper also said that the young gentlemen of Fort Benton were planning for the dances to be held during the winter season. Arranging for dances at the time was apparently left to the men. The ladies merely went and enjoyed themselves. The men exceeded the women in so great a ratio that every girl could feel like the belle of the ball.

Fresh oysters were regular fare in the frontier days, far from the bays and estuaries of the oceans, where the meeting and mingling of salt and fresh water provide the conditions in which oysters live and propagate. And fresh oysters they were, alive and well, thousands of miles from their habitat, with the only transportation the lumbering wagons and the slow boats. Fresh oysters are available in a present-day Montana cow town, with their transportation provided in a few hours by air freight, but how were fresh oysters available in Fort Benton in the 1800s?

The answer is that the oyster was conditioned to travel long distances at slow paces. By a process of sudden immersion and abrupt draining in a solution of brine that simulated the tides, the oyster was taught to close its shell tightly. This was followed by several erratic immersions. The oyster was then withdrawn, to simulate a long, low, dry tide, to which the oysters became able to accommodate themselves. During this period of simulated long, low, dry tide, with their shells clamped tightly shut, they were transported long distances, even to Fort Benton, Montana Territory. Here they arrived alive and fresh, tricked into the belief that they were still in Chesapeake Bay at the meeting of the river and sea.

Had 18-year-old Alicia Stanford been older and much less beautiful, she would still have found suitors in Fort Benton. But her beauty, talents, and open and friendly disposition soon attracted would-be husbands not only in Fort Benton but also in the outlying settlements, and even among young men passing through. Her only problem was in choosing one from the many available.

Charles Conrad started to court Alicia Stanford, but on a rather formal and restrained basis. Small though Fort Benton was, Conrad wrote his invitations and had them delivered by hand. On November 24, 1879, he wrote: "My dear friend. May I have the pleasure of your company to the concert tomorrow evening. Your friend, C. E. Conrad." This invitation was probably accepted, for on December 9, 1879, he was emboldened to write: "My dear friend. May I have the pleasure of your company to attend the hop on Friday evening? Yours truly, C. E. Conrad."

Charles must have agonized over a suitable Christmas gift, and the one chosen was probably quite elaborate. On December 25, 1879, he sent the gift with a note saying: "Merry Christmas with the compliments of your friend C. E. Conrad." The gift was evidently incomplete, for on January 1 he wrote: "My dear Miss Letty. I send you the necklace to complete my present of the 25th ulto. Yours truly, C. E. Conrad."

The courtship seems to have hit a snag following this Christmas gift. In an almost illegible letter to Charles from Letty she wrote:

> My dear Mr. Conrad. I am ever so sorry my note pained you but it was written on the spur of the moment and one of my sudden impulses took possession of me. It occurred to me that your beautiful present (given and accepted by me in the same spirit of friendship, not to you or I but to others) might appear as an obstacle in the way of your paying attention to other ladies — and I thought it would be better to act as I did. There you have it all in a nut shell and I know you will understand when I say — it was not that I valued your friendship less — *but I do not want to* lose it.

> About the other note of mine, is your large business so engrossing that you forget the school 'marm' on the way to the store for a perfect age — so long I don't wonder you forgot it. I did not think of mentioning it because I thought you would know. Let us shake hands since its a perfect understanding. Yours very sincerely, Lettie Stanford.

The patch held for a time, for on January 28, 1880, Conrad wrote:

> My dear Miss Letty. If you feel well enough and are not engaged, may I have the pleasure of your company to attend the hop on the evening of the 30th. Sincerely, your friend, C. E. Conrad.

> N. B. Dr. Powers leaves tomorrow. We are to call on you this evening when you can give me your answer.

After this flurry, Conrad was called to Canada, where his time was divided among Fort Walsh, Calgary, Fort Macleod, and Ottawa in connection with the Canadian contracts that had now become such a large part of their business. He had not told Letty of his Indian wife and son, although he suspected that she had received the information from the women of Fort Benton. He knew that he wanted to marry Alicia Stanford and knew that other men in Fort Benton had the same desire. He believed that Alicia looked upon him with favor, for she was holding at bay those suitors who had more time and opportunity to press their suits. Three things made him reluctant to propose. First, he was 10 years older than she. His second difficulty was his Indian wife, whom he had not seen or heard from since she left with her people. Third, he had the problem of his son, at school in Montreal.

Conrad did not believe he could propose marriage to Alicia while still married to his Indian wife. He had in his employ an Indian runner whom he used to carry messages among the various and far-flung places of business. He dispatched this trusted man to try to find his wife and waited anxiously for information. Some weeks later the runner returned. He had found the tribe in northern Canada and learned that the wife had taken another husband and died in childbirth. There was now no legal obstacle to his remarrying, if Alicia could accept the difference in age and the Indian son.

In the fall of 1880, Conrad returned to Fort Benton to make it his permanent home. The thing topmost in his mind was to make Alicia an offer of marriage, but he wanted her to be aware of the things in his life that might prove to be impediments. He called on her immediately and told of his life before her arrival in Fort Benton. Alicia listened intently as Conrad told her of his love and of his desire to have her as his wife. He told her also of his love and marriage to the Indian girl and of her death. He disclosed that he had a five-year-old son in a Catholic school in Montreal, for whose education and care he would be responsible. Then he departed, leaving Alicia to ponder these things. On September 15, 1880, Conrad wrote Alicia a letter of proposal:

> My dear Miss Lettie: Undoubtedly, you will not be surprised at me saying that I am very much in love with you, as my actions have betrayed me in this. Dear Miss Lettie I feel that there is a great barrier between us, and that is, my former character. Previous to the advent of ladies into the Northwest, I like many others, led a somewhat reckless life (undoubtedly of which you have heard) but meeting you and my love for you have made a new man of me. If you will consent to share your life with me, I will be to you a kind and true husband leaving nothing undone to make you happy. I believe you to be a liberal minded and unselfish woman, which I think you will find accords with my disposition. I have felt at times not worthy of you, and have tried to suppress my feelings (thinking I would lead a bachelor's life) but time only adds flames to my love for you, and I feel that my life will be a blank without you. Awaiting your reply with a great deal of anxiety I am as ever, Yours Affectionately, C. E. Conrad.

None of the things told her by Conrad was a deterrent to Alicia, and they became engaged. Nor did any of these things distress her during her life. In later years, at a tea in Kalispell, thinking to embarrass her, a jealous lady said, "I understand your husband was a squaw man." Completely unruffled, Lettie Conrad answered:

> My husband always chose the best that was available. His first wife was a beautiful Indian princess, the daughter of a Chief of the Blackfoot Nation. When she died and Mr. Conrad wanted to marry again he chose me. I have always felt honored to become the wife of a man who had married a princess and could have chosen any woman that he wanted.

The Conrads were married on January 4, 1881. On the wedding day, the temperature was 31 degrees below zero. This did not deter them from starting on the honeymoon they had planned. Following the marriage, they went by sleigh to Helena, an arduous trip in any weather. After a short stay there, they went by stage to Ogden, Utah Territory, where they took the train to the East. On their honeymoon they visited Washington, Baltimore, Philadelphia, New York, and Boston. From Boston they went to Halifax, where Conrad met Alicia's seven stepsisters, all still unmarried and all teaching in the world of arts, for which their upbringing had been such a splendid background.

After their visit in Halifax, the Conrads returned to the United States to visit the Virginia of his boyhood, but found all changed. William in later years would return to Virginia to live, but Charles was so affected by these changes that he never returned.

Both Alicia and Charles knew they would soon want to build a home and fill it with beautiful things. They spent much of their time buying articles of fine furniture to grace the home he had pictured in his mind to replace the gracious plantation home destroyed in the Civil War. Alicia finally found the piano she wanted. She knew the hazards of the trip it would take, so supervised its crating and started it on the long journey to Fort Benton. There it would sit on the dock, protected by sacks of grain covered by canvas until it was placed in the home they would build in Kalispell ten years later. Despite its long trip and the unlikely place and manner of its storage, it retained its beautiful tone and clarity.

Conrad had completed the transition of the Canadian business before he left, so the honeymoon was not at all hurried. The Fort Benton *River Press* on October 5, 1881, reported, "Mr. and Mrs. C. E. Conrad will return home in a few days from a somewhat lengthy trip in the East. They will be gladly welcomed by their friends." They returned on October 18 to spend 10 happy and prosperous years in Fort Benton.

CHAPTER 20
Frontier Parlors

The Conrads moved into a house that had been occupied by Colonel Guido Ilges, Commandant of the Army unit stationed at Fort Benton. Later they built a home which still stands in Fort Benton. This home was not as pretentious as the one built there by brother William. William's home was a Victorian-style mansion, beautifully furnished with fine pieces obtained in Virginia. For many years it was an outstanding example of the fine homes the wealthy merchants of Fort Benton built for their families. It fell victim to the modern craze for "ample parking." The Catholic priest, Father Carl Erickson, decided his parishioners needed more parking at the nearby church. Efforts to preserve this fine old home failed and, in 1978, it was burned by the Fire Department to provide additional parking in a small city where it would seem the only parking problem is to determine where to stop the car and turn off the engine.

Alicia Conrad loved the life at Fort Benton. She participated in all of the activities of the bustling little town and was surprised at the conviviality and quality of its social life. In later years she told her daughter, Alicia:

Much has been written and said about the hardships endured by the women of the frontier, but this was not my experience or that of the women I knew. Women at Fort Benton were cherished and coddled. The Indian women were respected by the white men, but the white women were almost deified and were probably the best treated women in the world. They were indulged and pampered in everything. Women were treated as a loved and fragile Christmas tree ornament, wrapped in cotton and handled with mild and tender care. For their women the men built large and comfortable parlors and furnished them lavishly, as the parlor was the place envisioned by the men as a worthy place for their women. Here were held brilliant social gatherings and parties which were as interesting as any in the world. Every man was a complete gentleman when he stepped into the parlor, and each man was interesting. There were doctors, lawyers, ministers, merchants, men educated and uneducated. Each had lived varied, dangerous and colorful lives. Their conversations about their

W. G. Conrad home, built in 1879 on corner of Baker and
Choteau streets Courtesy Montana Historical Society

experiences would have seemed braggadocio, except one knew the conversations concerned things that were commonplace to them and so
routine in their lives. Just to hear their conversations was an exhilarating
experience that could not be duplicated in any other parlor in the world.

According to Lettie Conrad, when a white woman walked down the
main street, the first man to see her would call out, "White woman
coming." All the men would remove their hats and stand with head and
eyes lowered to show their respect.

Lettie Stanford Conrad planted the first garden in Fort Benton. It was a
big garden located behind the new house. It had always been assumed
that Fort Benton's growing season was too short to raise vegetables.
Lettie, however, grew fine vegetables and, the following season, gardens
bloomed all over the town. The fresh vegetables were a delight to people
who had subsisted upon food brought in by the steamers. The steamer
trip was too long for the produce to stay fresh. Similarly, when the price
of eggs rose to $2.00 per dozen, Lettie proved that chickens could
flourish in Fort Benton, and the cackling of hens and crowing of roosters
became a familiar sound.

On September 29, 1882, a son was born to the Conrads. He was named Charles Davenport Conrad, the name Charles E. Conrad, Jr., having been given to the Indian son.

Then, on June 12, 1885, a daughter was born to the Conrads. She was named Catherine, after her Grandmother Stanford. This would have broken the continuous devolution of the family name Alicia, but another daughter was born on June 10, 1892. She arrived after the family had moved to Kalispell and was named Alicia, to continue the long line of Alicias which started in the year 1600 in England.

When James Stanford married, he moved with his bride into the brick house in which the Stanfords had been living since their coming to Fort Benton. Catherine Stanford and Hal then came to live with the Conrads, in quarters added to the new home in anticipation of their arrival.

A short time later, Charles Conrad's father, James, died from injuries sustained in a fall at the home of his daughter, Alice, in Great Falls. Following his death, the Fort Benton house was again remodeled, and Charles' mother, Maria, came to live with the Conrads. Except for the later arrival of little Alicia, after the move to Kalispell, the Conrad household was complete. Only death and marriage would change its composition, for the grandmothers lived with the Conrads until both died in 1904.

CHAPTER 21
The Profits and Perils of Freighting

The March 8, 1882 issue of the Fort Benton *River Press*, noted:

> I. G. Baker and Co. have again been successful in securing the contract for furnishing supplies for the various Indian agencies and posts at Walsh, Macleod, Wood Mountains, Calgary, Qui Appelle, Balleford, and Prince Albert Mission. The contract is an enormous affair amounting to $450,000. For six or seven years the I. G. Baker and Co. has had this contract and it is highly complimentary to the firm that it has again been awarded to them by the Canadian government.

The supply of the Canadian trade alone required a huge transportation system, and the Conrads became the largest freighters in the Territory. In 1880, 80 men, 576 oxen, 100 mules, and more than 100 wagons were employed in the Canadian operation alone. The Baker wagons were exceptionally strong. They were grouped together in threes, and a train contained 17 or 18 of these groups. Each group of three required 18 oxen or 14 mules. A single train of this character represented an investment between $25,000 and $30,000, which gives some idea of the capital required to operate just the Canadian business.

It is estimated that, from 1874 to 1883, I. G. Baker and Company hauled about 25 million pounds of freight from Fort Benton to fulfill their Canadian contracts. In the April 1, 1876 issue of the *Benton Record*, freight rates between Fort Benton and Fort Macleod were quoted at six cents per pound. On the Canadian haul alone the Company received nearly $2,000,000. This did not include the wagon trains going to Helena and other points or the revenue from return hauls. During the month of October, 1887, according to the *Record*, I. G. Baker and Company shipped to John Thompson and Company, Bridge Creek, 20,000 pounds of merchandise, to Helena 30,000 pounds, to Fort Macleod 336,000 pounds, and to Fort Walsh, 100,000 pounds.

In 1875 the *Record* reported that the Baker Company shipped into Fort Benton, 19,280 buffalo robes, 650 calf robes, 25 tons of antelope, deer, and elk hides, 503 wolf skins, 1,710 fox skins, 33 bear skins, and 1,300 pounds of beaver skins. The trade in buffalo robes was not to last long. In January, 1881, the *Record* noted that the lower Musselshell was black with buffalo. On January 1, 1882, the same paper said that the buffalo robes were in active demand at eight dollars each. On December 25, 1889, the *River Press* mourned that buffalo robes had become a curiosity. On October 1, 1890, the *River Press* quoted Professor William Hornaday, the noted buffalo authority, that only 1,000 buffalo were left in the world: 200 in National Parks, 245 in captivity, and 642 running wild. The editor said, "This seems scarcely possible to those who have seen the immense herds in the Yellowstone and Milk River Valleys."

The bull trains were slow but dependable. On October 24, 1871, the *Record* reported that a bull train loaded with lime for I. G. Baker and Company left Helena on September 17 and arrived in Fort Benton on October 23, only a month and six days out. On this run the freight rates must have been based on what the traffic would bear and there must have been more competition on the haul from Benton to Helena. On November 2, 1881, the *Benton Record* reprinted an article from the *Helena Independent* on the subject:

> Judging from the freight rates it must be a good deal farther from Helena to Benton than it is from Benton to Helena. Freight rates to Benton are $2.25 per hundred while from Benton to Helena they are only $1.00.

For faster freight, teams of horses were used. They were considerably faster, but freight charges were much higher, because grain had to be hauled with the train to feed the horses. No food was hauled for the oxen.

Bull train in front of W. H. Todd warehouse, circa 1870
Courtesy John G. Lepley

They kept in good condition by grazing on the nutritious wild grass during rest stops along the way. Oxen were not used in winter, when heavy snows covered the ground and the lumbering animals could not sustain themselves while traveling. Under these conditions, horses were used, their feed being grain, which was less bulky and burdensome to carry than forage for the oxen. All freighting diminished in the winter. By early fall the steamboats had unloaded their cargo and were headed back to winter quarters. Then came the rush to move the freight from the docks to its place of ultimate destination before the savage winter struck.

Fastest of all was the courier service between Fort Benton and Fort Macleod. The Record told of one dispatch, which arrived in Fort Benton with messages and orders for Captain Macpherson, that left Macleod Saturday evening and was only 30 hours on the road. The papers were passed from patrol to patrol along the way.

Slowest of all, in the eyes of the editors of the Fort Benton papers, was the United States mail. On January 23, 1881, the editor of the River Press fumed at the slow service. The mail had been so delayed that 26 mails arrived together in one delivery. On November 9, 1881, the editor of the Record was equally unhappy. He wrote:

> Uncle Sam's careless agents sent the Benton mail to Bozeman and we have no late news to give our readers. We have not had an Eastern mail since Sunday.

There were pitfalls in the freighting business which could be disastrous to the unwary and uninitiated. What appeared to be a successful haul from Fort Benton to Helena or to Virginia City could turn to disaster just from unfamiliarity with the method of payment. To be paid in greenbacks or paper money meant an immediate loss over payment in gold, due to the fluctuation in the values of these mediums. But even gold had different qualities of fineness and purity. The gold from each of the mining camps differed in value. The gold from Alder Gulch, near Virginia City, was the most valuable. If the contract for hauling did not specify Alder Gulch gold, then payment in Silver Bow, Last Chance, Frying Pan, or gold from the other mining areas would be substituted, resulting in a loss of from two to three dollars an ounce.

The source of the gold was not the only pitfall for the tenderfoot. When gold was weighed out it should be free of such impurities as dust and fine rock. To insure purity, those who knew gold required it to be "blowed" before it was weighed. This insured the purity of the gold taken in payment for the laborious and dangerous work of getting the wagon trains through the Indians, over the mountains, across the rivers, and against the snow and bitter cold of Montana winters.

In the June 9, 1976 issue of the River Press, Editor Joel Overholser wrote of the perils of those unfamiliar with gold and its use in trade.

Alder gold became the standard of value but far purer was the original Bannack of finer gold than U.S. coins at 99.9 percent. Highland City gold from near Butte ran Bannack dust a close race, but the inexperienced taking Silver Bow on a par with Alder was tempting bankruptcy. There was little currency except gold dust, and miners generally disdained what few greenbacks floated in.

That posed the problem for successful merchants of moving heavy parcels of gold out to keep merchandise coming in, and opportunity for the hard cases who flocked in too. The story of Henry Plummer and the road agents has been told too often to repeat, few tales of gold camps cover much else.

Enough merchants managed to get their gold and orders East, enough new speculators arrived to keep the mines supplied and business humming. Smallest price was two bits, which represented a delicate pinch from a poke, so barkeeps with big hands were favored. Also favored was a heavy carpet to put under the gold scales, and sweepings from the joints panned out heavily — swamping might involve paying the booze boss to do it.

Some of the independent freighters were entrepreneurs with great imagination. One who hauled between Corrine, Utah Territory and Helena, found himself with no load on the return trip to Helena. He bought all the eggs he could find in Utah for two cents each. He wrapped each egg with newspaper and nestled the wrapped eggs in boxes filled with oats. Over the top he piled hay and grain which he covered with canvas. In the dead of winter he started to Helena, guilding his wagon train over the rugged passes and through the deep valleys in bitter sub-zero weather. He arrived in Helena in early spring not knowing if he had fresh eggs or frozen omelet. When his cargo was unshrouded, ungrained, and unwrapped, he found them fresh and unfrozen. The egg-starved people of Helena paid $1.00 per egg without complaint, for they knew the hardship and danger entailed in getting the eggs through.

CHAPTER 22
The Indian Trade

In addition to supplying the Mounted Police and the settlements in Canada, the Conrads became the financial agents for the Canadian government and handled mail deliveries between eastern and western Canada, for there was no overland mail route between these points. Mail arrived in Fort Benton with United States postage, and then was carried overland to Canada by the Baker Company's freight wagons or riders. In 1881 the United States government granted a second-class postal permit to the *Fort Macleod Gazette* that allowed it to use the U.S. Mail Service to distribute papers to its subscribers in eastern Canada and the United States.

The Conrads also handled the money that the Canadian government paid to the Indians as annuities. The amount of the annuities and the time of payment, usually semi-annually, was established by the treaty between the Indians and the Canadian government, which took the Indians from their nomadic life and established them on the reservations.

George Overfield, an employee of the Baker store in Fort Benton, and also in Fort Macleod in the early 1880s, told of the procedure followed in distributing the annuities to the Indians in Fort Macleod.

When it was time for a certain tribe to get their quarterly or semi-annual annuity, the government would deposit the money in the I. G. Baker store, perhaps $20,000, all in one hundred dollar packages of one dollar bills. The clerks would arrange the stock of sugar, tea, crackers, calico and blankets on the counters so that every article could be seen. Everything was priced in dollars and no change was made. There might be two small articles such as a package of needles for $1.00, and any such bargain would be explained by sign language when the Indian handed over the dollar. Next, the clerks brought out from stock one or two wash boilers and filled them with water and put them on a big stove so there would be plenty of boiling water to make tea for their expected Indian visitors. Next, boxes of crackers to be served with sweetened tea were put on the shelves in readiness. A large clothes basket was placed behind the counter to serve as a cash register when the dollars were passed over the counter. Now all was ready. After watching the distant horizon for a short while, or perhaps for hours, the traders would catch a glimpse of the vanguard of the Indian caravan emerging from a cloud of dust on the brow of a distant hill. As the long, slow moving, trailing group advanced, its component parts gradually assumed their distinctive shapes, colors and sizes. First came some of the young braves riding ahead on their ponies, racing to get first place at the camp. Next came the chiefs and older bucks walking or lying on a travois, smoking their pipes. Bringing up the rear came the squaws laden with papoose or other burdens. They trudged along in their short, flat-footed gait, making sure that the children, dogs and the ponies came into camp. The squaws then put up the teepees and made the camp ready for their stay. That done, they made their campfires and spread their buffalo robes in their wigwams.

When the whole tribe had arrived, the trading post doors were unlocked. As many as could squeeze into the store were admitted and sat down on the floor while the others sat on the ground outside the store. The clerks then served tea and crackers until all were satisfied with their treat. The manager of the store then opened the safe and brought out one half of the annuity to be paid at this time and distributed it to the chiefs. The Indians took their dollars and sitting on the floor folded and refolded each dollar bill until it resembled a small finger, just larger than a match stick. When this proceeding was finished, the trading began. Either the chief or the head squaw chose the purchases. The Indian pointed to what he wanted and said "ungh" or perhaps "how much." The clerk would reply by holding up one, two, three or five fingers as the price might be in dollars. Then the Indian would hand over the number of rolled up dollar bills resembling fingers that matched the number of upheld fingers of the clerk. He was then given his puchase and the clerk tossed the dollar bills into the clothes basket behind the counter.

When the Indians were through trading for the day or longer and had used all their dollar bills, they went to their camp for the night. The store was locked and put in order for the next day's trading. The clerks counted the dollar bills, unfolded them and smoothed them out and put them into the safe. The next morning these same dollars were brought out and distributed to the Indians for the second half of the current annuity. By the end of the day or days of trading the store would have sold $20,000 worth of goods according to its prices, by using the first distributed bills twice, and would have $20,000 back in their safe. There was nothing dishonest about the transaction, though the prices were very high. It was just a clever way to handle the Indian trade and keep half of the money smooth and clean. When the annuity was all spent, the post trader told the Indians, "No more trade now. Money all gone. You come back three moons. You get more money then." The Indians would have another treat of tea and crackers, probably kill a dog for the last feast, then assemble the tribe for the long trek to their reservation. Some of the purchases were loaded on the crude wooden pack saddles that were so hard on the ponies' backs. Other loads were put on the travois or on the backs of the squaws. The blankets, the feathers and the brass rings in the braided black hair of the bucks and the beaded shirts and moccasins and the gay calico shirts of the squaws made a design of color as the tribe in a cheerful mood moved off in a straggling uneven column. They were visible for a long time in the clear western air, as they wound their way up the hills and finally disappeared.

Charles Conrad was an experienced and able Indian trader. Some of the Indians were shrewd traders also and even Conrad was sometimes discomforted. The December 13, 1902 issue of the (Helena) *Montana Press* carried a story of one of these incidents. Tail Feather, an old and grizzled member of the Piegan tribe, was a fine hunter, careful on the taking, preparation, and care of his skins and pelts. They were always of such fine quality that there was spirited competition for the catch he brought in each fall. Conrad had built a cabin to accommodate the Indian friends and customers. The *Press* story relates that Conrad:

... was in the habit of allowing Indian traders who were doing their annual trading with him to make themselves at home in the place without charge. Old Tail Feather came down one fall with an exceptionally large and valuable load of skins and furs and Mr. Conrad rubbed his hands in satisfaction when he saw what a nice deal he was going to make with the shrewd old Indian. He took the old fellow and his family into the cabin and told him to make himself entirely at home. He heaped up every favor on him that he could and made himself as pleasant as a day in June.

Tail Feather was both flattered and pleased and with a little parley made a very satisfactory trade with Mr. Conrad. Then in order to rest his ponies and give himself and family a little vacation he informed Mr. Conrad that he thought he would stay in the cabin a few weeks and enjoy himself. Mr. Conrad hinted that his usefulness having ended for the present it might be just as well to make his visit as short as possible as others might want to trade and use the cabin. Finally, when the Indian refused to take any hints, Mr. Conrad went to him and he said, "Look here, Tail Feather, I am very glad to have you here with us and I have enjoyed your visit while you have been here, but it is like this, there are several other Indians with their squaws and papooses who have come to trade and they want the cabin. You will have to go today."

"I will go," said the wily old red man, "but you have taught me a lesson. Next year when I come with a load of skins, I will trade when I get ready to go home instead of when I first come. I have noticed that you like me better before I have traded than you do afterwards."

It is not recorded how Tail Feather worked it the next fall, but Mr. Conrad always declared that Tail Feather taught him a valuable lesson not only in politeness, but also in dealing with Indians.

The Indians held Conrad in high esteem for they knew he was honest and could be trusted. It is likely that by the next trading season Tail Feather would place fairness and honesty above slight and return the next fall to trade with his friend.

CHAPTER 23
Approaching the Peak

The decade which began in 1880 brought Fort Benton the best business years in its history. Before the decade ended, Fort Benton would be finished as the most important transportation center in Montana, put in total eclipse by the railroads.

Some 12,100 tons of freight were brought in to Fort Benton in 1880, the largest tonnage to that date. This tonnage figure did not include 3,000 passengers and 1,500 head of cattle, sheep, and horses, all of improved blood lines. This was indicative of the importance of the agriculture and livestock industries in Montana Territory.

In this year, another newspaper came to Fort Benton. James E. Stevens, an employee of the *Benton Record*, joined with H. C. Williams and Thomas D. Wright, borrowed $1,700 and started publication of the *River Press*. Their backing came from Republican merchants who may have tired of the Democratic leanings of W. H. Buck, the outspoken and sometimes vitriolic editor of the *Fort Benton Record*. Buck started the *Record* in 1875 and had the field to himself for four and one-half years. During this period, he was cowed on only one issue: his penchant for a paper with temperance leanings. He did not conceal his political philosophy, partly because there was no competition and partly because some of the leading advertisers, including the Conrad brothers, were Southern Democrats whose memories of the Civil War insured their loyalty to the Democratic Party and to newspapers which espoused that political philosophy.

In 1876 Fort Benton's problems centered around shortages. Housing was scarce and building costs were higher than any place in the Territory. There was a chronic shortage of fuel, lumber, bricks, lime, and skilled workmen, made worse by the continual increase in population. But business boomed, money was plentiful, the fortunes of the Benton merchants grew, and in Benton there was never a shortage of optimism and hope. The new brick home of W. G. Conrad was completed in that year.

Both the house and furnishings were widely discussed in Fort Benton, not only in discussion groups but also in the newspapers. The furniture in the house and the shrubs and plantings on the outside were brought in from Virginia. One piece of furniture was described by the *Record* in its June 2, 1876 issue:

W. G. Conrad's house is furnished with new and expensive furniture. One special item, a French Walnut Secretary and bookcase, combine a most beautiful piece of furniture with a marvel of mechanical ingenuity and skill. Closed it resembles a small musical instrument. A more useful and elegant library ornament cannot be imagined, and it cost, it is said, a small fortune. As bachelors seldom take so much pains on furnishing houses it is but reasonable to assume that the Benton circle of brides will soon include a Mrs. W. G. Conrad, at least we hope so.

The editor's hope was realized later in the year, when, according to the biographical sketch of William Conrad in M. A. Leeson's *History of Montana*, "He espoused the daughter of Hon. Paul L. and Almira (Hopper) Bowen of Virginia, Miss Fannie E. Bowen." Fannie came to Montana and as a bride moved into the new home. Though totally different from that she had known in Virginia, Fannie Conrad grew to love her new life. At Fort Benton, five children were born. Later the family moved to Great Falls, and then to Helena, where Fannie Conrad died in 1911. An article in the *Helena Independent Record* noted her passing:

Mrs. Conrad was the embodiment of southern hospitality and whether it was at Fort Benton in the early days, in Great Falls in later years, or more recently in Helena, her friends always knew they were more than welcome in her home. In recent years Mrs. Conrad had not been physically able to take the leading part she did in earlier days in the social life and the philanthropies of the commonwealth in which she lived, but those who had the pleasure of her acquaintance and friendship in the early days recall the delightful way in which she did what she could to make others happy. But she never lost her interest in the welfare of those less fortunate than herself, and there were many, not only among her close associates, but among those who looked to her as a friend in time of need, who will sincerely mourn her. The legislature of Montana in session at the time of the death of Mrs. Conrad adjourned as a special mark of respect to her memory.

The Conrad brothers entered the banking field in 1880, when they opened the First National Bank of Fort Benton. Later they opened banks in Great Falls, Helena, and Kalispell. All of their banks were successful, for the reputation of the Conrads for honesty and fair dealing was well-established. An illustration of this integrity was pointed up in 1897, when they sold the Northwestern National Bank of Great Falls.

The buyers milked the bank and within a few months it was in the hands of a receiver. Upon learning of this, the Conrads notified each depositor that his claim would be paid in full by the Conrad brothers. They assumed the payment of potential claims amounting to nearly

$1,000,000, even though they were not legally obligated to do so. The brothers were unwilling that any depositor who had placed funds in the bank, relying on their established reputation, should suffer any loss. The Conrads superintended the settlement of the bank's affairs. Depositor panic ceased and no loss was suffered by any bank customer.

The *Helena Independent Record* of November 19, 1897, printed the story of this action and stated:

> We doubt if there is a similar National Bank case on record and if the depositors will comply with the circular letter issued, the affairs of the Northwestern National will be closed up in a shorter time than has ever been known in the case of a national bank. We wish there were 175,000 Conrad Brothers in Montana.

The winter of 1881 was a cold one, which brought high fuel prices during the heating season — wood going for $15.00 a cord and up — and low water during the navigation season. The winter was cold enough to cause the editor of the *River Press* to make this comment: "The late Chinook had a very marked effect on the mustache of a popular young gentleman of Teton. Better put it on again, old boy, the cold weather is not over yet." The flow of the river was so low that many of the boats had to unload at Cow Island, and the cargo was brought to Fort Benton by ox train over the long, expensive overland route. In spite of these difficulties, business for the year totaled $35 million, 1,300 passengers arrived, and 2,400 surrendering Sioux Indians were moved by the boats. In June, the *Press* complained that, while 3,500 tons of freight awaited shipment at Bismarck, the fleet was "carrying bands of Indians on a picnic." The boats were transporting Indians to reservations. This was no picnic for the displaced Indians, but to the editor, even letting them live was akin to a picnic.

The cattle business also was expanding in Montana, with thousands of cattle on the open range that had previously supported the buffalo. With the buffalo gone, there was nothing for the wolves and Indians to feed on except the white man's cattle, which they did in increasing numbers. However, the cattlemen flourished in spite of their losses.

Fort Benton continued to grow. More businesses opened, new buildings and warehouses were going up. Construction was started on the Grand Union Hotel, which was to be the finest hostelry between St. Paul, Minnesota, and the Pacific Coast. The population reached 1,618, of which 30 were Chinese, who brought a new problem to Fort Benton. In the January 19, 1881 issue of the *River Press*, the editor, under the headline, "Opium Den," wrote: "A new degradation to which Western towns are subjected through the introduction of the Chinese — low resorts for opium smoking. Stamp it out."

In 1881 Fort Benton did not have a telephone, but a resident of Montana had actually used one. The March 23 issue of the *River Press* stated that "James H. Wells, Commissioner of Beef at Fort Clagett, was introduced to a telephone a few days ago."

As more of the residents of Fort Benton began to die of natural causes, with their boots off, a new interest arose in the manner and place of burial. No longer were men satisfied with a shallow grave, a rude wooden cross, or a plank stuck at the grave head with perhaps a name and date of death. In some cases the site even had been obliterated, so that Indians would not dig up the reposing body and take another scalp to add to their collection. The sentiment now was for a permanent and lasting burial ground, with regulation graves and a stone on which could be engraved "Here Lies" and other vital statistics that preserve the memory of the dead.

On December 7, 1881, the *River Press* reported that,

> A meeting of a large number of prominent citizens was held to establish a new cemetery. It is proposed to divide the ground into four or five divisions setting apart a section for the Odd Fellows, Masons, Catholics, Episcopalians and other denominations and also to reserve a potters' field or place to lay to rest those who are buried by the county.

Surely this was a very fair and even-handed solution to the problem of preserving in death the sanctity of the groupings that had been maintained in life.

Despite a slow start and the problems brought on by weather, growth, and death, 1881 was the best business year in the history of the town. Fourteen thousand tons of cargo were brought up the river to Fort Benton. This was the largest tonnage for any previous year or any year to come.

CHAPTER 24
Fort Benton's Busiest Year

The last big year for Fort Benton proved to be 1882, but what a year it was. A mild winter permitted some building and business activities, and an early spring allowed both endeavors to take off with a frenzy. Building activity continued at a high rate. William H. Todd was pushing the construction of the Grand Union Hotel for an opening that year. J. R. Wilton was constructing houses priced at $1,600 for a one-story house and $2,000 for two stories. I. G. Baker and Company was awarded the contract for supplying the Northwest Mounted Police for the eighth consecutive year. In addition, they secured a contract to supply beef to the reservation Indians in Canada and the contract for hauling the mail between Fort Benton and the settlements of Western Canada. This firm was beating out not only the other Fort Benton merchants, but the Hudson's Bay Company as well. Trade tokens issued by that company, stamped H.B.C. and used in trading with the Indians, were over-stamped I.G.B. and put into trade for the Baker Company.

T. C. Power and Brother scored a first when it installed an elevator in its store in Fort Benton. Joel Overholser noted that in a February 10, 1872 issue of the *River Press*,

> A lessee of Nick Welch's Occidental promptly changed the name to Elevator Saloon, and Kitty Tonge was hired as Benton's first saleslady to put local men on their manners.

The school opened by Miss Tonge and Alicia Stanford closed when Alicia married C. E. Conrad and both young ladies started new careers.

The tourist industry also may have been born in 1882, when a group of ladies from Bismarck came upriver on the steamer *Big Horn* for a tour of Fort Benton. After seeing the sights of the vanishing frontier, they returned to Bismarck to report to their less venturesome husbands and friends.

In 1883 the Canadian Pacific Railroad reached Calgary. This cut down on that merchandise shipped to Fort Benton used to supply the Canadian trade, but had little effect on the Conrads' Canadian operations, at least for the next few years. They merely shipped their goods on the Canadian Pacific as far as they could and then used their bull and mule trains to supply the outlying posts and Indian reservations.

The year 1883 brought to Fort Benton the first demonstration of electricity as a source of energy. In July the steamboat *Rosebud* came for an exhibition of this wondrous source of light. Crowds gathered at the docks and when darkness fell the crude steam generator was started and furnished electricity to light a flood light which directed a beam over the town. The tallest building was the Grand Union Hotel. The beam was played on this structure to show its power and the distance it would carry. As the spotlight reached a balcony of the hotel, it brought into view a prominent bachelor of the town, amorously entwined with the wife of a leading citizen. This produced an electric shock that had not been anticipated.

Few would grasp the significance of the demonstration, not even the Conrads. The prediction of J. A. Kanouse in his speech at the Centennial Celebration in 1876 that Fort Benton would become the "Chicago of the West" even then was not firmly founded. However, the coming of electricity would destroy any chance that Fort Benton might become an industrial hub. The Great Falls of the Missouri, 30 miles upstream, which had insured the success of Fort Benton as the head of the river navigation, would now insure that it would never be more than the county seat of an agricultural community. When the falls were harnessed for the production of power, industry went to the new city of Great Falls, not to Fort Benton.

The opening of the Grand Union Hotel on November 2, 1882, was the greatest social event in Fort Benton's history. People came from all over the vast trading area. Even the Southerners came, shutting their eyes to the fact that the Hotel was named in honor of the Union Army in the Civil War. Mounties came down from Canada. Wolfers forsook their traps and strychnine. Wagon drivers held up their ox trains, swelling the crowd with drivers, mule skinners, bullwhackers, and roustabouts. Miners came from the mines, stockmen and cowboys left their herds, and Charlie Russell came over from the Musselshell. Best of all there were more than 100 white women from Fort Benton and the surrounding ranches. Less than ten years before, in 1872, the Reverend W. W. Van Orsdel had been preaching the Methodist gospel and reported that there were only two white women in Fort Benton, one of whom was George Baker's wife.

The Hotel was built and furnished at a cost of $200,000. Five hundred thousand bricks, all made at Fort Benton, went into its construction. The *River Press* claimed that:

The Grand Union Hotel in 1882, the year it opened
Courtesy John G. Lepley

Fort Benton can proudly lay claim to the best Hotel in the Northwest, the Grand Union. It has 50 rooms all well lighted and ventilated, and offering solid comfort to the sojourner at the river metropolis. Spelzley and Co. have furnished the house in fine style, rendering it first class in all its appointments, and the Grand Union has already earned an enviable reputation at home.

The grand opening culminated with a ball, at which the mode of dress ranged from the hide and skin garments of the wolfers and trappers to white tie and tails for the merchants and business men. The ladies were arrayed as they had never been before. Long before the event, special evening gowns were ordered from the fashion centers in the East, and opening night found the women of Fort Benton as elegantly attired and as beautiful as their sisters at Delmonico's in New York or the Willard Hotel in Washington, D.C. The frontier music did not attain that degree of elegance found in the East, but it was rhythmic, lively, and well-suited for the ball that opened the Grand Union Hotel in Fort Benton.

The brilliant social event provided by the opening of the Grand Union gave only a temporary respite to the merchants of Fort Benton in their ceaseless efforts to keep merchandise coming in and going out — not only to keep it moving, but protecting it along the long, difficult wagon trails from Fort Benton to destinations hundreds of miles away. Protection, too, was the responsibility of the owners. C. E. Conrad closed out the year on this type of a mission. On December 28, 1882, the *Fort Benton Record* reported that,

> Chas. E. Conrad, single handed and alone, made a raid on the camp of Chief Black Weasel and arrested the Chief's son for theft and depredation of I. G. Baker and Co. property.

The Indians stood in awe of bravery and had a deep respect for Conrad, whose reputation left no doubt of his fearlessness and bravery. The article stated that,

> Since the raid the Piegans have been making every effort to make a treaty with the house of I. G. Baker and Co. Robes, horses and peltries of all kinds are brought in by the friends of the prisoner for the purpose of securing his release as well as a guarantee of future good behavior.

CHAPTER 25
1883, The Beginning of the End

In the November 7, 1879 issue of the *Fort Benton Record*, the editor wrote: "Trade in Benton was never better. The nearer the railroads get to Benton the faster the town grows." The same editor reported in July, 1883, that business was gone, the levee was deserted, and "not even a dog fight relieved the monotony."

The 1883 season opened well and the Conrads hoped that business would be as good as during the previous year. How good that was and some indication of the business abilities of the brothers — then only 33 and 35 — are indicated in a letter from I. G. Baker. On February 13, 1883, Baker wrote from St. Louis:

> Messrs. C. E. and W. G. Conrad, Fort Benton, Montana. Dear Sirs: Yours of the 29th copy of inventory enclosed received. If it was a showing of $40,000 or $50,000 of profits I would say it was a splendid showing. So now when it is a quarter of a million I don't know what to say. Such results must produce a very enjoyable feeling and I know it must be gratifying to you that you have so far outstripped all other merchants and placed yourselves way up and beyond any that are now or ever were in the Territory. With such a start at your ages your possibilities are very great to rank high as capitalists. With me it is a very comfortable feeling to know that the four years passed over has year by year reduced the amount of responsibility and at the same time shown your increasing ability to meet the obligations you two assumed. I suppose you have heard the army contract for Mo. River and Montana are to be let at St. Paul the 1st of February. Yours truly, I. G. Baker.

The letter had reference only to the Baker Company business. Over and above this were the profits realized by the brothers from their cattle, mining, banking, and other businesses.

Each of the Conrads became a part of the political system in 1883. Charles was appointed County Commissioner to replace Joseph Hill, who resigned, and William was elected the first Mayor, after the city was incorporated in that year.

The steam boats made 35 trips into Fort Benton, with about 9,000 tons of cargo, during the 1883 shipping season. The trade into Canada was brisk. I. G. Baker and Company moved several wagon trains north to fulfill its Canadian contracts. A bull train to supply the Baker stores in Canada moved out of Fort Benton in July, 1883. The route of the Cana-

Railroad construction in late 1880s Courtesy Montana Historical Society

dian Pacific Railroad into Calgary from the East was completed on August 11, 1883. After this arrival, the railroad supplied more and more of the Canadian trade, but the Baker Company would continue to supply its Canadian stores out of Fort Benton until they were sold.

At about the same time, the lines of the Northern Pacific Railroad met in Montana Territory, at Gold Creek between Helena and Missoula. This cut the trade to Helena and beyond. The vast trade area of Fort Benton, which had extended from southern Montana to the Great Slave Lake in Canada, and west over the Mullan Road to Washington and Oregon, was now reduced to an area of less than a hundred miles around the city.

This was a severe blow, but it did not destroy the optimism of the Fort Benton merchants. Their philosophy seemed to be that, if railroads could hurt, they could also help. There was a general belief that the Canadian Pacific Railroad would be extended south to Fort Benton, and the Northern Pacific north from Billings. On this belief they built their hopes and concentrated their efforts. Railroad promoters drifted in and out of Fort Benton. It was thought that the Canadian Pacific line south was assured when Sir Alexander Galt, a Canadian railroad magnate from Montreal, expressed interest in the project and came to Fort Benton to promote it. There was also some interest in a railroad north from Helena to connect with the St. Paul, Minneapolis, and Manitoba (Great Northern), which James J. Hill was then building westward from St. Paul.

The Conrads believed that if Fort Benton could get rail connections to the north with the Canadian Pacific, south with the Northern Pacific, and maintain water traffic on the Missouri to keep rates competitive, Fort Benton could continue to be an important supply center. But all their wagons were not hitched to this star. They continued to expand their interests in cattle, mining, banking, and real estate, until their fortunes were secure — whatever the fate of Fort Benton.

CHAPTER 26
Great Falls Rises as Fort Benton Falls

During the 1884 season, only 15 steamboats came to Fort Benton, bringing 4,200 tons of cargo. With both the trade area and the cargo cut drastically, so was the need for the huge wagon trains to haul the freight. It required an enormous number of men, wagons, and animals to handle a peak year of 14,000 tons of freight. One three-wagon hitch could carry out eight tons of freight — four on the lead wagon, two and one-half on the swing wagon, and one and one-half on the trail wagon. Sixteen oxen were used on a three-wagon hitch. To move the 14,000 tons required about 1,740 wagons. A train might consist of 36 wagons, or 12 groups of three. One train would require 192 head of oxen and perhaps four bullwhackers, a cook, and roustabouts.

During the season these trains moved in and out of Fort Benton as fast as they could load, travel to their destination, unload, and return to load and start out again. At times there were 1,000 oxen stomping the dust or mud of the streets of Fort Benton. While they were waiting, the wagon crews were stomping around the saloons, gambling tables, and hurdy gurdys, which separated them from wages, usually $50 per month, for probably the hardest and most dangerous work on the frontier.

The freighters were a floating population and the main source of income for the saloons, gamblers, and prostitutes. When the freighting business declined, these establishments, which were open 24 hours a day to accommodate the baser desires of the freighters, were the first to suffer. From 14,000 tons to 4,000 tons of cargo spelled unemployment for a large number of freighters and disaster for a number of saloons, gamblers, and prostitutes. Many moved on in 1884.

Some of the older merchants did not survive. W. S. Wetzel went broke and Kleinschmidt and Brother closed its Fort Benton operation and moved the remaining stock to its store in Helena. The Wetzel bankruptcy had a sobering effect upon the business community of Fort Benton. The firm was well-established and thought to be financially sound. Wetzel had been a leader in the growth of Fort Benton. Only the year before he had constructed a home that eclipsed even the home of William G. Conrad in size and beauty. The fall of lesser men could be little noticed. When a giant toppled, it attracted wide attention and caused speculation as to who might be next.

The Grand Union Hotel, which had opened in 1882, seemingly destined for a brilliant future, went broke. It had been advertised, and was, the "foremost hostelry between St. Paul and the Pacific Coast." But even fine hotels need travelers, and the number of people traveling to Fort Benton was drastically curtailed. The Hotel was saved from the ignominy of being sold at sheriff's sale when it was redeemed by a group of local people who were willing to keep it open at a loss. This has been the subsequent history of the Grand Union. Each threat of bankruptcy brought forth some local family or group ready to save the historic old structure. When each believed that he had contributed enough, another rich cattleman or grain farmer took over. The result has been that the Grand Union remains operating as a hotel, and constantly is being renovated with the hope of ultimate restoration to its original grandeur, or at least of preservation as an historic site.

The City of Great Falls was founded by Paris Gibson in 1884. Fort Benton had not been kind to Gibson. He opened a lumber yard there in September of 1871, which was closed on October 10, 1871. His quick business demise was reported to have been occasioned by T. C. Power, who opened a rival business and intentionally froze Gibson out. Gibson had seen the Rosebud's demonstration on electricity. Its significance was not lost on him, but a lack of finances prevented his exploitation of this new idea. He went into the sheep business, in which he had some success, enough to provide money for moving around and exploring.

Gibson saw the potential of the Great Falls of the Missouri for the operation of power, but the project was too big for one man. He became friendly with James J. Hill, who was building the St. Paul, Minneapolis, and Manitoba Railroad and was looking for any opportunity to generate railroad business. Hill came to Montana and, with Gibson, examined that area of the Missouri River. They bought land along an 18-mile stretch of the river on both sides, which included the falls and cascades having such a vast potential for the generation of electric power.

Near the falls they platted a townsite, which they named Great Falls, in honor of the falling waters which they hoped to harness. The townsite prospered as a railroad division point and agricultural center for the storage and milling of grain. The new city was called the "Electric City" in anticipation of what was to come. The theme was carried even further when the new county was created and called Cascade County for the miles of cascades over which the falling water tumbled.

Financing a power development proved to be beyond the efforts of both Hill and Gibson. Hill was too busy raising capital for the construction of his Great Northern Railway, and Gibson was unable to find other financing. In the early 1900s, Cornelius Ryan, looking for power for the Anaconda Copper Mining Company, saw the falls as the answer to his problem. Hill agreed to sell, knowing that development would generate

Steamboat *Rosebud* at Drowned Man's Rapids
Courtesy John G. Lepley

business for his railroad. Hill and Gibson sold their river land to the Great Falls Waterpower and Contract Company at less than its cost. This company, the predecessor of the Montana Power Company, started construction of the dams, and Great Falls became the Electric City that Gibson had envisioned. Power produced at Great Falls was carried to Butte and Anaconda to produce copper, and for many years the Milwaukee Railroad was operated on power from the Great Falls of the Missouri.

Both Gibson and Hill were men of vision. In this instance the vision proved to be beyond their capabilities of realization, but they saw it realized by others. Hill said later that one of his greatest regrets was the inability to develop the land and waters along the Missouri River. Gibson had like regrets, but must have been consoled as he watched his town eliminate Fort Benton as the business hub of the area and saw the people of Fort Benton move upriver to settle in his new town.

CHAPTER 27
The Manitoba Comes to Fort Benton

Fort Benton's decline continued in 1885. Only 3,500 tons came by boat. The Coulson Line, once the largest on the river, sold its boats and went out of business.

The *Record*, Fort Benton's first newspaper, was sold at sheriff's sale and would never publish another issue. Later in the year, the *River Press* was destroyed by fire. The owners of the *River Press* acquired the equipment of the defunct *Record* and came out the next week, missing only one issue.

Building in Fort Benton came to a complete halt. The contractors, artisans, and a large number of people moved to Great Falls, which, from all appearances, would become one of the leading cities of the state.

Some merchants and businessmen hung on, still hoping for rail connections to the north and south. These hopes were not without foundation, for lines were being surveyed and money raised for railroad construction. There was still plenty of money in Fort Benton, and there seemed no hesitation in pledging it to secure a railroad. The greatest hope was the line from Calgary to Fort Benton. Sir Alexander Galt was still interested. If he continued his interest, the line could be built.

There was further decline in river traffic in 1886, with only 3,000 tons coming into Fort Benton. The I. G. Baker Company was still shipping cargo via the river. The Conrads were still supplying points in Canada with bull trains. In spite of the Canadian Pacific Railroad, the brothers maintained ties with the Mounted Police and had contracts to supply beef to the Canadian Indian reservations. Their stores in Calgary, Fort Walsh, and Lethbridge still provided the Hudson's Bay Company with the stiffest competition in any of its Canadian operations. The Baker Company was more popular with the Canadian government and the people than was the Hudson's Bay Company. The Conrad brothers could be counted on to supply any need at lower prices and in a more pleasant manner than the moribund Canadian company that retained many of the traits it acquired when it had a monopoly.

The Conrads maintained the I. G. Baker store and warehouse in Fort Benton, using it not only to supply the dwindling local trade area, but also as the distribution center for the Canadian operations.

Bull train on the old Macleod Trail in 1878 Courtesy University of Montana Library

Wool added a new dimension to Fort Benton trade. Falling cattle prices drove some ranchers into raising sheep. The sheep men remained loyal to Fort Benton and it became headquarters for the wool growers. When they met in Fort Benton in the fall, the town was filled with activity. The hotels were full and the docks busy, as over a million pounds of wool was loaded out on the steamboats for shipment down the Missouri.

Sir Alexander Galt's survey crews were out staking the rail-line to Canada, which raised further the hopes of the always optimistic people of Fort Benton.

The year 1887 was a bad one for Fort Benton. The hard winter, which had begun the previous fall, continued. The merchants were low on supplies; fuel was scarce and expensive. The asking price for coal was $60 per ton, and buildings were torn down for use as fuel. On January 19, 1887, the *River Press* reported: "Only 100 sacks of flour in town, coal oil is scarce, this community is in a bad fix." The severe weather conditions devastated the cattle herds. After the chinook in February, cow hides began pouring into Fort Benton in numbers that almost equaled the height of the buffalo-robe-trade days.

The steamship *Rosebud* arrived on April 26, 1887, bringing 300 tons of cargo. Thirty-two other boats arrived during the season, bringing in 5,800 tons in all, mainly equipment and supplies for the Manitoba Railroad being built west from Minot, Dakota Territory. Supplying the railroad made business good in Fort Benton most of the year, but it all came to a halt when the Manitoba Railroad, a part of Jim Hill's railroad empire, arrived at Fort Benton on September 29, 1887. The *River Press* reported the arrival with the following story:

> Fort Benton turned out with pomp and ceremony for its own funeral September 29, 1887, the day the Manitoba Railway reached the city. The Fort Benton Brass Band played, flags and bunting decked the carriages which transported the ladies of the town dressed in their finest gowns, and the men turned out in derby hats and polished boots. Mrs. James J. Hill, wife of the Empire builder, drove the silver spike in the coffin of Fort Benton's commercial supremacy. Three days later the first box cars arrived from St. Paul.
>
> Enroute to Fort Benton, sweating track crews laid 530 miles of track beginning April 2 at Minot. August 11, 1887, somewhere in the boundaries of Choteau County, the steel gangs laid eight miles and 160 feet of rails, a record that still stands. The Manitoba Railroad employed 9,000 men and 7,000 horses on the record job.
>
> Steamboats were busy all summer carrying supplies for the railroad and Montana settlements, then dropped down the river never to return. The big Fort Benton merchants quit business or moved to Great Falls or Helena. Stage coaches ran to Judith a few years longer but the steamboat era ended and freighters and rivermen drifted away.

The railroad did not come into the townsite itself but stayed about two miles out. It was built on the level prairie and was not extended down the steep slopes to the site of the town until 1900. For several years, freight arriving at or departing from Fort Benton still had to be hauled by wagons from the town on the banks of the Missouri up the long hill to the railroad, high above the city.

Once driven, the silver spike was removed and replaced by one of baser metal. Hill did leave the spike that his wife had pounded into the heart of Fort Benton. It is still on display at the city's museum.

The first freight brought in on the Manitoba arrived on October 5, 1887, a carload of groceries for I. G. Baker and Company, and a carload of whiskey for Gans and Klein. The gloom of the Fort Benton people was probably better assuaged by the Gans shipment than that of I. G. Baker and Company. The time required for the shipment told the story of Fort Benton's demise as a transportation center: the Manitoba, 6 days, 23 hours from St. Paul to Fort Benton; by steamer, 9 days, 23 hours from Bismarck.

The railroad brought Jim Hill and Charles E. Conrad together. They became friends and would become business associates when Conrad left Fort Benton to start another business career in western Montana.

CHAPTER 28
The Years of Transition

The years 1888 and 1889 were years of transition both for Fort Benton and for I. G. Baker and Company. The Conrads continued to maintain stores in Fort Benton and Canada. They were active in the business affairs of the city and prime movers in getting a plant for the generation of electricity at Fort Benton. This was accomplished in March of 1888, well ahead of any other city in the Territory. Their Conrad Circle Cattle Company became one of the largest in the Northwest. They were acquiring mining properties and expanding their banking systems. W. G. acquired a home in Virginia, where he stayed for longer periods, although he maintained homes in Great Falls and Helena as well. C. E. continued to live in Fort Benton and, in 1889, was a delegate from Chouteau County to the Constitutional Convention, which adopted an acceptable constitution and secured statehood for the former territory.

The convention introduced Conrad to the full political power of the "Copper Kings," who exerted considerable influence upon the writing of the constitution. Conrad and his group were able to exercise some restraint upon the appetites for power of the Copper Kings but, in spite of all efforts, the constitution contained clauses protecting what the companies conceived to be their interests. One clause required all metals to be taxed only on their value in place in the ground. Another provided that cities in Montana should have only the powers given to them by specific act of the State Legislature. By these provisions metals could only be taxed in their least valuable state, and the mining companies could control the action of all the cities and towns in the state at one central point, the State Legislature, which met for only 60 days every two years.

Following a battle that shook the state to its very foundations, the taxation provision was finally amended to permit taxation of the net proceeds of mining operations. But cities and towns in Montana are still hampered in their exercise of legislative power by vestiges of the philosophy by which the copper interests sought to control the legislative power of the state.

The cattle operations of the Conrads were increasing in size and importance, and the cattle industry was significant in the state. In 1889 a report from the Governor's office gave the livestock population of the state as 1,250,000 cattle, 230,000 horses, and 2,150,000 sheep. On October 30, 1899, the *River Press* reported, "Two train loads of beef for the Chicago market were loaded out at the Fort Benton stockyards today. Two train loads a day have been shipped out from these yards every day of the week."

In May of 1888, Canada honored its beloved Queen Victoria. In the *Calgary Record* of May 23, I. G. Baker and Company ran an advertisement which said, "God Save the Queen." It was the only business firm in the city to note the event. The Hudson's Bay Company, the most English of them all, gave no public recognition of this important celebration.

In 1889 the new water system at Fort Benton commenced to deliver water to the residents of the city. It was another first in which the Conrads played an important role.

With the decline in business, Charles had time for other activities. The October 30, 1889 issue of the *River Press* reported:

> Hon. Chas. E. Conrad, accompanied by his wife and Mr. T. J. Todd, made up a hunting party last Friday and went to Harwood's Lake. They enjoyed the trip and "camping out" immensely and were very successful in bringing down wild geese and ducks. The most interesting event was that of Mrs. Conrad taking her first shot at wild geese on the wing, in which she scored a point, bringing down a fine bird by breaking its wing at the first shot. Like all hunters she determined to bag the game unassisted which she succeeded in doing in handsome style. Her good fortune did not end here, for two more unlucky birds flew within range of her trusty gun and fell a prey to her good marksmanship. It is safe to say that Mrs. Conrad enjoyed the sport full as well as the gentlemen of the party and her good luck will probably tempt her to try again.

The local social life continued, as noted by the *River Press* on December 11, 1889:

> The young gentlemen of Fort Benton propose to give one of their pleasant social dances Friday evening at Stocking's Hall. They plan to keep up these dances during the whole winter season.

By 1889 the Indians had been pacified. Stated in another way, they were completely cowed, broken in spirit, and confined to reservations. They were, however, beginning to adapt to their new lives. On November 11, 1899, the *River Press* printed an article titled, "Blackfeet Becoming Civilized." It stated that the Blackfeet Reservation comprised 1,760,000 acres. It was populated by approximately 2,000 Blackfeet, Blood, and Piegan Indians, most living in log homes. A few farmed on a small scale. The *River Press* article continued:

> For a period of ten years from 1888, the annual appropriation for them is $150,000 for supplies, wagons and implements, horses, cattle and buildings and used for maintenance of schools.
>
> 2,000 brood mares and ten stallions were bought last summer. With

126

wagons 30 Indians engage in freighting from Fort Benton and receive $1.25 per cwt. in cash. For other labor for the government they receive $1.00 to $1.50 per day paid in tickets exchangeable for supplies.

Chief White Calf and other big and little Indians get a weekly ration of 4 lb. of beef and 5 of flour paid every week. The sick and infirm get an extra ration every week which takes about 20 good Montana beef steers. White Calf does not like the presence at the Agency of the colored troops. He said, "I don't want them here. Let them go back to the place where they grew up and turned black. My people are dark enough for me and I want them to turn white."

Chiefs White Calf, Big Nose and Tearing Lodge constitute a police tribunal to try misdemeanors committed on the reservation. Thirty days on the wood pile is the fate of the Indians caught drunk or having liquor. Despite all precautions some Indians get whiskey. When caught the liquor is spilt by one of the police breaking the bottle on the Agency flag staff. Shortly after one of these breakings an old squaw picked up a glass fragment and sorrowfully licked it.

Lately some rich quartz has been found in the main range of the Rockies directly west of the Agency and in the opinion of old timers, there will be several mining camps before long. Prospecting and mining are forbidden but the prospectors and miners get there just the same.

Coal is used at the Agency from a vein on Two Medicine Creek.

On January 1, 1890, the *River Press* had more to report on the Indian situation:

The Piegan braves are fast becoming civilized. They were once the fiercest and most warlike of all the Northwest tribes. The other day Captain Aubrey came to Fort Benton with 20 wagons, each wagon driven by a Piegan brave, owner of his outfit, who is paid by the government for the freight he hauls.

Not all Indians were so fortunate. On October 30, 1889, the *River Press* said:

Justice George Crane sent an erring sister of Indian ancestry to the county refrigerator yesterday to abide therein for 30 days. She had been made drunk by whiskey furnished by some disreputable white men. The officials should arrest some of the men for furnishing whiskey to these poor creatures which is also against the law. Give them a little of the same kind of law medicine administered to their victims.

These Indians continued to trade at the I. G. Baker and Company stores both in Fort Benton and in Canada. Charles E. Conrad's strong ties with the Indians would continue until his death.

CHAPTER 29
An Empire Dismantled

The census of 1890 was an undeniable confirmation of what the people of Fort Benton knew, but hated to acknowledge. The population of the city had fallen from 1,618 in 1880 to 624 in 1890. Meanwhile, Great Falls, which had not existed in 1880, had grown to 3,979 in the six years since its founding. Other census statistics revealed that Montana had a population of 143,000. Of these, 93,000 were males, 50,000 females, and 1,000 Negroes. Indians were not given the dignity of a separate classification, but were lumped into a grouping as "others, 14,000."

The steamboats confirmed Fort Benton's drop in business. The *F. Y. Batchelor*, the only remaining boat of the once great Block P Line, came to Fort Benton on June 12, 1890, and unloaded 300 tons of cargo. When the *Batchelor* departed, sounding its mournful whistle for the last time as it passed from sight around the bend, effective steamboat traffic into Fort Benton was ended forever. The people of the town had pleaded with the Corps of Engineers and the U.S. Congress for 20 years to make channel improvements in the river. On the last trip of the *Batchelor*, Captain Tom Mariner, aptly named for his profession, announced that there was 100 percent improvement in the river channel because of work recently completed by the Corps of Engineers. He said bars and impediments on which the steamers had frequently grounded had been removed. Had the work been done in the 1870s and 1880s, when it was needed, thousands of tons of cargo, several steamers, and untold hours of labor and steamer time could have been saved, as well as the long overland haul from Cow Island. Completed at the end of the water-transportation era on the Missouri, its only navigational aid would be to make easier the passage of the huge paddle fish up and down the river.

The merchants and townspeople of Fort Benton suffered through the long, hot summer doldrums, still hoping for railroad connections to restore prosperity. By fall it was evident to even the most optimistic that Fort Benton had the only railroad it would ever have. With the abandonment of this hope, the dream of Fort Benton continuing as an important transportation center collapsed and more businesses closed and more people moved to Great Falls. C. E. Conrad appeared to be unworried, for, on June 18, 1890, the *River Press* reported that he and his family had gone to Helena for a few days stay at the Broadwater, a famous and luxurious health spa then at the height of its popularity among the more wealthy people of Montana.

In August, 1890, I. G. Baker and Company decided to close its store in Fort Benton. An advertisement in the *River Press* announced that the selling-out sale would commence on September 1. The entire stock of general merchandise, groceries, dry goods, clothing, gents' furnishings, boots, shoes, hats, caps, wagons, and agricultural implements would be sold at net cost, for cash. The same ad was run in every issue of the paper until January 7, 1891. On September 10, 1890, the *River Press* reported:

> The rush at the I. G. Baker store is unprecedented in history. The army of clerks is kept busy from morning until night and goods are going like hot cakes.

Fort Benton had been able to stand up to the closing of small stores and the departure of lesser merchants, but losing I. G. Baker and Company was devastating. The firm had been the bulwark of the city's prosperity since 1865. With its closing, only T. C. Power and Brother remained as the last of the pioneer merchants. This store would remain open until 1932, when the Great Depression forced its sale. Although his store survived in Fort Benton those many years, T. C. Power, the founder, had moved to Helena in 1878. Helena became his center of interest and, in 1889, he was elected to the United States Senate.

Power was elected to the Senate by the Montana Legislature, which then held the authority to select United States Senators. During the fall of 1889, W. H. Todd, the editor of the *River Press*, offered the only diversion from the calamitous events that were befalling the people of Fort Benton. Power, so Todd thought, had run as an advocate of the free coinage of silver, then almost universally favored in the West. Following the election, Todd accused Power of reversing this position after he had promised to support free silver. Todd was a fiesty and gutsy man who, like most frontier editors, said what he thought in colorful language.

The *River Press* became a very vocal opponent of both T. C. Power, then in the U.S. Senate, and his brother, John Power, who was aspiring to a seat in the Montana Senate. The attacks became so annoying to the Powers that they pulled all of their advertising from the *River Press* and boycotted it completely. This might not have been so serious a few years before, when Fort Benton had lots of merchants, but the Power store was fast becoming the paper's only potential advertiser.

Still, the loss of the Power advertising did not deter Todd from his criticism. As a stronger persuasion, the Power brothers started a rival newspaper in Fort Benton, the *Review*. When Todd accused the Powers of owning the new paper, they denied it, but the denial did not convince the editor. In December, 1889, Todd called the *Review* a "Pavrick." He

Mule team in front of the T. C. Power & Brothers store
Courtesy John G. Lepley

said this was the nearest thing to a maverick, which means Ma-less or motherless, and went on to say:

> The Power brothers denied they had anything to do with the paper and the editor, who has been nursing the organ to keep it alive, would not acknowledge the poor little thing. It had no mother and was denied by its father and was in turn disowned by the pa.

> As near as we can get it T. C. Power and Bros' Fort Benton organ is a pavrick, a pa-less or fatherless animal.

Todd continued his opposition, but could not overcome the advertising boycott. The next month he sold the *River Press* to T. C. Power. He left Fort Benton, a thorn removed from the Power side.

On October 22, 1890, the *River Press* reported that, "The old levee warehouse of the I. G. Baker and Co. was yesterday torn down, its days of usefulness over." That note of finality was followed by yet another. On February 2, 1891, the *River Press* carried the story of the removal of the Fort Benton Bank that the Conrads had opened in 1880.

> Jos. A. Baker of the First National Bank of this city went to Great Falls to arrange for the removal of that Bank to Great Falls. It began its career here over ten years ago and was one of the most useful in the Northwest.

> The move necessitated a change of name since there is already a First National Bank of Great Falls. (It became the Northwest National Bank.)

The close-out sale of the I. G. Baker and Company store in Fort Benton ended in January of 1891. The records of the Company's operations since 1865 were stored in its only remaining warehouse, with little concern for their care or preservation. John Lepley, a lifelong resident of Fort Benton, recalls that, as a boy, he watched the destruction of the old warehouse. Hundreds of boxes of records were thrown into the Missouri River, which washed away any contribution they might have made to history. The records of the Power store, which did not close until 1932, were preserved. Descendants of T. C. Power gave the records to the Montana Historical Society, and they are now in the archives of the Society, in Helena.

The pioneer merchants of Fort Benton had set their minds on destiny, not history. The burden of the preservation of history too often falls on the descendants, the ancestor having been too occupied in the making of history to bother with its preservation. Luckily the Power records were still in existence and could be saved. The Baker records were largely destroyed, but a few remain. These are now preserved, part of them in the archives of the University of Montana, in Missoula, and others in the archives of the Montana Historical Society, in Helena. They are pitifully few to record the history of the firm that probably made the greatest contribution to the settlement of the area in which it operated.

The I. G. Baker and Company stores in Canada, at Fort Walsh, Calgary, and Fort Macleod, were sold to the Hudson's Bay Company in 1891. The stores were still showing a profit, but not one of the dimensions to which the Conrads were accustomed. More money could be made on cattle, banking, and land development, and those interests occupied all of their time. The stores had become something of a nuisance.

The Hudson's Bay Company was pleased to be rid of the Conrad brothers as competition. In an article in the *Great Falls Tribune*, on December 16, 1906, W. G. Conrad was quoted in recollection of the sale:

> We gave the Hudson Bay Company such keen competition in the purchase of furs that they finally concluded to buy us out and we abandoned our trading posts and this portion of the business. If I may relate an incident without subjecting myself to a charge of immodesty it will throw some light on the success with which Fort Benton business men carried the war in competition with the great Hudson's Bay Company. At a dinner given by Sir Donald A. Smith, at his country place, Silver Heights, Winnipeg, after we sold out to the Hudson's Bay Company, and which was attended by a score of notable guests, including Cyrus Field, who laid the Atlantic cable, the manager of the Bank of Montreal, the general manager of the Canadian Pacific Railroad, one of the high officials of that company proposed the health of the writer as the man who had scaled the value of their stock down from pounds to shillings. Of course, the compliment would have been more justly applied to the hardy and adventurous men who did the trading, pushing forward always into new territory, my part being only in planning and directing operations from Fort Benton. Our operations in furs were very large and widely extended, a good many being sold in Europe, and I remember getting sales accounts from St. Petersburg,

I. G. Baker Courtesy John G. Lepley

expressed in rubles, which pleased me greatly at the time as I took them for
dollars until I inquired into the account further. In one year we shipped
30,000 tanned buffalo robes and 25,000 wolf skins to St. Louis by our boats.

I. G. Baker and Company was always more popular with the Canadian
government and the people than was the Hudson's Bay Company. The
withdrawal of the Conrad brothers from the Canadian business scene
was a loss that was felt deeply. On February 25, 1891, the *River Press*
reprinted the following editorial from the *Macleod Gazette*:

> It is now known beyond a doubt that the mercantile business of I. G.
> Baker and Co. in the Northwest has been transferred to the Hudson's Bay
> Company. Two or three months will probably elapse before all the details
> of the transfer are completed and the time honored firm of I. G. Baker and
> Co. is numbered with the things that are passed. The *Gazette* will echo the
> sentiments of every man in this country when it expresses the deepest
> regret that the I. G. Baker and Co. have decided to give up business. The

highest tribute that we can give to this firm is necessarily poor and small when we consider what the country and the settlers of the country owe to them. Their whole business course in the Northwest has been marked by almost prodigal generosity and kindness to those who have done business with them. To the struggling ranchman first starting business they have never refused to extend a helping hand. Many a business man in the country has been enabled to tide over his difficulties through timely assistance from I. G. Baker and Co. To enumerate the thousands of instances in which they have ungrudgingly helped the struggling business man and settler would be unnecessary. Their record in this country is too well known to require that, and words fail us in attempting to voice the general feeling of gratitude to I. G. Baker and Co. which exists in this country.

With the closing of the stores in Fort Benton and Canada, the honored and respected name of I. G. Baker and Company passed from the business scene of Canada and the northwestern part of the United States. Thereafter, the Conrads would operate as a partnership under the name of Conrad Brothers, with the Bakers having no interest in any of the numerous business enterprises of the partnership. Joseph Baker retained a beautiful ranch in the Highwood Mountains, where he spent considerable time. I. G. Baker, the founder of the Company, loved to spend a part of each summer at the ranch, and did so as long as his health permitted. When he was there, the ranch became a haven for the remaining pioneers. They gathered to reminisce about the early days and to enjoy the company of I. G. Baker, who was a much-loved part of the scenes they recollected.

CHAPTER 30
Search for a New Frontier

The sale of the store and the removal of the bank to Great Falls would sever the business ties of the Conrad brothers to Fort Benton. They would still own one warehouse and some vacant lots, for which there would be no demand for many years. They had some questionable accounts, as indicated by a letter written by William to Charles, which also provides some insight into the working of their minds and the future that lay ahead. On April 12, 1891, William wrote to Charles from White Post, Virginia:

> I am glad to get your letter telling me who Comstock and A. A. White are. (They were two of the men chosen by James J. Hill to work with C. E. Conrad in establishing the townsite of Kalispell as a division point on Hill's Great Northern Railway.) I hope we will make some money out of this business as we have made none since the Canadian grub contracts. Am glad you say we are going to collect up and you are right. As soon as an account gets old and if we don't get them this summer, we will lose them. We have no favors to ask of these parties and we should make them pay if they are worth anything. In reference to contracts this would be a good time to buy grain. I have always noticed that when beef was high and scarce we usually bought it low in the fall and that grain gotten at present prices we would feed it next fall and winter at a profit. But I don't know that it is best to bother with it. When we have a lot of trashy things to attend to, it bothers us and occupies our minds so that we do not look after things that could be of more importance.

The brothers could make a complete break with Fort Benton and with ease move on to other things. While residents of Fort Benton, they were among the city's most loyal and useful citizens. The break would not be so easy for Fort Benton. The activities of the Conrads had been too important not to be missed in many ways. They left gaps in the lives of Fort Benton and its people that would never be filled.

The Methodist Episcopal Church wrote Charles after he had moved from Fort Benton to the Flathead Valley in western Montana:

> Fort Benton, Sept. 8, 1891. Hon. C. E. Conrad. Dear Sir and Bro. At the last official meeting of the M. E. Church of Fort Benton you was again elected as one of the trustees of said church. And as the conference has sent us Rev. H. D. Wadsworth formerly of my state and as you know that was the meeting that his salary came up and as Sister Bell did the collecting of the

funds last year she said you always gave 30 or 40 dollars each year for the support of the minister. I was directed to write you as to your willingness to give this year and as you know we need your help now more than ever before. So the Church is hopeful of your doing toward it. Will you please write to me in relation to it so I can report to our next meeting. And if you are desirous of paying any portion of what you may give please send a check to Rev. H. D. Wadsworth, Fort Benton, and you can rest assured that the Church will be very grateful to you for your kindness toward her. Signed W. C. Schecker, Recording Secretary. M. E. Church, Fort Benton, Montana.

In 1891, $40 would pay the salary of a minister for a large part of the year. The loss of C. E. Conrad as a contributing member would create a burden hard for the M. E. Church to sustain.

Trouble, too, seems to come when the master is absent. News of it travels fast and sometimes in short and cryptic terms. Witness the following letter:

Mr. C. E. Conrad, Kalispell, Montana. Dear Sir: Your calf has been stolen and the smallest Shetland pony died Saturday. We have been unable to tell from what cause. Yours truly, (James) Stanford.

The paths and interests of the brothers would now diverge for the first time since they stepped ashore at Fort Benton in 1868. Something in William's nature seemed to demand that the family name be restored to prominence in their Virginia homeland. A few years before, he had purchased and renovated a pre-Civil War mansion at White Post, Virginia, which he named Montana Hall. He gained some prominence in that community as a man who had gone to the western frontier and returned a millionaire. William reestablished himself in Virginia and even disinterred the members of his immediate family who were buried in Montana for reburial in Virginia. The mansion he restored in White Post is still called Montana Hall and is remembered as the home of a man who had conquered the West and made his fortune. It is not now owned by a Conrad descendant, but has been designated a national historical site and is described as one of the beautiful plantation homes representative of the Civil War Period.

Charles had no interest in returning to Virginia. That life now seemed to him sterile and uninteresting. He knew that William was losing some of his taste for the fierce competition that had characterized their business lives for more than 20 years. They now had greater wealth than they had ever expected or could hope to spend. William seemed somewhat inclined to withdraw from the business world and enjoy his wealth. Charles had an unquenchable thirst for empire building, which drove him to the day of his death, with sufficient momentum to carry William along.

Charles had always influenced the various enterprises, well back from center stage, leaving to William the political and public aspects of their activities. William loved the role and played it well. In the relationship of the brothers, it is interesting to note that I. G. Baker, who knew the brothers and their abilities, always addressed Charles first, although he was the younger. All of the correspondence between the brothers indicates that, in business decisions, William deferred to the judgment of Charles.

Charles was uncertain regarding his future, but he knew that he must establish himself in some location other than Fort Benton, and he knew that the course of empire lay to the west. Jim Hill was pushing his railroad ever westward. Soon it would cross the Continental Divide, snake down the course of the Middle Fork of the Flathead River and, once free of the mountains, enter the beautiful Flathead Valley where, building from both east and west, the trails would meet. With the railroad went progress and prosperity. Conrad's friendship with Jim Hill would make easier the tapping of the opportunities being created.

During the summer and fall of 1891, C. E. Conrad made trips westward to explore for a new location. Every place offered opportunities, but initially Spokane, Washington seemed to offer more to people with the tastes and means of the Conrads.

Alicia Stanford had come to Fort Benton in 1879. The change from a life of cultural pursuits in Halifax, Nova Scotia, to the rawness of the Western frontier was at first quite a shock. She grew to love the life at Fort Benton and was somewhat loath to leave. As business after business closed, it became evident that a dying Fort Benton could never satisfy the questing spirit of Charles E. Conrad in its pursuit of an ever-expanding empire. Lettie Conrad knew that a change was necessary. Her only choice was to steer it in a direction compatible with her tastes and the type of life she desired for her family, especially the children.

Spokane, situated in the rich agricultural area of Eastern Washington and near the new mining area of the Coeur d'Alene Mountains, was rapidly becoming a hub of growth and opportunity. It offered cultural attractions that were important in the eyes of Lettie, for she wanted her children to have every possible advantage. Charles also looked with favor upon Spokane. Business opportunities abounded. Fortunes were being made and empires created in banking, mining, cattle, and merchandising, all areas where Conrad had a proven competence. Moving to a new home could be accomplished by the Conrads with ease, but was out of the question for Fort Benton. Unable to change its location, the little city needed to search for a new life. The life it found was somewhat a blend of the lives of William and Charles Conrad. From William it took the tendency to relive and glory in the past. From Charles it took the ability to change course and keep building, however different the direction. The lives of Fort Benton and the Conrads were inextricably interwoven and entwined and will always remain so.

CHAPTER 31
Not Even a Dog Fight
Relieved the Monotony

The history of Fort Benton carries a haunting sadness and a sigh of what might have been. The Great Falls of the Missouri, 30 miles upstream, which impeded further upstream water traffic, insured that Fort Benton would be the head of navigation for the steamboats on the River. It is ironic that these same falls, together with the railroads, would put Fort Benton into near total eclipse. It was Paris Gibson, not the enterprising merchants of Fort Benton, who saw the potential of the falls for the generation of electricity. He founded the city of Great Falls, which became the industrial center of that area which Fort Benton had hoped to serve.

In 1891 the future of Fort Benton was bleak and unpromising. There was speculation that it would not survive. Business was at a standstill. There was no longer the thrill of the steamboat whistle as it rounded the bend and headed for the levee to unload all manner of things and new people. Gone was the time-honored custom of meeting boats to look over the new arrivals. No haystacks or oxen impeded traffic on Front Street, nor was the levee piled high with goods. The quiet of death settled on the town, to echo the editor of the *Fort Benton Record* when he wrote, "Not even a dog fight relieved the monotony."

Yet Fort Benton held more resilience than some had predicted. The hardy little city shook off the near knockout blows that had rained upon it. It now thrives as the county seat of Chouteau County, one of the wealthiest agricultural counties in the nation. With a population of approximately 2,000, it is as large or larger than at the peak of its prosperity as the head of commerce on the Missouri River. It is the home of numerous millionaire farmers and ranchers, who live well and comfortably with themselves, their neighbors, and others whose lives they touch.

The Missouri still runs in the same course past Fort Benton. It still curves to the right as it passes from view about one mile to the east and continues on its way to join the Mississippi far downstream. It is a much changed and regulated river and would scarcely be recognized by the boat captains of old as the wild, free-flowing stream that had thwarted all but the most skilled navigators.

The people of Fort Benton claim that it is the birthplace of Montana. In all of Montana there is no more historic place, nor one that, with all its history, is so little visited. Great Falls is a thorn in the side even in this aspect. The tourist speeds by on the way to lodging in Great Falls, seldom realizing that a few miles off Interstate 15 lies historic Fort Benton. History buffs seek out Fort Benton, revel in its legendary past, sleep in the old Grand Union, and get an eerie feeling that soon a steamboat will whistle at the bend or an ox train appear at the top of the river valley, where the prairie begins. This feeling was greatly intensified in those fortunate enough to talk with Joel Overholser in his cubbyhole at the *River Press*, where he has reigned as editor and chief writer. The entire history of Fort Benton marched through his mind, a knowledge he was willing to share with an unselfishness that belied the years he has devoted to collecting it.

The Conrad brothers would not be happy in Fort Benton today, for their natures required the excitement of empire building. Joseph Baker might, for he was a gentle soul who did not need a dog fight to relieve the monotony.

CHAPTER 32
Farewell Fort Benton

Charles and Alicia Conrad temporarily left Fort Benton in the early fall of 1890 to find a new home and a new life. Their intended destination was Spokane, Washington, with a stop enroute in the Flathead Valley of Western Montana to visit with Hal Stanford, Lettie Conrad's brother.

The trip from Fort Benton was long and circuitous. The Manitoba (Great Northern) Railway, which had reached Fort Benton in 1887, was extended to Helena, and this was the first leg of their journey. At Helena they changed to the Northern Pacific Railroad, which had been completed in 1883. Building from both the east and west, the rails met at Gold Creek, about 80 miles west of Missoula, in August of 1883. Their rail journey ended at Ravalli, the closest railroad point to the Flathead Valley. Here Charley Allard operated a hotel and restaurant famous for hospitality and good food. From Ravalli the stages left for the journey northward. Unhurried passengers stayed overnight at Allard's before boarding the stagecoach for a bouncing journey of about 35 miles to the south end of Flathead Lake.

After an overnight stop at Allard's, the Conrads took the stage to Polson to begin the most pleasant and beautiful part of their journey. On a sunny fall day, the Conrads boarded the steamboat that took them from the foot of the lake up its entire length to Demersville, located on the banks of the Flathead River a few miles up above its point of entry into the Lake.

Lettie Conrad always remembered the beauty of the trip. She described it many times to her daughter Alicia. At Fort Benton the trees grew only along the banks of the Missouri River, and even these had been cut for wood to warm the homes of Fort Benton and to make steam for the boats that plied the river. All around the town was treeless prairie. Lettie Conrad said later that the scenery viewed from the boat made it seem they had entered paradise. Compared to the muddy water of the Missouri River, the waters of Flathead Lake seemed crystal clear. The

Steamboat *Klondike* on Flathead Lake Courtesy Montana Historical Society

entire shoreline was lined with huge, green trees with few breaks for habitation. The colors of fall marched up the foothills and mountains, blazing in the bright fall sun. As the Conrads watched the passing scenery, there began a love affair with the Flathead Valley that would warm their hearts and glow within them for as long as they lived.

CHAPTER 33
The Flathead Valley

In 1890 Demersville was the largest and most prosperous settlement in the Flathead Valley. It was founded by Jake Demers, a Frenchman from Frenchtown, Montana, who hauled goods and supplies by pack train from Fort Missoula to Fort Steele, about 25 miles from Kimberly, Canada. In 1881 a town called Ashley was built at a point where the present Meridian Road in Kalispell crosses Ashley Creek. Jake's pack strings passed through Ashley both going to and coming from Fort Steele. He decided to open a store and way station at Ashley, where business was brisk as new settlers moved into the Valley. Jake searched for a suitable location but found none at a reasonable price. The meanest lot was selling for $5,000, with prices going up from there. When Jake learned that the Ashley merchants had ganged up on him to keep him out, he became angry. With anger and stubbornness mixed in about equal proportions, Jake resolved not to be thwarted by the Ashley merchants. As he looked over the prospects of the Valley, it became evident to him that water transportation on Flathead Lake might soon make Ashley's location untenable.

Jake searched out the most feasible location for a town that would take full advantage of the possibilities of Flathead Lake. The site he decided upon was owned by Uncle Billy Gregg. When Uncle Billy heard Jake's story, he sold him a portion of his homestead, which was located on a big bend of the Flathead River a few miles above the head of the Lake. Here Jake built Demersville. When it was finished, it very quickly became the trade center of the Valley. This left Ashley merchants the choice of closing or moving to Demersville, where they had to deal with Demers for locations.

One of Jake's first buildings was a hotel, which he named the Cliff House, to offer hospitality, at a Frenchman's profit, to the increasing number of people coming into the Valley by way of Flathead Lake. Jake's hotel was a good one, and people staying at Allard's got the word that the Cliff House was the place to stay. This was the message the Conrads received and, at the end of their beautiful boat trip, they checked into the Cliff House to stay during their visit with Hal Stanford.

The Conrads loved what they had seen of the Flathead Valley and wanted to see more. Both liked to ride and, with rental horses, they roamed the Valley exploring it in all directions. The Conrads did not see the Flathead Valley in its pristine state. Since 1883 construction workers from the then-completed Northern Pacific Railroad had drifted in to change the Valley's face. But their impact had been small and, in 1890, one could still see the Valley pretty much in the condition it had been prior to the coming of the white men. George F. Stannard, an early settler, wrote a description of the Valley which can be found in Sam John's book, "The Pioneers." Stannard wrote: "The Indians had given a name to the country lying north of Flathead Lake, interpreted from the Indian language, we have, 'The Park Between the Mountains.' "

Stannard said that the Valley was heavily timbered with cottonwood, tamarack, and fir, and with some spruce and birch on the bottom lands. The higher lands were covered with yellow pine. Brush was thick around the lake shore and river banks. Scattered throughout the timber were prairies, some large and some small. These prairies were interspersed by scattered groves of yellow pine and pot holes. There were two principal landmarks which could be seen from the prairies. One was the Point of Rocks, north of the current Somers, through which the cut was made for Highway 93. The other was Bad Rock Canyon, where the Flathead River enters the Valley. No matter how lost an early settler became, if he could get to a prairie spot, then the two landmarks loomed up to provide bearings.

Some of what is now considered the area's best farm land was then too wet and swampy to till. This was true of the Smith Valley to the west of Kalispell, and the Creston area to the east. For this reason the high ground to the north and northwest of Kalispell was the first settled.

When the Great Northern came to Kalispell in 1892, its right of way, commencing from outside Columbia Falls, was a straight line, 14 miles long, through a dense stand of timber. The tracks seemed to be in a tunnel of trees for as far as the eye could see.

The Conrads' visit with Hal Stanford stretched and stretched, until it grew a little stale. Still the Conrads stayed on, riding out each day to a different part of the Valley. Two weeks went by, and they were still loathe to leave. Finally, Conrad told his wife that they should be moving on to Spokane, which they had thought might be their future home. At the thought of leaving, Lettie Conrad began to cry and said, "Why must we leave this lovely valley? Couldn't we make our home here?" Conrad told his wife that they had the means to live anyplace they chose, that he too loved the Valley and would like to make it their home. He could see that with the coming of the Great Northern Railway, the Flathead Valley

142

would no longer be isolated. Opening it up would provide many opportunities for building a localized empire large enough to challenge and excite Conrad's business and money-making instincts. These had been well-honed by the activities at Fort Benton, and Conrad was anxious to get back into the excitement of the business world from which he drew such stimulation.

Conrad knew that the railroad was the key to opportunity in the Flathead Valley. With this in mind, he contacted Jim Hill to tell Hill of his decision to make his home in the Flathead. He told of his desire to work with Hill in establishing a townsite for the division point that would of necessity be located in the Flathead Valley. Hill told Conrad to come to St. Paul to discuss the matter. The Conrads returned to Fort Benton, with Charles going to St. Paul to see Hill. A deal was struck, and Conrad returned to Fort Benton to prepare his business interests and his family for the move to the Flathead Valley.

Others sensed the opportunity and came seeking land for the same purpose. D. R. McGinnis, a shrewd speculator, believed he had an inside track. He had an accomplice in the engineering department of the Great Northern who told him of the approximate proposed route for the right of way. Armed with this information McGinnis came to Demersville. He must have felt a need for concealment for he wore rough workman's clothes and darkened his skin with walnut juice. For days he roamed, surveying the area from Bad Rock Canyon, where the railroad would enter the Valley, to the hill west of present-day Kalispell, where the right-of-way would leave the Valley and cross Haskell Pass, just beyond the current Marion.

McGinnis found land he thought would have to be the townsite. He then removed his disguise and, dressed as a businessman, bought the land, concealing from the owners his purpose. McGinnis left for Helena in high spirits, thinking Jim Hill would have to deal with him.

McGinnis did not realize that he had been playing the game with a cold deck. When Conrad was in St. Paul, he evidently did not see Hill personally. But a deal must have been struck on the basis that Hill would locate the division point at whatever site Conrad bought land. On October 10, 1890, Hill wrote to Conrad.

> I was sorry not to have seen you in regard to the Flathead matter, but this will keep as we will not locate any station or town until you have time to examine the situation. The party who has gone in there to receive land will get no aid or encouragement of any kind from the Company, and without it they can do nothing. You may be able to buy them out at a fair price in which case the matter would be made much easier. I think it would be well for you to run over and get the situation in your mind. It would be well for you to look up the crossing of the Stillwater and, in fact, look over the entire good agricultural country. Whatever you do, the location is one that can be easily built up without unnecessary expense, as it will be much

easier to build a town on a good location than on a rough and uninviting one. Let me hear from you when you have anything of interest.

Blind luck subsequently helped McGinnis far more than his planning. The land he had bought was located at the northwest corner of what is now Kalispell. On it was located a hill of the finest gravel in the Northwest. When the railroad and the town were built, gravel was in great demand. McGinnis opened a pit and began to sell gravel. The pit provided him with a good living all of his long life. It is still providing for various nieces and grandnieces, since McGinnis never had a wife or child. Most probably there will be gravel on the McGinnis land long after there is McGinnis progeny to benefit from it.

Following his trip to St. Paul, Conrad returned to Fort Benton where the liquidation of the business of I. G. Baker and Company was still in progress. He had been home only a short time when he received Hill's letter of October 10, 1890. This caused him to return to the Flathead. On this trip he investigated the things Hill had requested and decided on the land for the new townsite. In his land dealings, Conrad employed no secrecy or guile. He told the landowners his purpose and offered a fair price. In this manner he was able to get options on the homesteads of Alex LeBeau, George McVey Fisher, and Tyson Duncan. Duncan refused to sell a part of his land and later platted that portion as Duncan's Addition to Kalispell.

Closing a business in Fort Benton and getting things started at a new location required frequent trips. When he travelled between the two places, Conrad stopped at Allard's hostelry in Ravalli. He became well-acquainted with a Mrs. Larivee, who was the cook and presided over the hostelry. Like others who knew her, Conrad grew to admire and respect Larivee. By December of 1891, the land for the townsite was acquired. Conrad went to Fort Benton for Christmas and went then to St. Paul to form the townsite company. On this trip Conrad told Larivee that no name had been chosen for the new town and asked her for a suggestion. She offered the name "Kalispell," for an Indian tribe that had been respected by whites since the days of Lewis and Clark.

Before the Lewis and Clark Expedition, the Indian tribe, now called the Flatheads, were, according to Duncan McDonald, called the Kalispels. McDonald, one of the earliest settlers, said that Lewis and Clark called this tribe the Flatheads because they flattened the heads of their children. McDonald said that this was not true. He felt that this mistake of Lewis and Clark maligned the finest Indian tribe in the West. Perhaps Larivee was trying to atone for the wrong done the Kalispel tribe by Lewis and Clark. Conrad liked and respected all Indians and took this name with him to the meeting in St. Paul where the matter would be decided.

On January 20, 1891, articles of incorporation for the Kalispell Townsite Company were signed at St. Paul. The incorporators were Conrad, A. A. White, J. B. Conner, and W. P. Clough. White, Comstock, and Clough had been named by Hill, who must have thought that odds of three-to-one would be sufficient to protect his interests. Hill had accepted the name "Kalispell," and so the new town was named. Conrad returned to the Flathead. When he stopped at Allard's on the way home, it must have pleased him to be able to report to Larivee that the new town would bear the name she had suggested. Once back in the Flathead, Conrad faced the formidable task of getting the townsite surveyed and platted. He wanted to be ready to sell lots at the earliest possible date to the people who would flock into the area with the coming of the Great Northern Railway.

CHAPTER 34
A Town Is Born

Conrad returned to the Flathead Valley during the first part of February, 1891. In the middle of winter he began to consolidate the land holdings and to assemble a crew for the survey work. The deed for the first purchase — 30 acres from William E. Doggett — was recorded February 24, 1891. On March 9, 1891, a deed for 160 acres from William J. Sear was recorded. On March 19, 1891, deeds were recorded from Alexander I. Fraser, for 80 acres, from George McVey Fisher for 160 acres, and from John Tell for 160 acres. Fisher was the first preacher in the area. A Presbyterian, he conducted the first church service ever held in Ashley, in Jack Graves' saloon. The saloon was the only public place large enough for a church meeting until a place of worship was completed. It is not reported what effect the saloon had on the church business, but both seemed to prosper in the presence of the other, since holding church services in a saloon was not uncommon in the frontier West.

On March 19, 1891, Harriett M. Hunt conveyed 160 acres to the new Kalispell Township Company, Tyson B. Duncan transferred 120 acres, and Alex LeBeau conveyed 120 acres. In about a month and a half, Conrad acquired 990 acres for the new townsite. He later deeded 40 acres back to Fisher, who platted it as the Fisher Addition to Kalispell. The money Fisher made from the sale of lots gave him an affluence not usually associated with ministers in the early West. And finding surveyors was no problem. For Jim Hill sent in as many of his Great Northern crew as were needed.

The subdivision proceeded at a pace a developer today would find unbelievable. There were no planning boards or restricting regulations. In the beginning each owner was responsible for his waste and water. If he wanted his privy beside his house or his well, he could have it there. Business lots were 25 feet in width and residential lots were 50 feet. In the original townsite of Kalispell there were 1,116 residential and 1,080 business lots. The last land was acquired on March 20, 1891, and the first lot was sold on April 21, 1891. The Townsite Company conveyed to

Kalispell in 1891. Photo taken from corner of First Street and First Avenue East. Courtesy First Interstate Bank of Kalispell

Salomon G. Comstock, as trustee, Lots 13 and 14 of Block 74 and gave him the right to construct and operate water works, street railways, and electric lights in the new city. Comstock was Hill's man and, through him, Hill's control could be exercised over future municipal services.

The first deed to an individual was made on April 30, 1891. Frank Shernborn acquired Lot 8 of Block 51, Lot 22 of Block 66, Lot 13 of Block 74, and Lot 14 of Block 70. The deed stated the consideration as $1500.

The sale of lots to the public was started in April of 1891. Emma A. Ingalls, wife of the editor and founder of the *Inter Lake*, wrote an article entitled, "Trails of the Past," found in Sam Johns' "The Pioneers." Ingalls wrote:

> "Kalispell was platted and lots placed on sale in April, 1891. Owing to the great rush of buyers a map of the townsite was simply placed upon a table and each purchaser, often a dozen of them, would crowd up and point out the lot they wanted. The agent sat near and took down the number of the lot and name of the buyer, it being impossible to draw any kind of contract at the time. $400,000 worth of lots was sold in a few days. The cost to the townsite company was $60,000. Besides, they reserved all of the choice lots.

The $400,000 referred to by Emma Ingalls was made in the first few days of the sale. Not only were the choice lots reserved, but there remained unsold hundreds of lots to be doled out as they became more valuable.

147

The profits of the Kalispell Townsite Company augmented considerably the already large fortune Conrad had acquired at Fort Benton.

Kalispell boomed. Ed O'Conner bought the *Ashley Graphic* and moved it to Kalispell in the spring of 1891 to become the new town's first newspaper. A great rivalry soon developed between the towns of Demersville, Columbia Falls, and Kalispell, aided and encouraged by their newspapers: The *Graphic* at Kalispell, the *Columbian* at Columbia Falls, and the *Inter Lake* and the *Journal* at Demersville. According to Emma Ingalls,

> Everything boomed until about June and then a rumor started that it would be two years before the Great Northern would arrive. Everyone footloose left town, those who stayed had their all invested and must perforce stay. The town went on the rocks.

Any misfortune suffered by Kalispell pleased C. O. Ingalls, editor of the *Inter Lake*. He wanted desperately for Demersville to retain its supremacy and so predicted in colorful and thundering terms. In July of 1891 he wrote: "We understand that a meeting was held in Collapstown, formerly known as Kalispell, for the purpose of building a fly screen over the town."

Ingalls' thunder and rhetoric could not stay the coming of the Great Northern Railway. As winter approached, the rails came nearer and nearer, building from both the east and the west. When the line emerged from Bad Rock Canyon, construction speeded. On the Sunday before it reached Kalispell, crowds of people walked up the right-of-way, as reported by Emma Ingalls, "to see with their own eyes that it was really coming." At six o'clock P.M., on December 31, 1891, the rails met at Main Street in Kalispell.

A celebration was held the following day for which preparations had been under way for weeks. An arch of evergreen was built over the tracks bearing a sign: "Welcome to Jim Hill, the first man to build a railroad across the continent without government aid." The parade consisted of everything that could move, with Indians brought up from the reservation, not only to parade but to dance. Steers were roasted all night in a trench 30 feet long. According to Emma Ingalls,

> There was no snow and the celebration lasted all day, all night and all the next day. Liquor flowed like water down the river in flood time. Still it was a good natured crowd because everyone was so happy over the arrival of the long looked for road.

The high point of the celebration was the driving of the silver spike that joined the rails. From 18 silver dollars, contributed by the women of Kalispell, George Stanford fashioned a silver spike. This was driven by the wife of J. J. Kimmerly, the first white woman to settle in the Valley, and by Nicholas Moon, one of the early settlers who operated the first irrigation project in the Valley and who proved that vegetables could be raised there. The contrary notion had been fostered by the early cattlemen, who wanted to discourage any settlement that might interfere with maintaining an open range for grazing.

Nicholas Moon was a bachelor who hated all women when he was sober, but loved prostitutes when he was drunk, which was quite frequently. About 1887 Nick and a partner struck a rich vein in Wolf Creek, west of Kalispell, from which they extracted about $80,000 in gold. They wintered in Spokane and returned broke in the spring. Nick panned enough from the leavings to buy a little ranch up the creek from Ashley. Here he installed the first irrigation system and raised vegetables, which he sold to the settlers. Soon after the celebration, Nick sensed that civilization was closing in on him. He sold his ranch and bought a grubstake for moving on. He spent the night in the red-light district, where he was relieved of most of his money. The next day he left town, riding his buckskin horse with his worldly goods loaded on a pinto pack pony. When asked where he was going, Nick replied, "I'm headin' for British Columbia where there is some peace and quiet. There's jest too many petticoats on the clothes-lines in this town."

The arrival of the railroad spelled doom to Demersville. Despite all his predictions and bombast, Ingalls, in January of 1892, moved his *Inter Lake* to Kalispell. During the same week from Demersville came the *Journal*, Stevens Drugs, The Tivoli Saloon, both banks, Cannon Clothing, Braunbergers, Gates and Newcomb, Lang and Malcolm, The Herring Fruit Stand, The Hubbart Livery, The Miller Harness Shop, and the Knights of Pythias Hall. On one day in January, 1892, 12 buildings could be seen moving across the prairie from Demersville to Kalispell. After the move, Kalispell had no more loyal and enthusiastic citizens than C. O. and Emma Ingalls.

The future looked bright both for Kalispell and for Charles E. Conrad, but a blow was yet to fall. In the spring of 1904, Jim Hill announced that the division point for the Great Northern would be moved from Kalispell. The grade over Haskell Pass was too steep for efficient operations. A lesser grade would save both time and expense. Time was important, for the railroad that could announce the fastest time schedule between St. Paul and the West Coast would gain an advantage in attracting business.

F. O. Williams, an early resident of Kalispell, told of the discovery of the new grade. Williams and a small group of Kalispell businessmen had discovered a rich coal deposit in southeast British Columbia. Rich as it was, it was useless without transportation to get it out. The group contacted Ed Boyle, who had guided C. F. B. Haskell to the discovery of Marias Pass in 1889. He was engaged to find a route to bring out the coal. Boyle found an excellent route, with a moderate grade, that could be

Kalispell Fourth of July Parade, 1896 Courtesy Conrad Mansion Directors

used to build a spur from the Great Northern line to the coal deposit.

The group went to St. Paul to try to persuade Hill to build the spur that would take out the coal and make them rich. Boyle presented his plan and Hill became intensely interested. He called in engineers, who went over Boyle's survey, and they too became interested. Hill and his engineers discussed the proposed route, apparently forgetting the Kalispell group. Williams finally asked if Hill were interested. He replied that he had no interest in the coal, since the Great Northern had plenty of that, but if the grade figures were correct, it was a great improvement over the present route. He would have it checked and, if it proved out, a new line would be built to take advantage of the better grade.

Williams and his group returned to Kalispell thoroughly chastened. They knew Boyle's survey was accurate. They knew also that if the new route were used, Kalispell might lose the division point, so important to the new city. The group pledged themselves to secrecy and returned to Kalispell where they waited to see if the worst would happen. They did not have long to wait.

When Hill made the announcement, he was no longer a hero in Kalispell. The papers called him a tyrant whose thirst for power should be curbed. Hill was hanged in effigy at about the same spot where he was lauded only 12 years before. The businessmen tried to get an injunction

150

to stop the move. None of the measures was successful, but the agitation started the move for the Montana Railroad Commission, which later was created to exert some control over the railroads.

The sad blow finally fell. On October 4, 1904, the *Kalispell Bee* carried a rather mournful story of the move:

> The railroaders were all off in a bunch Saturday, two trains hauling the unwilling employees to the wilds of Whitefish where they will again make their homes subject to the arbitrary moods of the railroad tyrant. In the afternoon a train of cabooses, flat cars and railroad repair machinery, also the goods of the railroad families, were started for the junction. The men occupied their cabooses on this trip and left their wives and other encumbrances to follow them on the late east bound through train.
>
> Probably 300 people left Kalispell today and swelled the population of Whitefish to that extent. Some unearthly whistling at a late hour noted the departure of some light engines, and the round house, the rip track and yards are all gloomy and very much deserted. Some of the old timers and many responsible citizens were among the departing crews and are a distinct loss to the business and social life of the community.

A great gloom settled over Kalispell. There were those who thought Kalispell might suffer the same fate as Demersville. Emma Ingalls stated it well when she wrote:

> The removal of the division point to Whitefish meant a big loss by taking away the railroad payroll, and all things considered, we thought we were ruined. Apparently we had a sound foundation and have continued to grow in spite of these adverse conditions.

The division point was moved after Conrad's death in 1902. It is unlikely he could have prevented this loss, but he had built his town well and gave it a foundation strong enough to survive even a blow of this magnitude.

CHAPTER 35
The New Home

Charles E. Conrad brought to the businesses he started in Kalispell the same commercial acumen, organizational ability, and willingness to delegate authority to competent people that had made him so successful in Fort Benton. In 1891 he started a bank at Kalispell, which at first was a branch of the Conrad Brothers' Bank at Great Falls. Soon it was chartered as a national bank called the Conrad National Bank of Kalispell. The bank's first home was a rude, one-room frame shack, located at the corner of First Street and Main. Whatever the location or manner of housing, any bank owned by Charles E. Conrad would prosper. His reputation as a banker was summed up by one old-timer who said, "All you needed to deal with Charlie Conrad was a decent reputation and your word of honor." From this one-room shack, the bank grew to the largest in northwest Montana. It operated under the Conrad name until 1981, when the name was changed to the First Interstate Bank of Kalispell.

By the middle of 1892, Conrad's affairs in Kalispell were pretty much under control. The bank was started and had competent management. The construction of its new home at the corner of Second Street and Main was under way. The business of the Townsite Company had progressed to a point that a competent clerk could sell the lots and collect the money. Conrad was free to think of other things, and the first was a new home. Since they were first married, the Conrads talked of the new home they knew would come, but it had been more in the nature of dreaming than planning. When Conrad thought of a new home, his mind was filled with visions of the gracious plantation home he had known as a boy. Lettie Conrad's mind was dominated by her English heritage, and ran more to the Tudor tradition. They had heard of the new homes being built in Spokane for the Coeur d'Alene mine owners. With the lull in business, the Conrads went to Spokane to get ideas for their new home.

Spokane had many lovely new homes, and the Conrads spent several days inspecting them. Almost every home they liked had been designed

Conrad Mansion Library Courtesy Conrad Mansion Directors

by Kirtland K. Cutter. Cutter had been born in the East. His parents were wealthy and had encouraged him to study architecture in Europe, which he did. Yet he chose to settle in the West. Here everything was new, and he could impose his style on the development taking place there. In addition to Spokane's most beautiful homes, he also designed the Spokane Club and the Davenport Hotel, both handsome examples of the Cutter style.

Cutter came to Kalispell to look at the building site before agreeing to accept a commission. When he saw the 72 beautifully wooded acres, with the majestic Flathead Range of the Rocky Mountains rising in the east, he wanted to start at once. The Norman style plans that he drew did not fit the dreams of either of the Conrads, but both knew that Cutter's plan was perfect for their dream home. He was hired with the understanding that he would have a free hand and no restrictions on cost.

In 1895 there was no builder in Kalispell with experience in the construction of homes of the size and quality called for by the architectural plans prepared by Cutter. Conrad, at Cutter's suggestion, employed Michael C. Conley, a Spokane contractor with experience in building similar homes. The contract was dated May 18, 1895. By its terms, Conley agreed to provide all materials, and do all labor necessary for the erection of a two-story frame residence, with attic and basement, on Block 195 of Kalispell Townsite Company's Addition Number Two in the City of Kalispell. The work was to be done under the direction of Arthur E. Parmain, Architect, of Kalispell, according to drawings and specifications prepared by Cutter and Malmgren, Architects of Spokane, Washington and Cleveland, Ohio.

The consideration was $9,465.00. The whole of the work was to be completed and the entire building ready for occupancy by October 15, 1895. If not completed by that date, Conley was to forfeit $5.00 per day for each additional day required to complete the contract. The contract required Conley to use local materials and labor when possible, but gave him the right to use outside labor for any work requiring skills not to be found locally.

Construction started in 1895. Workmen were imported from Germany for the inside finishing work, especially the great hall and the stairway,

Great Hall of the Conrad Mansion Courtesy Conrad Mansion Directors

for Cutter demanded the best artisans to work with his beautiful oak. The lighting was done originally with gas, but the house also was wired for electricity, which was yet to come to Kalispell.

Cutter's plans required the use of oak in the interior panelling of the new home. He went to the Midwest where he not only selected the individual trees, but also supervised the quarter-sawing of the logs to get the grain that he wanted. The rock for the foundations and fireplaces came from an argilite formation near Essex that Cutter had spotted from the train. All of the stained glass was specially ordered from Tiffany's in New York, and all of the other materials were obtained under Cutter's personal direction.

The agreed consideration of $9,465.00 and the construction period of six months both seem totally inadequate today. However, in 1895 the workday was more or less co-extensive with the daylight hours. In addition, wages were so low a builder could hire as many workers as could be usefully employed on a given project and insist that they work continuously throughout all the long working day.

The building was evidently finished on time, but the consideration proved to be too low. These facts are gleaned from the complaint in a court action filed by Conrad in the Superior Court of Spokane against Conley and his bondsmen. The action was for the recovery of $1,497.34 for materials Conley had purchased in Spokane but failed to pay for. Conrad had been required to pay this amount in addition to the $9,465.00 consideration of the contract.

There is nothing to indicate that the house was not ready for occupancy on time. The fall was cold and rainy in 1895. In a letter dated September 19, 1895, Conrad wrote from Havre urging Lettie to move to the West Hotel with the children until they could move into the new home. Whatever the weather, the Conrads moved into the new home early in November, 1895, never again to experience inadequate housing.

Conrad was so anxious to get started on the new home that he commenced construction even before he owned the land. The home was not in the original townsite of Kalispell but in the Second Addition, the plat for which was filed on May 18, 1895. Conrad did not receive the title until December 24, 1895, about a month after the family moved in. On June 29, 1898, he deeded the home to his wife, and the title remained in Lettie Conrad's name until her death in 1923.

The mothers of both Charles and Lettie Conrad had lived with them since early in their marriage. The design of the house gave full consideration to their comfort. Each had a room on the first floor, separated by a bathroom, which they shared. The bathroom on the second floor was directly above. Both bathrooms shared a common plumbing tree. This arrangement made it impossible to install additional bath and toilet facilities without changing the basic design of the house and tearing out the walls to install and conceal plumbing pipes and fixtures. Many times the house was full of company, filling not only the eight bedrooms but spilling over into the third floor as well. However many people, only the two bathrooms were available. They seemed to suffice, and the Conrad home was considered the ultimate in luxury and comfort. The youngest daughter, Alicia, remembered that some of the guests, who had known only outside toilets, were awed by the magnificence of the facilities and hesitated to use them for the intended purposes.

Cutter was a man of many talents. He wanted to design not only beautiful buildings, but to plan their settings so that they were presented to the best advantage. The landscaping of the Conrad house was designed by Cutter, in keeping with the style of the architecture. The formal south garden was outlined with paths and juniper trees, which were formally sheared. Native and imported species of trees and plants were placed to blend with the setting, yet to stand out in beauty. The lawn and gardens were laid out with geometric precision. A gazebo, made of cedar and roofed with cedar bark, was made the focal point of the south lawn. The entire landscaping was designed to require a minimum of maintenance and care, even to the installation of an underground water system to water the lawn, trees, and shrubs. Alicia said the system was made of galvanized pipe. At intervals pipe was extended upward to make fountains. On sunny days, the sunlight made rainbows in the fountain spray. On bright moonlit nights the water system was sometimes turned on, and the spray of the fountains catching the moonbeams created a scene of incredible beauty.

During the period of construction of the home, the Conrads lived in a number of places. The first buildings and homes were those moved from Demersville. Building was proceeding at a frantic pace, but housing was scarce, and that available had a minimum of comforts. Conrad was gone much of the time, but letters to his wife show that he followed very carefully the construction of the new home as it progressed from one stage to another. During the cold winter months, the family lived at the West Hotel, then the best in Kalispell. It was housed in a frame building and run by Auntie Walker, whom Alicia remembered with great fondness. Despite the crudity of the building and its facilities, Auntie Walker gave to it an air of homeyness and refinement that radiated her goodness and the few nice things left from her better days.

There was little for Lettie Conrad to do in the infant city with her husband gone for long periods. She spent much time watching the progress of the new house, when the weather permitted. Winter came early in 1895. In September, Conrad was at the Blackfeet Agency on business with the Indians. On September 19 he wrote:

> It commenced snowing here this morning and there is now 4 inches of snow and quite cold. I fear you have the same conditions or else cold rain. Hope you will move down to the West (Hotel) if you have. I do hope you will not all get colds before moving.

Construction continued until the fall of 1895 and finally progresed to the point that furniture could be moved in. Curtains and drapes were hung and the house made ready for occupancy. In November of 1895, all was ready at last for moving into the new home that had been so long in building. A few days before Thanksgiving, Lettie Conrad moved the family in, even though her husband was not home. So great was their joy and so deep an impression did it make upon the entire family that Alicia, then three years old, remembered the event in some detail. She recalled toddling after her mother from room to room with everyone exhulting and exclaiming. Especially she remembered her sister, Kate, eight years older, who — after three years living in close proximity with the rest of the family — was so delighted to finally have a room of her own that she cried with joy and kept repeating, "At last I have a room all of my own. And never again will I have to use an outside privy or chamber pot." The whole family, from the grandmas on down, must have felt the same way.

The Conrads had been wise to allow Cutter complete freedom in the design and construction of their home. The Southern Plantation style of architecture that Conrad had carried in his mind for so many years would have been incongruous in the Flathead Valley, with its rugged setting and sweeping views. Such a setting suggested to Cutter the chateaus he had seen in Europe during his studies there. The Norman style mansion that he conceived pleased the Conrads, and they were thankful they had abided by the decisions of Cutter.

The house contained 22 rooms in three stories, built over a full basement. The first floor had a large kitchen and a commodious pantry and serving room. A barrel pass-through from the kitchen to the dining room facilitated serving. The large dining room had ample windows on the east, which framed a view of the Rocky Mountains. On the south wall of the dining room was a huge fireplace. To the west of the fireplace, a door opened onto the fernery. This room contained a fountain flanked with ferns and green plants that gave a hint of summer throughout the year.

Leaving the dining room, to the north, one entered the library. It had no fireplace, but the windows allowed a beautiful view of the mountains to the east. Next on the north was the Great Hall, which was the centerpiece of the house. The main entrance door was situated in the northeast corner of this room. The east wall was a massive fireplace. What would have been the west wall was the beautiful oak staircase going to the upper floors. To the north of the Great Hall was the music room.

To the west of the music room was Grandmother Stanford's room, which had north and west exposures and a fireplace. Next was the bathroom, which connected to the room of Grandmother Conrad, having a western exposure but no fireplace. On this side also was an entry which opened onto a porticoed driveway. The driveway entered from a gate on the north side of the property and exited on the south, making a half-circle.

The dining room, library, Great Hall, and music room had magnificent beams and wookwork of the beautifully grained golden oak.

The stairway led to the second floor and opened into a hall which radiated to the south and the north. On the west from the head of the stairs was the billiard room. Next on the north was the second bathroom, which was immediately above the bathroom of the grandmothers. North of the bath was Kate's room, which had a northwest exposure and a fireplace. To the east of Kate's room was the master bedroom. This had a northeast exposure, with a view of the mountains and a large fireplace. A little balcony opened into the hall from the master bedroom. From it, Lettie Conrad claimed to be able to hear sounds from any part of the house. South of the master bedroom, facing the east, was young Alicia's room, which had an eastern exposure and a fireplace. The rooms of both Kate and Alicia had doors opening into their parents' room and into the hall.

From the head of the stairs the hall extended south, flanked by rooms on either side. On the east were three bedrooms, the first of which was Charley's and the other two were guest rooms. At the southwest corner was another guest room. To the north were a hall and stairs that went down to the kitchen. Last was the sewing room, an important room in the house, for most of the clothes for Lettie Conrad and the girls were made there by local seamstresses.

The third floor was unfinished. Initially the laundry room was in the basement. When Kalispell acquired sewers, the basement was lower than the sewer line, so the laundry room was moved to the third floor where the wash water drained out with a whoosh.

This was the Conrads' new home. Moving in made a never-to-be-forgotten impression on those who shared the event.

Alice Waitman, whose father ran a livery stable in Kalispell for a number of years, was a friend of Kate. When hospitalized once in Kalispell, Alice waved Alicia into her room to talk. She told Alicia,

I want to tell you something. You won't remember moving into your new home, but I do. I was there with Kate the day you moved in. I was her friend and was invited to spend the night. I was with the family when they moved into the house and want to tell you about it. Your mother, marvelous that she was, had the house completely furnished, completely equipped in every way. You might go in and think you had been living there for years, and that would be the night that everybody moved in. So your Father had nothing but complete at-homeness. There wasn't even a handkerchief misplaced or any indication that the house was being occupied for the first time. You might have lived there for years.

That is the way Alicia remembered the house. Everything seemed geared to making her father feel at home.

CHAPTER 36
Solving the Servant Problem

While the Conrads lived in Fort Benton, they had as household help a Chinese man named Wong. There was no room for Wong in any of the places the Conrads lived during the construction of the new home but, as soon as the family moved in, Wong came to resume his former position. It soon became evident that more help was needed. Relatives came to see the new home from as far away as Virginia. These visits were neither casual nor short. In 1895 travel was still slow and arduous. To make a trip worthwhile, one stayed not days, but for weeks, even months. In addition to relatives visiting, the Conrads also entertained with frequent, large parties. This required more help than just Wong.

Conrad's brother, William, and his family arrived for a visit. When he saw the need for household help, he offered to send out some Virginia blacks, insisting that they were the finest help available. He found and arranged passage for three women. When they arrived, the help problem seemed to be solved. All went well for a time, but then Lettie Conrad noticed that cooking brandy was showing up on the grocery list quite often. As time went on, it became evident that the brandy was being put to uses other than cooking. Strange things started to happen in the kitchen. Soon Lettie Conrad realized that her new help was drunk a good part of the time. She cut off the supply of brandy, but the Virginia women were resourceful. Somehow they maintained enough of a liquor supply to keep themselves happy, but hardly competent. The three were put on the train and returned to Virginia, where, as William's recommendations made it seem, their talents were appreciated.

Lettie Conrad had a preference for Scandinavian girls, who came from those countries either alone or with their parents or relatives. These girls were also preferred as wives by the young Scandinavian men coming in to find jobs in the woods. The new maid might be a new wife soon after she was trained and had worked for a short time. Good help was a continual problem, until a Japanese man named Hori came to the Conrad home looking for work.

Hori was hired as a house boy and quickly demonstrated that he could run the house. Lettie Conrad grew quite dependent upon him and was stricken when he told her he had to make a trip to Japan and would be gone for several weeks. Somehow they survived his absence, and he returned with a proposition for Lettie. If she would pay him a certain monthly sum, he would provide all of the household help. The Conrads would give them board and room, and Hori would pay their salaries and provide for their other needs. Lettie Conrad accepted and, within weeks, the help started to arrive. They were all young Japanese men, eager both to learn and to please.

The Conrad home, with Hori in charge, was now run efficiently and well. The young men would stay for about a year. Then would come a day when one would be gone and another, who looked and acted like him, would take his place. There were always from 6 to 15 servants, all beautifully trained, most efficient, and very desirous of speaking English to the Conrads and their guests. But no one knew how many servants would be there from time to time, except that there would always be six.

The Japanese lived in a house built for servants at the northeast corner of Fourth Street and Woodland Avenue. Under Hori's direction, the young men built a beautiful Japanese-style garden at the back of the house. This became a showplace which Hori exhibited proudly to the Conrads' guests. A stile was built over the stone wall on the south side of the house, which was used by the Japanese to go back and forth from their house to the Conrad home. It is still visible and useable today.

This highly satisfactory situation continued for a number of years, with Hori taking periodic trips to Japan to visit his family. Then Hori began to be absent a great deal of the time. He would disappear in the morning and return at night. The house still ran smoothly, but Hori was hardly ever there.

Lettie Conrad heard that Hori had bought, and was still buying, land near the railroad at Whitefish. Then she learned that he had developed extensive vegetable gardens on the land. Still the home ran efficiently, even though at times Hori might use the Conrad help in his vegetable gardens, if they could be spared from their duties.

Lettie was intrigued and suspicious. It did not seem possible that Hori could do all he was doing on the salary she paid him, when part of that went to pay the Japanese men he furnished. Where did the money come from? There was nothing amiss at the home. It was still being run as efficiently as ever, even though Hori was not living at the house where the others lived.

Curiosity finally overcame caution, and Lettie Conrad sent word to Hori that she wanted to see him. At the meeting, she told Hori that she was mystified by his activities and apparent affluence. She could find nothing dishonest, except that he was never on the job, though he was being paid. But even this created no real problem in the running of the home. Hori told her that he too was disturbed by the situation. He knew that it could not continue unexplained, but he did not want to be the one to bring it up.

Hori said that he had bought considerable land. He now had extensive vegetable gardens, from which he sold vegetables all over the country, even some to the Great Northern. He said he was now bringing coolies over from Japan. Hori guaranteed them passage and a job and worked them in his vegetable gardens. When asked about the source of his funds, Hori said he had never been dependent on his salary alone. The young men who came to work for the Conrads were all graduates of universities in Japan, who wanted to do graduate work at the Ivy League colleges on the East Coast of the United States. Before entering these colleges, they wanted to learn English. Hori had made a deal to furnish them board and room and an opportunity to learn and speak English. For this, each young man paid him a certain amount. Hori had not only the money from the Conrads, but also the amounts paid him by the young men. All this was clear and sufficient to enable Hori to invest in land and acquire considerable land holdings. He said that his interests now required too much supervision, that he knew he could not continue with the Conrads, and that he welcomed the opportunity to get things out in the open and to arrange for the break.

When the group of Japanese working at that time went on to their chosen college or university, there was none to replace them. Lettie Conrad went back to the former practice of training and losing household help, until a change in the family fortunes made help not so great a necessity.

CHAPTER 37
The Stables

Charles Conrad needed little help in planning the stables. He allowed Kirkland K. Cutter to give the buildings an exterior design that blended with the house, but the interior was almost pure Conrad.

The stable area was outlined, along Woodland Avenue, by a rock fence that extended south from Second Street to Fourth Street. An arched gateway located facing Woodland, across from the end of Third Street, gave entrance to the stable area. The stone pillars of this gateway still stand. The openings for the incoming and outgoing traffic lanes seem narrow today but were more than ample for the carriages then used. The road from the gate ran into a breezeway that was open to the east, affording a view of the mountains. To the south of the breezeway were the stables; to the north was the carriage house. The structure's middle section, between the carriage house and stables, was two stories high. The second story held living quarters for the stable hands and gardeners.

In front of the building's middle section, on the stable side of the breezeway, stood a three-story Norman-style tower, which faced Woodland Avenue. At the very top of the tower, there was a little room for a night watchman. This location afforded a view of the home and all of the buildings. It was manned all night for the protection of the home, the horses, the cows, and the stable buildings.

From the breezeway, two heavy doors opened onto a corridor that ran through the middle of the stable building for its full length. At the corridor's south end were two other heavy doors that opened into a large corral. There were stalls on both sides of this corridor.

The stalls provided rather plush accommodations for favored horses. According to Alicia,

> They were not really stalls but more like rooms. A solid wall extended from the floor to the height of about four feet. Above this was a railing supported by fanciful little pillars. The horses could put their chins over the top of them. For instance, if you took sugar over to them or apples or if they liked bread, and held your hand out, the horses could take it out of

Conrad stables, circa 1896 Courtesy Conrad Mansion Directors

your hand without having to reach over something high.

The first two stalls housed a team of blacks which Alicia described as,

> . . . coal black, high spirited and beautiful and they were the cherished team of horses for both summer and winter driving and would be the lead team with the conveyances that took four or six horses. They had stalls on opposite sides of the corridor so they could see each other. They were friends 'cause they were a team and could talk to each other. The next stall was Champ's, Father's saddle horse, and across from him was Rex, Mother's saddle horse. Mother's was a bay and Father's a chestnut. Then came two small stalls for the Shetland ponies, Merry Legs and Pansy. They had rooms together so they could talk to each other. They were very mischievous, merry little people, full of tricks and they always ran away with people they didn't like. I don't know if they couldn't be controlled because they had only rubber bits, but they would come racing and swinging around the corner in the surrey. The two-seated surrey would tip over on two wheels and go galloping and the driver, who was trying to control them with the reins, sawing on the reins which didn't hurt the ponies at all, but the people who understood didn't tighten the reins, just talked to them and they minded the voice command.

The stable's north-south corridor ended in two large doors that opened on the corral. At a point opposite Champ's stall was another corridor, opening off of the north-south passageway, to the east. The east-west corridor had stalls on either side, but these were just ordinary box stalls. They housed Fog and Mist, a team of dappled greys with white manes and tails. Alicia recalled these as,

> ... a team and they were so-called work horses. They weren't dress horses but they were a beautiful team and could have graced any conveyance. They were driven summer and winter — for instance on the camping trips and pulling the Gladstone wagon and all the supplies.

Some years after her husband's death, Lettie Conrad gave Fog and Mist to the Kalispell Fire Department. Alicia remembers the splendid animals pulling the fire wagon at a fast gallop, with tails and manes flying and siren screeching. Alicia believed that the horses knew they were performing an important service and loved it.

After the stalls for Fog and Mist came the stalls for the cows. Alicia said that they "always had a herd of no less than 20 cows," which furnished milk and cream, not only for the Conrads but for many of the townspeople. The door at the end of this corridor opened into the same big corral that covered the land behind the stable building, all the high ground to the east and all of the land south of the stables. Alicia recalled,

> The horses and cows were allowed to run together in the corral. The south side of the stables, where it was sheltered and sunny, was a favorite loafing place for all of the stock. The horses and cows would be in there together and they all got along well for the enclosure was big. And Merry Legs and Pansy held their own with the bigger animals, for they were so feisty and full of fun that they acted like entertainers and the larger animals seemed to understand that and not take advantage of their size to bully the ponies.

At the south end of the corral was a silo for storing feed for the animals. Alicia remembered it as,

> ... a beautiful building of concrete with a tower on the top. Around the tower was a wrought-iron platform with a filigreed wrought-iron railing and cast-iron steps leading up to the platform. The silo was enclosed by an intricately designed wrought-iron fence with an elaborate wrought-iron gate.

Of the tower, Alicia said:

> The platform around the tower gave a beautiful view of the pens for the poultry, ducks and geese, and the stream below the hill, which we called the Crescent River. It was a beautiful stream then, big enough to canoe on and we would canoe far up and down the river. It's just a little piddling stream now, whose course has been changed and it only drains the Woodland Park lagoon. But once it was a branch of the Stillwater River and flowed westward from Cemetery hill, past the back of the stables, rejoining the Stillwater before it flowed into the Flathead.

At a point east of the stables were steps leading down to the river. This was a substantial stairway of three flights, with a little landing station between flights. Along the stairway were cages for the birds and fowl. These were large, wire cages to the east of the steps, roomy enough for the flying birds to exercise their wings. As one descended the stairs, the first cage was for guinea fowl. These birds were not allowed to roam, but their distinctive cry could be heard all over the grounds of the house and stables. Next were the pheasants, which were also kept penned. The next pen housed the peacocks, which were allowed to roam. Alicia remembers that their favorite perches were the pillars of stone on either side of the gates and the pillars interspersed through the stone fence that surrounded the house and stable. One fine, sunny day Alicia looked out and saw a sunning peacock on each pillar of the fences along Woodland Avenue both on the house and on the stable sides. Alicia, who believed in fairies, thought the little people must have placed them there for her pleasure.

The eagles were kept in the last pen along the descending steps. They were acquired on a camping trip in Glacier National Park. A nest with two baby eagles was found by a member of the party. Their mother did not return, and the nest was reported to a Park Ranger. When he had satisfied himself that the mother would not return, the Conrads were permitted to take the baby birds home. With good care and lots of red meat, the babies thrived and grew into huge, bald eagles. The pair remained healthy and was a great attraction for several years. After the death of her husband, Lettie Conrad felt sorry for the freedom-loving birds and released them. They flew away, but for some time returned at feeding time. Eventually they learned to hunt for their own food and never returned.

The ducks and geese were not penned, but roamed the river banks and flatlands along the river. Wild birds would join the group, and it became difficult to distinguish the permanent flock from the sojourners.

A large, two-story log house was built at the level of the river as a winter home for the birds. An opening between the first and second stories allowed the birds plenty of flying space. On the first floor, were four rooms to house different kinds of birds that needed separation, but many were allowed the freedom of the whole structure. Small windows on the first floor and big windows at either end of the building were open in the summer and closed in the winter. The pigeons thrived and multiplied in this building. Their number was kept manageable by the Conrads' frequent serving of squab, which also were given away.

The river was spanned by a footbridge for passage to the 45 acres of park-like woodlands lying on the east side of the Stillwater River. The woodland area was unfenced until about 1917. The International Workers of the World (IWW) was organized at Chicago in 1905, and became a very militant labor group, prone to violence in some areas. It became strong in the lumber camps of the Northwest and, in 1917, called a timber-worker strike which produced some local violence. The 45 acres was a natural camping site for the roving "Wobblies," as members of the organization came to be called. To combat this development, Lettie Conrad had the area fenced. Then she somehow acquired a herd of elk which were placed within the enclosure. The combination of the fence and the elk herd destroyed the popularity of the area as a camping site, and the Wobblies were seen no more.

Alicia remembered that the stables were the heart of the family's life and activities, for horses then played such a big role in every-day living. Also within the stable area were the vegetable gardens, the asparagus and herb beds, and the berry and fruit orchards. The stable buildings provided the storage area for all of the food used by the family.

A stairway descended along the south foundation wall of the carriage house, into a large basement room. From this room, doors opened into smaller rooms, each designed to store and preserve the various food-stuffs grown in the gardens and orchards. The humidity and temperature were controlled by windows placed in window wells. Every window contained a screen both on the outside and on the inside. Each room had windows that were opened and closed according to the outside temperature, to maintain the proper temperature within the room. The air flow into the rooms was carefully controlled by the people working in the stables, and produce would keep and stay fresh for months.

Apples were stored separately, because they would absorb the taste of the root crops. Potatoes, cabbages, rutabagas, and turnips were stored in large bins. Carrots could be buried outside, but if kept inside required more careful treatment. Cured hams and bacon and dried beef hung from the rafters. Peas, beets, green beans, tomatoes, and other vegetables, all grown in the gardens, were put up in quart glass jars. Apples, apricots, and plums were both canned and dried. The dried fruit would last well into the winter and, when gone, the canned fruits were used. Raspberries, currants, and gooseberries were also canned. In addition, Lettie Conrad had planted and canned buffalo berries, a wild fruit which she had learned to like when living in Fort Benton, where wild fruit was all that was available. Sauerkraut and pickles were prepared and stored in great crocks, with wooden tops, kept on the floor.

In response to the question, "Did your folks depend on the garden and put up enough vegetables to last until the vegetables came on the next year or did they buy canned stuff?" Alicia answered:

> I don't think they ever bought any. I can remember being so amazed at the first canned fruit and vegetables I ever saw and I was a good big girl

before I ever saw any, but even this did not prepare me for seeing a canned ham, which I thought had to come from the rafters.

The gardens and orchards also were located in the stable area. From the north of the carriage house, a gravelled path ran through the middle of the garden area all the way to Second Street. The planting and care of the garden was supervised by Lettie. She planned everything and directed the work of the stable hands who during the growing season, also took care of the garden. Immediately to the east of the path was a huge asparagus bed. Alicia remembered that it was rectangular in shape and at least 50 feet long. It had been prepared by digging out the old soil and replacing it with rich, black dirt and manure. The bed could be cut repeatedly and Alicia recalled that, "You could cut asparagus for the whole town, cut it every day. It was very fine asparagus, and Mother always made a point to give that to people who enjoyed it or were in the hospital."

Next came the herb garden. Here Lettie Conrad planted every variety of herb that would grow in Montana. Alicia remembered that her Mother always had a large and varied collection of fresh herbs. It pleased her greatly to be able to furnish almost any herb to those who came to borrow.

Beyond the herb garden were located the berry patches: raspberries, red and black; strawberries in big beds; the buffalo berries, which thrived with careful cultivation. Along the north end of the garden were cherry and pear trees. Alicia recalled that the gardeners would cover the cherry trees with cheesecloth but, when they were not looking, her Mother would make little openings in the coverings so the robins could get a few cherries.

To the west of the path were the vegetable gardens. As with the herbs, Lettie tried to grow every vegetable that could be raised successfully in Montana. The garden produced so heavily that it supplied all the needs of the Conrad table, enough to preserve for the winter season, and plenty to give away. All this was accomplished without the insecticides that gardeners depend upon today.

At the extreme, south end of the stable area were the apple and plum trees. This was called the South Orchard. Some of the original apple trees are still there bearing fruit, but not of the quality grown by Lettie Conrad and her gardeners.

When asked, "You remember the canning. Did they keep it up all summer and did you have extra help?" Alicia replied:

I don't think we had extra help, but the family all worked at it and it was a gay time and a happy time. For instance, pea shelling and cutting string beans and snapping string beans, and, of course, the asparagus would be

168

canned, with great perfection, cut and canned right away so that it was very fine, in quarts. We didn't have two-quart jars. I never saw a two-quart jar in those days, there were pints and quarts. Canning time was a happy time. It was something we all did together, from the grandmothers down to the newest stable hand. With everyone having a good time, it just didn't seem like work.

One of the smaller rooms in the stable basement was a wine cellar. Wine must have been made by the Conrads in far greater quantities than it was consumed. In the winter of 1924, the year following Lettie Conrad's death, the stable area was left virtually unwatched and unsupervised. A group of high-school boys were snooping around the deserted buildings and found the wine cellar. They took what they could carry and spread the word of their find around the high school. One who received the word was Kenny Adams. With a group, he sneaked in from the east, through the snow, to find almost every boy in school waiting his turn. Kenny said that, when he got in, there seemed to be hundreds of bottles of wine, mostly marked as being bottled in 1895. Like the others, Adams was wearing a suit and overcoat, and he found pockets and carrying places for several bottles. Kenny remembered that some of it was good and some of it spoiled. Enough was good to change the pattern of living at the high school for a few days, and Kenny said, "The whole high school got drunk."

When the source of the wine was learned, the supply was cut off. The culprits were all known, but nothing was done. The Volstad Act, which made alcoholic beverages illegal, had become law in 1919, and everyone involved wanted to forget the matter as quickly as possible. Such things would be forgotten, but people interested in history seem to dig them out and keep them alive.

The stable buildings still exist, but are scattered and severely altered. In 1929 Charles D. Conrad, the son, engineered a sale of the stable buildings to A. J. Dean, manager of the first J. C. Penney store in Kalispell. Dean did not dismantle the buildings, but simply cut them into pieces. The two-story area in the center of the stable complex, with the round tower, was cut from the structure and moved across the street. It was remodeled into a house and is now the residence located at 244 Woodland Avenue. The stable and carriage buildings also were cut into house-sized pieces and moved. One now stands at the corner of Main and East Oregon Streets, and other pieces are the residences located at 615 and 623 Third Street East.

Merry Legs and Pansy would never be able to find their stables now, for no one knows who is currently living in them.

CHAPTER 38
Christmas at the Conrad Mansion

The Conrads' first Christmas in their new home was in 1895, about one month after they had moved in. They were delighted with their new home as it was a dramatic change from the West Hotel and from the smaller houses occupied during the long period of construction. They were the leading citizens of a young and growing city that owed its existence primarily to Charles E. Conrad. Both of the Conrads by nature were kind, generous, and caring people. They appreciated their material blessings and truly wanted to share with the less fortunate. They were even more conscious of all these advantages because they had moved in at the approach of the Christmas season. For the first time they were housed in a manner that befitted their wealth and position, and they felt a little uncomfortable about it. They were bothered about how they would use the new home, which loomed as a mansion against the background of the Western frontier.

The Conrads did not take the problem lightly. Essentially they were humble people who had no desire to give the appearance of the lord and lady of the manor. Both wanted to fit into the life of the community as comfortably and with as little pretension as possible. They did not wish their home to be viewed as an unapproachable castle on the hill, but wanted to share both it and their good fortune. Christmas of 1895 was approaching. This would offer the first opportunity to extend the kind of hospitality that they hoped would become synonymous with their name and home.

The Conrads had strong spiritual beliefs. Engrained in Lettie Conrad was a love of pageantry, which sprang from her British heritage and from memories of Christmas in England. Charles was steeped in Southern hospitality and was willing to participate in anything that pleased his wife. The Conrads decided that they would open their house for Christmas and follow that with a New Year's Eve ball. For Christmas, the guest list would comprise people who otherwise would spend the holiday alone or in a hotel or boarding house. This was a prime consideration, for loneliness at Christmas haunted Lettie, who remembered the early life of her orphaned mother.

The number of guests was limited only by the sleeping capacity of the house, which was strained to include every niche that could accommodate a body with any degree of comfort. Requirements for comfort were considerably diminished by the knowledge that loneliness would be dispelled. Alicia remembered that by using the third floor in almost dormitory-style, as many as 25 guests could be accommodated. The celebration all began when the family went to the woods to select a Christmas tree. Their choice was almost unlimited in size, for they would put the tree in the Great Hall, with the top extending into the second story. Once the tree was chosen and placed in the Hall, both the tree and the house were decorated until they carried the festive air envisioned by Lettie. Dozens of beeswax candles were fastened to the tree, ready for lighting. When all was done, Charles Dickens and Tiny Tim together could not have conceived a more beautiful or appropriate place for the celebration of Christmas.

The guests arrived in the early afternoon of Christmas Eve. Each guest was assigned a sleeping space and then was free to ride, sleigh, visit, or just enjoy the atmosphere of the home.

The dinner hour was timed so that the visitors could attend both the evening church service and the midnight mass. Dinner was not a sit-down affair but was served buffet style to accommodate the schedule of the guests. On the menu were meat, fish, and game, all done with a blend of England and the Old South.

When everyone returned from church, they gathered in the Great Hall. The fireplaces blazed and the flickering lights reflected the ornaments on the tree and the decorations of the room. Lettie Conrad then told the story of Christmas and spoke of the Christmas Spirit. In essence she said,

> When you go to your rooms, please stay there, so the Spirit of Christmas will come to our house. I must say that I have never seen Santa Claus nor ever known anyone who has seen him. But after you go to bed, if you hear sleigh bells and noises on the roof that might be the sound of prancing reindeer, well, who can tell? In the morning when you go to the Great Hall and see presents around the tree, and traces of soot and footprints encrusted with ashes leading from the fireplace, again who can tell?

> If people say there is no Santa Claus, or wonder why they have never seen him, I am sorry for them. There is nothing more real in life than the Christmas Spirit; nothing stronger to carry with you for all of your life; nothing more joyous to give, to receive, and to share. If some people think that Santa Claus looks like the Spirit of Christmas, for them he undoubtedly is that Spirit. We should pray that the Spirit of Christmas will be with us

always.

When Lettie finished, Charles Conrad sent two men to the top of the stairs, where they stood with fire hoses. Then the candles on the tree were lighted with everyone participating. When all of the candles were glowing, the lamps and other house illuminations were extinguished and the Great Hall was illuminated with a blaze of light reminiscent of the glory that shown over the manger of the Christ Child. After the beauty of the scene had impressed itself upon the minds of the watchers, never to be forgotten, Grandmother Catherine Stanford started to play Christmas carols and hymns on the piano. All joined in singing, some finding voies that they did not know they possessed.

When Grandmother Stanford stopped playing, the candles were extinguished, the lights turned on, and the Conrads asked everyone to go to bed. Lettie repeated the admonition not to get up, no matter what Christmas noises they might hear. Everyone went to bed with the words and music ringing in their ears. They did, indeed, hear sleigh bells, and sounds like prancing hooves on the rooftop, and a voice that could have been that of Santa Claus. All stayed in their rooms. When everything was quiet, sleep came to the Conrads and to their guests.

Sleep did not last long. As soon as daylight came, footsteps were heard in the halls, and then shrieks of delight, as the children peeped over the bannister at the sight below. Those guests still asleep were awakened by the sound of violin music floating up from the Great Hall. As the violinist played the familiar Christmas music, people in nightdress and robes stepped quietly to stand at the railing and look down on the scene of Christmas morning. Again their voices gathered in singing and the house rang with the sound of hymns and carols until the music stopped.

After dressing, the guests gathered in the Great Hall. The fires still burned brightly. The tree had taken on a new beauty with the addition of the gaily wrapped presents tied here and there on the branches and piled on the floor under and around the tree. There were traces of soot and footsteps encrusted with ashes that led from the hearth to the tree. No one spoke but, with these sights, everyone remembered the sleigh bells and the sounds on the roof during the night. All was quiet, but the true spirit of Christmas seemed a sound that reverberated around the house, from room to room, floor to floor, and even from the rooftop where the sounds of the night before might well have been the feet of prancing reindeer.

Reluctant to break the spell, Charles Conrad invited the guests to gather around the tree to open gifts before breakfast. Daughter Kate, never one for self-restraint, had crept down during the night and opened her own presents by the light of the fireplace, but she joined in the joy of others as they opened their presents, and she was as excited as if each gift were her own.

Each of the women received a box of long-stemmed violets. These flowers became the traditional gift for the ladies and were grown especially for the Christmas party by the local florist. The gifts for the men varied from knives and pipes to small articles of clothing, which were more practical and bespoke the taste of Charles. When all the gifts were opened, he announced breakfast, which was served buffet style to those persons not too excited to eat.

When breakfast was over, the Christmas Day guests were again invited to ride, sleigh, skate, or just relax to await the dinner, which was served in the early afternoon. This was the festive Christmas meal. Lettie Conrad and her mother loved the English traditions, one of which was the Christmas goose. All food traditions seemed to be followed, for there also were turkeys, ham, and roast beef. Charles carved at the table and Lettie served. As the plates were filled, according to the directions of each guest, they were delivered by a serving woman. When all had been served, C. E. Conrad gave thanks to God and then asked the guests to add their blessings. When all who cared to had spoken, the meal began and was as festive and convivial as beautiful surroundings, good food, and high spirits could make it.

Everyone was reluctant to have the dinner end, but end it must, as darkness came early on that December day. There was a final gathering in the Great Hall, where goodbyes were said and the guests expressed their appreciation for a Christmas they would always remember. When the visitors were ready to leave, Charles had two large sleighs waiting in the driveway to take them to their residences. With sleigh bells ringing, the horses moved off, bringing to an end the first Christmas at the Conrads' new home.

Charles Conrad died on Thanksgiving Day, November 27, 1902. Until then, the pattern for the celebration of Christmas remained essentially the same. Immediately following the death of her husband, Lettie Conrad was too grief-stricken to undertake the Christmas party alone, so there was none in 1902. By the Christmas of 1903, however, Lettie had thought of a new plan for the commemoration of Christmas. It still would help many deprived and lonely people, yet would be so different that it would not evoke such powerful memories of her husband's part in the first Christmas at the Conrad Mansion.

CHAPTER 39
The Christmas Pudding

Of all the ceremonies and traditions that were celebrated at the Conrad Mansion, the making of the Christmas pudding was probably the most revered. Certainly it was looked forward to with great anticipation, since custom required the participation of everyone connected with the Mansion, from the grandmothers down to the newest stable hand.

On the first day of Advent, Lettie Conrad would announce that it was time to commence preparations. Grandmother Catherine Stanford would get her book containing the old English recipe handed down in her family for generations. The recipe had been born in the beautiful apple country in the County of Kent, through which trod the pilgrims of Geoffrey Chaucer on their way to the Canterbury Cathedral. Grandmother Stanford always thought that the apples for the pudding must be of some Kentish variety. She believed the McIntosh must have come from Kent, for it was the only apple that Grandmother Stanford knew was durable enough to withstand the severe testing of apples chosen to become an ingredient for her pudding recipe.

The family and staff would gather in the Great Hall in front of the fire. Lettie would begin the Advent season with a prayer of thanksgiving and would ask God's blessing for the coming activities in preparation for Pudding Day. From then on, the religious significance of each act was recognized and made a part of the preparation.

The recipe was read aloud by Lettie, and someone always seemed to know which ingredients were on hand and which must be ordered from the grocery department of the Kalispell Mercantile. Each year fresh spices were ordered, so the taste of the pudding would be full-bodied and bold. And these had to have been ordered in ample time for the KM to have the varied array of spices, some quite exotic, on hand for the day of preparation.

From the first day of Advent to Christmas Eve, the pudding ingredients were gathered under the watchful eyes and close supervision of Lettie Conrad and Grandmother Stanford. The butcher was alerted to save sufficient suet from the kidneys of veal calves, since only kidney suet was considered proper for the Stanford family recipe. It was handled with great care and cut with precision. The suet had to be cut, not crumbled, since crumbling made inexact pieces, and no deviation in size was tolerated, either in the Kent County of old or by Lettie's recipe.

Candied peels of oranges, citron, and lemons were kept in the great storeroom under the stable. The McIntosh apples were carefully selected, wrapped in double folds of paper, and put aside in the coolest place. The markets were scoured for the best raisins, currants, and dates, which also were placed in the storeroom with the other segregated items that were homegrown or homemade. Well before Christmas, all the pudding ingredients were either on hand or ordered.

Pudding-preparation Day would be well before Christmas, and word of the date was passed to all. On this day, only the absolutely necessary things were done, so every person could participate in the Pudding-making Ceremony. Everyone first gathered in the kitchen or the Great Hall for prayers, begun by Lettie Conrad and followed by anyone who wanted to ask God's blessing upon the activities that were about to begin.

Following the prayers, the stablemen brought up the supplies from the storeroom and placed them in separate heaps in the kitchen. The food chopper was made ready and each ingredient was chopped to the proper size. The aim was to maintain uniformity. From experience, Lettie knew how much each ingredient would shrink or expand in the later boiling. Dates would almost cook away, but citron would withstand the boiling without shrinking.

While the cutting, chopping, and mixing went on, there began the singing of Christmas songs from the different nations represented. The stablemen, who were mostly German, sang the songs and told the Christmas stories of their homeland as did the Norwegians, Swedes, and Yugoslavians. Grandmother Stanford brought the England of Dickens, and Grandmother Conrad that of the Old South.

As the mixing went on, Lettie Conrad watched every movement. Everything was done under her supervision. But everyone made suggestions, which were carefully considered and discarded only if they did violence to the treasured recipe. Each song and story brought on more. The people who were at first hesitant caught the spirit and made rich additions.

When the chopping and cutting and mixing were almost completed, a fire was built in the huge kitchen range, and on it was placed a large copper boiler, containing the proper amount of water. After the water began a furious boil, the mountainous pile of mixed ingredients slowly was added, as someone stirred the mixture.

The recipe required the participation of all for, as one stirred the others blended into the pudding the thoughts and memories of Christmases past and the hopes for those to come. If the stirrer or anyone else had thoughts to be shared, he spoke them. If one sang, the others joined in. And the air was filled with the smell of pudding — and the spirit of Christmas — as it emanated in word and song from the pudding mixture.

The recipe required that the boiling be continuous, so everyone took a turn at stirring. The singing and storytelling went on and, the thicker the consistency of the pudding, the harder the job of stirring became. But everyone stirred, even if he had to be helped, for this was the most important part of all. If the people in the kitchen knew the words of the stirrer's song, they would join in, and they listened with interest to the stories of the Christmas customs and ways of other nations and homes.

No pudding could be properly made without tasting. Big wooden tasting spoons were provided. As the cooking progressed, each person would taste and either close the eyes in blissful agreement or cock an eye toward the array of spices and opine that it might need a pinch of this or a dash of that. If Lettie agreed, the pinch or dash would be added. If she did not agree, in her most kindly manner she would say, "I believe you may be right, but we can't depart from Grandmother Stanford's recipe."

When the mixture finally reached the proper consistency, Lettie had the pudding that she wanted and that was called for by the recipe. For Lettie's idea of a Christmas Pudding was that it should contain not only the finest ingredients, but also the feelings, beliefs, memories, recollections, and reminiscences of all of the Christmases that had ever been experienced by those who helped with the pudding — both Christmases past and those hoped for, and all of the joys and all of the sorrows that had touched each life. But most important of all were the stirring in of the love that each had for his fellow men and the hope that the compassion and forgiveness promised by the Christ could be shared by all mankind.

This was the true spirit of Christmas: the spirit of Him whose birthday the pudding was intended to celebrate. Only with this spirit, blended in by the thoughts, prayers, and expressions of those who stirred, did a pudding become a Christmas Pudding, no matter what the quality of the ingredients.

The pudding done, it then had to be wrapped and stored. First, a big bolt of new, heavy, unbleached muslin was put into boiling water to remove the sizing and to make it soft and pliable, since the muslin was almost as heavy as canvas. Then the muslin was torn into pieces of the proper size. It was always torn, rather than cut, since cutting would leave tiny threads that might get into the pudding. The muslin was so heavy that the tearing required two strong men, but it was finally reduced to the proper sizes.

The largest muslin piece was laid flat on a huge bread board on the kitchen table, then covered with white flour sifted to a depth of about one-quarter inch. Next the hot pudding was ladled from the boiler, placed in the middle of the muslin piece, and piled up until Lettie Conrad signaled. The four corners of the muslin piece then were raised and the pudding jounced gently to settle it into the bag. If the quantity was right, the four corners of the bag were tied. More pudding was added if necessary, watching that the correct amount of room was left at the top for the pudding to breathe and expand, and Lettie knew exactly the amount of room to leave. If any of the mixture remained, it was placed in smaller muslin bags in the same manner.

The stablemen then carried the bags to the storage room in the basement of the carriage house, where they would hang to mellow and age. On Christmas Eve of the following year, the stablemen would bring the pudding to the Mansion, where all were participating in the making of the pudding for the next Christmas. This done, each employee was given a piece of the pudding made the year before — a piece commensurate with the size of his family. The rest was saved for the Conrads' Christmas dinner.

On Christmas Day, the pudding was brought out about two hours before serving and steamed until it was hot all through. At the conclusion of dinner, the pudding was placed on an enormous silver platter, which, with a bottle of fine brandy and sugar lumps, was set before Charles Conrad. All eyes were on C. E. as he piled sugar lumps on top of the pudding, until it would hold no more. Then slowly he poured brandy over the lumps, until the lumps and the pudding were soaked. A servant then handed him a taper, lighted at the blazing fire. With this he ignited the brandy, and it flamed in beautiful colors. As the pudding flamed, he dipped brandy from the platter with a silver ladle and poured it back over the flaming pudding, until the flames turned blue and lowered and lowered until they died out with a final blue flicker.

During the time Charles was flaming the pudding, the guests sang Christmas songs, first started by Lettie. As one song ended, another person would start his favorite, and the singing would continue until each person was served.

Charles served the pudding with a great silver spoon and it reached the plate retaining the shape of the spoon. As he filled a plate, it was handed to a servant who carried it to the waiting guest. When the last guest had been served, the Fairy Sauce was passed. This white sauce, laced with Barbados rum, was also made according to a recipe from Grandmother Stanford's recipe book.

The Christmas Pudding, and all that went into its preparation and serving, provided one of the greatest joys in Lettie Conrad's celebration of Christmas. To her, every event of that season was meant to celebrate the birth of Christ. The fervor of her faith made Christ an almost tangible presence at the table.

Even though Grandmother Stanford's recipe is lost, taken by a vandal who stole her cookbook, Lettie could recreate her cherished pudding were she here next Christmas. No matter what ingredients might be on hand, after she had stirred in her Christian love and the devotion and the compassion she held for every living thing, it would be a true Christmas Pudding that was ladled onto the muslin and hung in the basement of the carriage house.

CHAPTER 40
Life at the Conrad Mansion

The year following the completion of the Mansion, the Conrads commenced construction of a rather elaborate summer home at Foy's Lake, about four miles west of Kalispell. When completed, this became the summer residence of the Conrads and their guests. About the first of June, the home in town would be closed, leaving only a caretaker and a gardener. The entire Conrad entourage would then load up in buggies and wagons to be off for Foy's Lake, where they would stay until about the first of September, except for trips back to town to participate in the canning and preservation of fruits and vegetables. The trip to and from the lake was a long one and not made often. In fact, such a trip was considered newsworthy by the Kalispell papers. Included in the social news are items telling who had gone to Foy's Lake for a visit with the Conrads.

Alicia recalled that the house was on a big island.

There were eight bedrooms and a great dining room and kitchen, and ice chests, and there was a barn and stablemen and riding horses and carriage horses. The ice was put up from the lake and stored in the big ice house there. It was quite an establishment. There were tents around through the forest. It was an uncut and beautiful forest, with ferns and moss and shade, and the lake was good for swimming. There was a ford of built-up rocks to go back and forth from the island to the mainland. The ford was kept at a certain height by adding rocks to it, but the lake would often be so high that the Shetland ponies would have to swim, but the surrey was all right if you sat on the back of the seats with your feet and knees in the water.

The summer place was a haven for guests. Both Charles and Lettie Conrad had many brothers and sisters, who produced a great number of nieces and nephews, all of whom wanted to spend the summer with their uncle and aunt at the lake. The two older Conrad children, Charley and Kate, did not attend high school in Kalispell and were gone except for the summer months, when they brought friends home for the summer vacation. Travel conditions did not encourage short visits. Those people

179

who came were not only summer visitors but usually visitors for the summer. The Conrads truly welcomed their guests. Both had a great appreciation for their home and the surrounding area and were filled with a strong desire to share these things with their friends and guests. Sharing seemed to be their greatest pleasure and the greater the number of guests, the more pleasure it gave the Conrads.

The Conrads also were among the first to use what is now Glacier Park as a recreation area. Charles organized pack trips to show his guests the magnificent scenery. Men and wagons were sent ahead with camping gear, supplies, and horses to establish camps. Those persons who wished could ride horses to the rendezvous point, or they could take the train to Belton (West Glacier) and ride or be driven from there. A base camp was set up at Lake McDonald. From there, the guests covered the area either by one-day or by overnight hikes or rides.

Alicia remembered one trip that was a thriller. The party rode to Sperry Glacier. From there they were let down by ropes into the Avalanche Lake Valley and hiked back to the base camp. Kate — who was well on her way to the 250 pounds she eventually weighed — caused quite a lot of speculation as to whether the rope could withstand the strain, which was funny to everyone except Kate. The expense of those trips must have been enormous, but Conrad evidently believed that the pleasure and satisfaction derived justified the money spent.

C. E. also established camps on Flathead Lake. The guests went from camp to camp by steamers, which provided the most comfortable north-south transportation. When the Conrads' guests left, they would have seen everything in the Flathead area considered worth seeing, and in a style as luxurious as could be provided at that time.

The Conrads' guests were primarily family, friends, famous people, and scientists doing exploratory work and research. The hotels of the day were not too comfortable, and word of the Conrads' hospitality spread among travelers. Dr. William T. Hornaday, the noted naturalist, came to the Flathead Valley to study the Conrad buffalo herd and to select animals as the nucleus of herds by which to save the buffalo from extinction. He spent weeks as a guest of the Conrads. Alicia remembered an ornithologist who came to the Flathead Valley to determine the number of its bird species. From the length of his stay, the Conrads concluded that the variety of bird species in the Kalispell area must be the greatest in the world.

One of Alicia's favorite visitors was Teddy Roosevelt. A. W. Merrifield, an early resident, had served in the "Rough Riders" with Roosevelt. The two had become great friends, and they were partners in a ranch in Dakota Territory. From there, Merrifield came to Montana and eventually settled on land which is now Mission View Terrace on Flathead Lake. After Roosevelt became President, he appointed Merrifield a U.S. Marshall for Montana. When Roosevelt came to visit Merrifield, he also visited at the Conrads.' Alicia remembered him as very talkative and very vivacious.

> My father was very fond of him and a great admirer of his. He would be a guest in our home, depending on which way he was traveling. He would hold the floor with his delightful way of speaking, because, of course, he was an accomplished speaker and had a lot to talk about. So I could remember him best at dinner at the dinner table, and this is my early memory because this must have been important. I had my food, my meals, in the nursery, but I always came down and sat in a high chair at my Father's left side for dessert. I was very quiet and listened and got a lot of vivid memories that way. I felt a very great warmth of friendship for Roosevelt, but I expect he brought that out in everybody.

The oil painting of Roosevelt that now hangs in the library of the Mansion was given to Merrifield, probably by Roosevelt, and hung in his home at Flathead Lake. It was in this home when it was purchased by Jack McCarthy, who then operated the Montana Hotel in Kalispell. When McCarthy sold the Hotel, the picture was left hanging in the lobby, where it stayed through other changes of ownership. After the hotel operations ceased, the picture hung in a local law office for a number of years, until it was given to the Mansion to preserve that part of the Conrad history.

In 1896 the first New Year's Eve ball was held at the Mansion. At that time Kalispell was small enough that a blanket invitation could be issued to the whole town. The ball became the social event of the year. The dining room, library, Great Hall, and music room were cleared of furniture. The orchestra sat in the music room. The punch bowls were placed in the alcove under the stairs. The ball started at nine o'clock, and the guests arrived on time, for they did not want to miss anything. It was never known how many people would attend, but the house seemed able to handle any number. Charles and Lettie Conrad danced the first number, then the dancing continued until midnight, when tables were set in the dining room and filled with the finest food that the Conrads could provide. One hour was given over to eating, then the music started again and continued until the most determined dancer had had enough.

Charles loved to dance and was always happy at the sight of people dancing at the ball. In his last years, he would dance until tired, then slip away to rest. Once, going upstairs, he saw Mary Murphy, the little family seamstress, crouched on the stairs, watching the dancing crowd by peering through the bannisters. Conrad took her hand, led her to the dance floor, and they danced a waltz so beautifully that others stopped to watch. Little Mary Murphy was then in demand as a partner and spent a very happy evening, because of the kindness of a generous man who wanted everyone to know happiness and pleasure.

Alicia remembered most vividly the visits of the Plains Indians whom her father had known, befriended, and advised when he lived and did business in Fort Benton. So great was their confidence in him that the chiefs still sought his advice. A date would be made for a visit, and the Indians would arrive in their finest regalia. Alicia recalled their great courtesy and refinement. The meeting always began with a dinner at which Lettie Conrad used her best china, linen, and silver. The Indians recognized and appreciated this display and sought to live up to the honor. They watched Lettie in her choice and use of the various pieces of silverware and china. Then they would make the same choice and proceed as though they had eaten in this manner all their lives.

When dinner was finished, Charles and the Indians would adjourn to the Great Hall. Here the Indians squatted in a semi-circle around C. E., who sat with his back to the fireplace. With the lights out and the flames making moving shadows of the Indians and illuminating their bronze faces and arms, they would reminisce. Conrad spoke several Indian dialects fluently, but if there was a chief from a tribe whose language he did not speak, the beautiful and expressive sign language would be used.

When things were well under way, Lettie and Alicia would slip quietly to the outside of the circle, where in the semi-darkness they could hear and watch the Indians, fascinated by the flickering shadows of bodies and moving arms, the musical language of the Indians, and the spontaneous roars of laughter when someone recalled an amusing event that they all remembered.

At a time determined by the most important chief, some problems considered serious by the Indians would be discussed, and Conrad would give his opinions and advice. Satisfied that they had secured the best advice that their trusted white brother could give, the ranking chief would stand, indicating the end of the powwow. All the Indians would thank the Conrads for their hospitality and, with great grace and gravity, shake hands with Charles and Lettie and little Alicia. They then would go out the front door in single file in the order of rank, the highest chief leading the way with the dignity befitting a chief taking leave of a good friend and brother, and his beloved family.

In her eighty-sixth year (1978) Alicia's most vivid memory was that of the half-circle of Indians seated in the semi-darkness with the lights from the flaming fireplace highlighting their bronzed and glistening faces, giving them a look of dignity, which was matched by the manner in which they conducted themselves in totally unfamiliar surroundings.

182

Although Charles Conrad was away frequently, during his time at home he and Lettie loved to spend time in the library. Lettie would read aloud from the works of Rudyard Kipling, from the classics, from books on art, music, and architecture, and from *Harper's Magazine*, which they both enjoyed. Alicia would sit quietly in the library, listening to them as they discussed what they read and delved into the encyclopedia and other reference books on any subject that particularly piqued their interests. Alicia recalled that, on one occasion, her father was talking on some topic when he stopped and said,

Lettie, just imagine me knowing about all these things. Before we were married, I knew nothing except business. But you have led me to a knowledge of many things. You remember when I brought you the India shawls? The owner of the shop told me that I had chosen his finest pieces and complimented me on my knowledge and taste. You taught me that, Lettie. You taught me that a Hepplewhite was not something you attached to a wagon tongue. The things you have taught me and aroused my interest in have so enriched my life and expanded my knowledge that I no longer feel deprived by my lack of formal education.

Life in the Conrad Mansion was rich and varied. Its hospitality was legendary. No traveler was turned away and the Conrad name became synonymous with generosity and sharing.

CHAPTER 41
The Grandmothers

Grandmother Conrad

The grandmothers were an important part of the Conrad household. Grandmother Conrad, who was born Maria Ashby on October 20, 1846, descended from one of the first families of Virginia. Her father was the great-great-grandson of John Ashby, a loyal subject of King Charles I of England. John Ashby was one of the first to land in Virginia and was with George Washington in the Braddock Expedition (1755). The father was also the great-grandson of Benjamin Ashby, who served on Washington's staff during the Revolutionary War.

Maria Ashby's girlhood was spent on a pre-Civil War plantation. She lived in the pleasant and comfortable style of the Southern belle. At an early age she was married to James Warren Conrad, who lived in the Shenandoah Valley of Virginia, where they made their home.

Conrad was descended from Joseph Conrad, an early emigrant from Germany, who had settled in the Shenandoah Valley. James Conrad acquired a large plantation in the Valley and later became a district judge and a colonel in the Virginia State Militia.

Her first years on the Wapping Plantation were happy ones for Maria. Slavery was still the backbone of the economic system of the South. Even her bearing of thirteen children did not interrupt the gentle flow of plantation life. No matter how many children were born, there were always plenty of mammies to care for them. As the children were born, they were named: Mattie E. (Mrs. T. S. Todd); William G.; Charles E.; James, who died at birth; Mary, who died at birth; Nannie M. (Mrs. Joseph A. Baker); John Howard; Joseph Hunter; Mollie Blanche (Mrs. Charles Price); Warren Ashby; Alice Agnes (Mrs. F. J. Adams); Arthur Franklin, who died at 15; Ernest, who died when a baby.

This pleasant life continued despite rumors of war between the states, which most Southern plantation owners did not really believe could happen. But the Civil War did come, and with a savagery no one expected. Colonel James Conrad and his two eldest sons — William G. and Charles E. — went off to war expecting to return in a few weeks. They stayed through the entire war (1861 to 1865) and all escaped serious injury.

Maria Conrad had kept her brood of white and black children together in spite of General Sherman and the whole "Damned Yankee Army." How this tiny, genteel lady managed the horrors she must have seen and the sickening fright she must have felt for what might happen to her children, no one knows. Her responsibilities eased when her husband returned. They managed to hold the plantation together for the first years of the Reconstruction, but it was clear that the life they had known had ended and would never return. William and Charles established themselves in the frontier town of Fort Benton with a financial success no one had anticipated. By 1879 they were able to reunite the whole family in Fort Benton and thereafter the two elder brothers provided for the rest of the family in all of their needs. After the family was reunited, Maria put the past from her mind and gave herself over completely to another way of life.

The horrors of the Civil War left few scars on Maria. Only two things ever returned to trouble her thoughts and dreams. The first was the miscarriage she suffered when she was forced to gather fuel, cook, and serve a meal to a company of Union soldiers, without any help either in the preparation or serving of the dinner. The second was the ever-returning question of what had happened to the black children who had been deserted by their parents. The large, beseeching, white eyes that followed her as she left the war-ravaged Wapping Plantation followed her for the rest of her life. She never ceased to be troubled about what had happened to them, even though the Emancipation Proclamation (1863) had ended her responsibility.

Maria Conrad, with her husband and remaining family, arrived at Fort Benton in June of 1879. They had traveled overland from Virginia to St. Louis, Missouri, and then came up the Missouri River by steamboat to Fort Benton, Montana Territory, to begin a new life. This was to be a life of ease and comfort, reminiscent of the Old South, because the success and wealth acquired by their sons, Charles, and to a lesser extent William, would be shared with the family as long as they lived.

Grandmother Stanford

Grandmother Stanford's ancestors were entirely English. She left England at an early age and never returned, but she retained a keen interest in her English heritage and the family that remained there.

185

Although called Catherine, she was named Alicia to continue a family name that started in 1600. The first Alicia married an Englishman named Tyson, starting a new blood line that produced some venturesome people.

Grandmother Stanford kept informed about her English family by taking newspapers published in England and she probably subscribed to a clipping service. Among her things was a newspaper article from an English paper about James Tyson, a millionaire whose death was reported from Sydney in January of 1899. The clipping does not show the name of the paper or its date, but she wrote in the margin of the page that the clipping was sent to her by someone in England. The date was not given but other articles indicated the date of January 2, 1899.

The news story reported that one branch of the Tyson family had emigrated to present-day Australia at an early date. The first English settlement on that continent was a penal colony established in 1788. The Tysons must have arrived soon after that for in 1822 a son, James Tyson, was born. He was an unusual man. When he died at the age of 70, he was able to say that he had never entered a church, a theatre, or a public house; that he had never tasted wine, beer, or spirits; that he had never sworn or washed with soap — he used sand instead; that he had never worn a white shirt — or a glove; that he had never married or been in close proximity to a woman.

Yet James Tyson made a huge fortune in the cattle business. After three failures, he finally established a successful cattle station in the outback. He then multiplied his holdings into stations scattered all over the continent, with some locations extremely remote and lonely. This did not bother Tyson, but it was difficult to find help who would live in such isolation. At one station the help wanted a church and Tyson was the only source of money for its construction. When approached, Tyson said that he would provide funds for the building of the church, but only on the condition that the whole bill of costs be made out and presented for payment in one sum, so he should not be bothered by requests for further contributions. The condition was accepted, the money given for the estimated cost, and construction started. When Tyson returned to the station the following year, he was requested to give 20 pounds for the installation of lightning rods on the church. His reply was, "I will not. I have given a church to Almighty God, and if He cannot take care of it for Himself, He does not deserve to have it."

Tyson's fortune was estimated at five million pounds at his death, but the money did not interest him. He was content to leave it behind and let it go where it might. Fighting the desert had been his only interest. He said,

I have been fighting the desert all my life, and I have won. I have put water where no water was, and beef where there was no beef. I have put fences where there were no fences and roads where there were no roads. Nothing can undo what I have done, and millions will be happier for it after I am long dead and forgotten.

These were the blood lines upon which Catherine Alicia Coogan descended, but she did not thrive on adversity in the same manner as did some of her early ancestors. Catherine Stanford did not cope well with the genteel poverty into which the family fell following the collapse of the businesses which had been established by her husband. The family was scattered: George in Australia; James in Canada; Alicia, or Letty, in Chester, a small town in Nova Scotia far from Halifax with the transportation system of those days; and Catherine and the youngest son, Harry Penn. Harry, called Hal, was named for William Penn, Catherine's cousin, who founded Pennsylvania.

The decision was made that the family would regroup in the West. In a hand written note, Mrs. Stanford recalled:

Our journey of nine weeks from Pittsburg to Fort Benton, Montana, was 3600 miles long on the Steamer Montana.

The June 6, 1879 issue of the *Fort Benton Record* reported that mother, daughter, and son arrived in Fort Benton on May 30, 1879 to become permanent residents. The two refined ladies were beginning a new life in a dusty, brawling, little frontier settlement. It must have been frightening to them and to the 11-year-old boy, whose eyes grew larger at each new and unfamiliar sight. Catherine Stanford would find peace and a life of comfort and ease in this lusty land. The daughter, Lettie, just eighteen, would establish in the rugged and uncouth West, a home that would become a symbol of refinement, elegance, and hospitality. The gentle and sensitive Hal would grow to love the natural beauty of the West and begin a career as a taxidermist that would bring him recognition throughout the United States.

In Fort Benton, both grandmothers settled in houses provided for them by their sons. Their relationship became closer when, on January 4, 1881, the young Lettie married Charles E. Conrad. The marriage proved to be a most happy one, not only for the young couple, but for the two grandmothers, who began their lives together at almost the same time as did their children.

Grandmother Stanford was a widow when she arrived in Fort Benton. Grandmother Conrad became a widow when, a few years after reaching Fort Benton, her husband, James W. Conrad, died in Great Falls, where he was visiting their youngest daughter, Alice. He fell down the basement steps and broke his neck and was buried in the Highland Cemetery in Great Falls. The Civil War and its aftermath were still so distressing to the Conrads that there was no thought that any family member would be returned for burial in their homeland.

When Charles and Lettie Conrad brought their family to Kalispell in 1891, they also brought the two grandmothers. While the Mansion was being constructed, the family's housing was varied and inadequate. This probably had an influence on the design of the Mansion. It appears that, from the outset, the comfort of the grandmothers was one of the principal considerations of the Conrads. When the new home was completed in 1895, the grandmothers moved in with the rest of the family. They had the freedom of the entire house, but their quarters were dedicated to their privacy, and no one entered unless invited.

Following the move into the Mansion, the grandmothers were able to develop their individual lifestyles. There was never any feeling that the grandmothers were a burden or that they in any way interferred with the family life of the Conrads. They were a loved and treasured part of the household. Both were warm and understanding people, but were different in most other respects. Each loved and respected the other, but each was careful not to intrude upon the other's privacy or life. Each enjoyed the companionship of the other, but developed an intuitive awareness of the times when she wished to be alone.

Grandmother Conrad was a tiny woman, with soft gray hair, who rather looked like a grandmother in miniature. Alicia Conrad held fresh and vivid memories of her grandmothers. Outstanding in Alicia's mind were the vivacity and gaiety of her Grandmother Maria Conrad. She refused to be cast as an old woman, and she did not demand to be respected or revered because of her age. The word "grandmother" did not seem to fit her, nor was she too fond of it. She was "Muddy," a companion in fun and frolic, a great player of practical jokes. When she told a story, she held children and grown-ups enthralled. She was a mimic who brought tears and laughter as she became, in mimicry, the people and characters that the children knew. Alicia remembers her Muddy, seated on the floor of the Great Hall, surrounded by children of all ages — cousins, grandchildren, friends — listening wide-eyed and breathless to her tales.

Maria Conrad told of the life on Wapping Plantation in Virginia before the Civil War. She recalled how, early on Christmas morning, the black children would come to the plantation house, where they would hide. Then they would peep around the corners and doors, peek-a-boo style, and shout, "Christmas gift!" If the child shouted before a Conrad said, "Merry Christmas," the tot received a gift. This went on until each black child had a gift, and it continued until the gifts ran out.

188

She pictured the woebegone look of the little black child, whose duty that day was to keep the chickens, ducks, and geese out of the flower and the vegetable gardens. This was a duty that no one liked and did with the greatest reluctance.

Grandmother Conrad also told of a very special event in the life of the plantation: a beaten-biscuit festival. It was held only when one of the big oaks was felled. The tree was cut, leaving a stump about table-height. The top of the stump then was sheared and leveled off as smooth as a breadboard. This work was done with large, double-bitted axes. The stump then was cleaned and scrubbed until it shone. On this makeshift breadboard was placed flour, lard, and water, with no leavening. The ingredients were kneaded into a big lump. The Negroes scrubbed the axes until they were clean and bright, then pounded and beat the dough with the flat sides of the axes. Grandmother Conrad did not remember how long the beating took, but it must have been a while — for, even with the machine used to make beaten biscuits for the Mansion, it took quite some time to get the dough to the right consistency.

As the dough was beaten, the Negroes gathered around the stump in a circle and sang. No one worked on the day of the beaten-biscuit festival. They sang the old spirituals so beautifully that they could never be forgotten. The most popular was "Swing Low, Sweet Chariot," and this remained the favorite hymn of C. E. Conrad as long as he lived.

When the dough finally reached the proper consistency, the participants pinched off pieces, which they rolled into balls between thumb and fingers. Each ball then was flattened to a one-inch disk and a cross was made on it with a fork. After this, the disks were taken into the house and cooked on the huge kitchen stove. Everyone ate until he could eat no more. The celebration lasted almost the entire day and, when it was finally over, the help returned to their quarters full and happy, and they continued to sing far into the night.

The children also heard about "Uncle Jeff," the bearded Negro patriarch. Uncle Jeff was too old to work but remained a man of great importance, for he was the historian to the Negro children. He told them of the life in Africa before he was captured by the slavers. He was a link between them and a life they would never know. More important, Uncle Jeff gave them a reason to have pride, even in slavery.

Muddy talked so much of plantation life that the children believed that they knew the slaves, could call them by name, could distinguish the field hands from the household help, and understood whom could be trusted. She told how some of the Negro girls possessed what was called "the touch of healing." Those girls who held this talent manifested it at an early age, and they were trained by Grandmother Conrad to help with the care and nursing of the sick.

These "healers" became adept at manipulating the "palate lock," or the tuft of hair on a slave child's head. When the child would not open his mouth for a dose of medicine, the nursing girl would jerk on his palate lock, his mouth then would pop open, and he was dosed before he could shut his mouth again. These girls also possessed an instinctive knowledge of herbs, of their medicinal value, and of how they must be used to produce the best results.

Another of Grandmother Conrad's favorite narratives concerned the black mammy who was more strict with the Ashby girls than was their mother. The mammy always went with the girls to parties to help them to arrange their hair, to get into their hoop skirts, and to lace up their tight stays to achieve the hour-glass waist. She then would return with reports of the girls' behavior and manners. After one party, she brought two of the girls home and reported, "Miss Liddy (Mattie), she et like a lady at de pawty, but Miss Dumps (Nannie), she et like she was etin' shoats' legs and squirrels."

Muddy also mimicked people whom the children knew. In spite of her size, she became the overly fat lawyer waddling to the Flathead County Courthouse and puffing and blowing his way up the stairs to the courtroom. Despite her age, the children could see in her mimicry the little pigtailed girl who winced and pouted when some mischievous boy gave those pigtails a yank.

Muddy loved to help plan the many social functions held at the Mansion and loved better to attend them. She was always a charming and welcomed addition, and the group of which she was a part was never dull. The breakfast-in-bed or dinner-in-her-room routines were not for Muddy. She liked to be where the action was and, if there were no action, she created some.

Grandmother Maria Conrad preferred to have people around her and did nothing alone. When the vegetables ripened and were ready for canning, Muddy would have pea-shelling and bean-snapping parties. Mountains of peas and beans could be made ready for canning without anyone seeming to work. As the beans were snapped or the peas shelled, Muddy told stories or mimicked. She arranged contests, promoted sing-alongs, or sometimes had someone read favorite stories aloud. Always the pile of vegetables was gone before anyone tired of snapping and shelling, and most of the time the group kept ahead of the kitchen crew in charge of the canning.

Muddy further was an expert at picking the feathery down from geese. She would station herself on the Mansion's front porch and a stableman would bring from the pens a goose, its legs and wings tied. The goose was placed breast-up on Muddy's lap, and there was always more goose

190

than lap. She then would move both hands in a circular direction around the goose's breast, her nimble fingers picking the fine down until the goose was plucked. The down was put in a sack held by someone sitting beside her. When the proper amount was in the sack, it was hung in an apple tree in the south orchard to sun and dry, for the downy pillows used by the Conrads and their guests. Grandmother Conrad kept at her work until all the geese were plucked and turned loose to grow a new crop of down to keep them warm during the winter. With the coming of spring, the stablemen would start again the procession of geese to Grandmother Conrad, so another crop of down could be harvested.

The granddaughter Alicia shared a real intimacy with her Grandmother Stanford, but this was an affinity tinged more with veneration than with the comradeship and ease she felt for Grandmother Conrad.

Grandmother Stanford continued to love her music and books, and to pursue her interest in learning. When she was fifty-one years old, she had suffered a stroke that restricted the use of her legs. After her recovery, she always carried a cane and could never keep pace with Grandmother Conrad. Although she did not enter into the social life of the Mansion with the same gusto as did Grandmother Conrad, she did entertain the family and guests by playing the piano. The stroke had not affected her ability to play, and her music retained some of the concert quality of her youth. She delighted every audience, for fine music and other cultural advantages still were lacking in the pioneer West.

Grandmother Catherine Stanford spent a great deal of time in her quarters, reading and writing. She enjoyed some supervision of the library, and its books reflected somewhat her literary tastes. Faithfully and with great care, she kept a journal in which she recorded her thoughts, the life in the Mansion, her views on the contemporary scene, and random speculations on life itself. She read the journal to the young Alicia, and her grandmother's thoughts and views exerted a great influence upon Alicia's life.

The journal reverted to Alicia after Grandmother Stanford's death, and it became one of her greatest treasures. She was heartbroken when, during the years that the Mansion was not occupied, a group of young boys broke into the home and stole the journal, and thus this valuable historical document was lost. Sometime later, in downtown Kalispell, an unknown woman approached Alicia and said, "It was wonderful of you to give my boy your grandmother's diary. We have enjoyed it so much and it is my son's greatest treasure." Alicia replied, "I did not give the diary to your son. It was stolen and I want it back." Alicia said the woman immediately disappeared. She did not know the woman and never saw her again, although she looked for her constantly, whenever on the streets or in a crowd in Kalispell.

Grandmother Stanford did not enjoy the rugged outdoor, recreational trips that took up much of the Conrad family's summers. As long as her health permitted, she attended summer school, alternating between the colleges at Bozeman and Missoula. She loved the university life and was able there to enjoy some of the cultural events that had played such a large part in her life before she came to Montana.

Grandmother Stanford also followed closely the careers of her sons. James ranked high in the Royal Canadian Mounted Police; George was a successful businessman and banker; Hal became a recognized naturalist and taxidermist. The mounted birds currently in the Mansion were done by Hal. These works of art were saved by Alicia. After Hal's death, vandals kept breaking into his taxidermy shop to steal the valuable specimens, so Alicia took some of the better pieces to the Mansion for safekeeping. Finally the shop was burned to the ground, and the remainder of the beautiful collection was destroyed.

In her later years, Grandmother Stanford suffered another stroke from which she did not recover. Her mind was not affected and remained clear and sharp, but her ability to move about the house was severely restricted. She began to spend most of her time in her room, with Alicia as her devoted companion. Alicia read to her grandmother, took care of her correspondence, helped to keep up her personal journal, ran her errands, and, in general, replaced the legs Grandmother Stanford could no longer use.

For many years the two grandmothers spent the winters at the Coronado Hotel in Coronado, California. Each year, after Christmas, the ladies went to Coronado, where they moved into the lovely old hotel that is still in operation. The two ladies today would feel perfectly at home in their rooms and in the dining room of this gracious hotel, so well has it been maintained. But they probably would be horrified at the multistoried condominiums that surround the beautiful structure and seem poised to engulf it at the first oppotunity.

Both of the grandmothers died in 1904. In the spring of that year, Grandmother Conrad learned that her daughter, Alice, was planning a trip around the world in a sailing vessel. Alice's husband, Dr. F. J. Adams, was an avid traveler. Although they had made two trips around the world, Dr. Adams wanted to go again, and he wanted Alice to go with him. Grandmother Conrad did not think that Alice was physically up to a trip that would entail some hardship and would take nearly a year. So she boarded the train to Great Falls to try to dissuade them.

Grandmother Conrad seemed to sense that, if Alice left, she would never see her again. But Dr. Adams was adamant in his desire to go, and Alice decided that she must go with him. They sailed from San Francisco, leaving Grandmother Conrad to live in their Great Falls house during their absence. Maria Conrad soon became ill and sent for her daughter-in-law, Lettie, whom she told, "I didn't want Alice to go, but she has gone. I don't want to get up again, ever, and I don't want to live." A few days later, she died — almost as though she had willed it.

The *Bee*, an early Kalispell newspaper, in its issue of June 3, 1904, quoted the *Great Falls Tribune*, which reported that:

> At the funeral, every carriage in the city was pressed into service and it was one of the largest turnouts ever seen at a funeral in this city. The floral offerings were superb. Undertaker Mr. Allister who had charge of the funeral says that he has never before seen such a showing of flowers at a funeral since he came to Great Falls. There were spray pieces and cut flowers innumerable. Every variety of beautiful and expensive flowers was to be seen on the casket which was buried eight inches beneath them. It required a separate wagon to transport them to the grave. The local florists' supplies were exhausted as well as those of the Helena greenhouse men.

The story ended on this poignant note:

> All of her children were present except Mrs. F. T. Adams, who was on the ocean journeying toward Japan.

Tiny Grandmother Maria Conrad, aged seventy-eight, was buried beside her six-foot, six-inch husband in Great Falls' Highland Cemetery, and the dynamic spirit that had contributed so much to the life of the Conrad Mansion was forever stilled.

Not long afterward, Grandmother Catherine Stanford suffered another severe stroke. She lingered for almost two months and died on September 1, 1904, at age seventy-four. She, too, had a large funeral, which was held at the Mansion that had been her home for the last years of her life. She was buried in the beautiful cemetery that her daughter, Lettie, had created as a memorial to Charles. Her grave, marked by an obelisk, is located to the west of the mausoleum in which Lettie and Charles Conrad are buried. The tall grave marker seems a little aloof — somewhat recalling Grandmother Stanford in her room, apart from the activities of the family, as she had been so much of the time during the last of her life at the Mansion.

With the death of Grandmother Stanford, the saga of the grandmothers ended. Lettie Conrad would continue to live in the Mansion until her death in 1923, always feeling the presence of the two gentle ladies who had moved into the home with the family and who had influenced so strongly each life that they touched.

CHAPTER 42
The Conrad Buffalo Herd

Charles E. Conrad played a significant role in the drama of saving the American bison from extinction. The 40 million buffalo that had roamed the land from the Mississippi River westward were all but obliterated by the year 1879. In 1830, there began a systematic, if unrecognized, destruction of America's buffalo herds. Particularly after the Civil War, hunters and skinners descended upon the Great Plains buffalo. These men were driven by the demand for fresh meat created by the railroad construction camps as the transcontinental railroads pushed westward. In addition, there appeared to be an insatiable demand for buffalo hides and tongues, which were shipped to buyers in St. Louis and Chicago.

It was estimated that in 1882, there were 5,000 hunters and skinners working the western plains. An efficient hunter could kill 250 buffalo a day. Skinners could remove a hide in about five minutes. In addition to the professional hunters, the transcontinental railroads organized excursions enabling sporting men to shoot buffalo from the trains just for the joy of killing, since the slain buffalo were left to rot or to be taken by human and natural scavengers. In 1900, only about 300 buffalo remained on the North American continent.

A substantial portion of the Conrad fortune had been derived from the trade in buffalo hides and tongues, carried on by the I. G. Baker Company in Fort Benton when the herds were so immense that there was no concern the buffalo might one day become extinct. At that time money could be made from a dead buffalo but not a live one, so the buffalo were almost gone before any thought was given to saving them. Charles E. Conrad was one of the few who became alarmed when the danger became apparent and embarked upon a project to preserve the buffalo, giving to it the same energy and purpose that he gave to any project he undertook. The interest of Conrad would have been too late had it not been for Walking Coyote, a Pend d'Oreille Indian brave whose efforts to save the buffalo came almost inadvertently.

In 1873, Walking Coyote wintered with the Piegan Indians on the Milk River in eastern Montana. In the fall of that year a buffalo hunting expedition was organized in which the Pend d'Oreille brave took part. At the end of the hunt, four calves -- two bulls and two heifers — became separated from the herd and were lost on the prairie. The calves — as seems to be characteristic of lost buffalo calves — followed Walking Coyote's horse back to camp. He succored them through the winter of 1873-1874. In the spring of 1874, he headed back to the Flathead Valley with the four calves following like puppies. All the way across the plains and through the Rocky Mountains, the calves trailed the horses, until they finally reached the Catholic mission at St. Ignatius, which was to be their home.

When they were 4 years of age, the heifers produced calves. The herd increased slowly, numbering 13 in 1884, just 10 years later. By this time, Walking Coyote found that his herd was increasing beyond his capacity to care for them. Charles A. Allard, a Flathead Reservation rancher, foresaw that buffalo would become profitable, as the demand for them would outpace the supply. With a fellow rancher, Michael Pablo, 10 of Walking Coyote's herd were purchased at $250 per head. This stock became the nucleus of the Allard-Pablo herd, which was to insure the survival of the buffalo.

Allard and Pablo were capable ranchers, and the herd increased. When Allard died, in 1896, the original 10 head had increased to about 300 bison. The herd then was divided between the Allard estate and Pablo. After further division among the Allard heirs, Mrs. Allard sold her share to C. E. Conrad. These animals became the famous Conrad herd, which would supply the nucleus of the herd at the National Bison Range in Moiese, Montana, and would contribute to the herd at Banff, Alberta.

Conrad secured from the federal government a lease of Wild Horse Island, a large island in Flathead Lake. Here he brought his buffalo herd, and they remained for about one year. When the federal government refused to renew the Wild Horse Island lease, Conrad bought a ranch in Smith Valley, west of Kalispell. This ranch contained the hilly terrain, flats, and springs which the buffalo seemed to prefer.

While Charles Conrad lived, the herd was allowed to increase — yet Conrad died in 1902. The inventory of his estate property, filed in the District Court of Flathead County, Montana, listed 46 buffalo: 11 bulls; 23 cows and heifers; 12 calves born in 1902, each appraised at $50 per head. After his death, Lettie Conrad assumed the management of the herd.

The buffalo, however, is a hardy and fecund animal. Twins are not uncommon, and the calf-survival rate is high. The Conrad herd soon became too large for the available facilities, and some disposal program became a necessity. Lettie Conrad decided that 100 head was the maximum number that the operation could sustain. She then established a pattern of marketing the herd down to that maximum each year. The calves were kept, and the older, mature animals were sold.

By the year of 1906, the demand for buffalo was growing. From all over the United States and Canada came zoo curators, government researchers, representatives of conservation organizations, and persons seeking to establish herds, to study the Conrad herd and to puchase animals. Naturalist William Hornaday and a Mr. Lawrence, the Commissioner of Canadian Parks, spent an entire summer at the Conrad home making studies of the Conrad buffalo herd.

The animals were sold to zoos, to parks, and to other herd owners for new blood infusion, and to persons wanting to establish new herds. Alicia Conrad recalled that the sale price was about $250 to $300 per head, crated and ready for shipment, which was no small task.

The buffalo were shipped in heavy wooden crates. The crates were designed by Lettie Conrad and her buffalo hands, following the process of trial and error. The crate, as it finally evolved, was large enough to allow the buffalo a slight freedom of movement, but not big enough to allow the generation of sufficient momentum to break out of the crate. Each crate was built to the specifications of the individual buffalo to be shipped and was fitted with the care usually associated with the crating of a valuable piano. Since a buffalo lies with his legs folded under him, the animal could lie down in the crate. Containers for food and water were provided and kept supplied. All sides of the crate, as well as the top and the bottom, were heavily padded with burlap to prevent injury.

The safety record was remarkable. Of all the buffalo crated and shipped by Lettie Conrad and her buffalo experts, not one died or sustained a serious injury. This feat is even more remarkable because shipments were made all over the United States and Canada, using as many as five different railroads, to points as distant as zoos in New York.

Building the crate could be reduced to a science. But science was little help in getting the buffalo into the crate. Many times specific buffalo were purchased, especially when the animals were chosen for zoos and as breeding stock to start new herds. So specific buffalo had to be crated and shipped.

These buffalo could not be driven or cut out from the herd. When loading time came, the animals to be shipped, and as many others as wanted to go along, were drifted into a stout, buffalo-proof corral on a railroad siding. The crate was placed in the railroad car. A loading chute led from the corral to the crate. This chute was wide at the opening and narrowed down to fit the door of the crate.

Buffalo crates at C. E. Conrad ranch Courtesy University of Montana Library

Working quietly and smoothly, the hands would try to partition off the unwanted animals and eventually to separate the chosen animal. Even when separated, little effort was made to drive him into the crate. The buffalo's natural curiosity was one of the most important loading factors. With the proper mixture of coaxing and curiosity, the chosen animal eventually entered the chute and then wandered up the chute, until it was aware of the feed and water in the crate. Men stationed atop the crate and out of sight then let the door fall, closing the crate the instant the buffalo was inside.

The crate door might drop shut an hour or so after the herd entered the corral. Or it might be at the end of the day. No one went home until the buffalo to be shipped were in the crates and the crates were chained to the car walls to prevent any movement or slippage enroute.

In 1908 Lettie Conrad sold 34 head of carefully selected buffalo to the American Bison Society. Primarily through the efforts of this Society, the National Bison Range was established at Moiese, Montana, on lands purchased from the Salish Indians. William Hornaday, then the Society's director, supervised the acquisition of the lands and of the animals that were the nucleus of the herd.

Alicia Conrad remembered well the crating and shipment for this sale. She was allowed to watch it from beginning to end. She accompanied

Crated buffalo being hauled by wagon Courtesy University of Montana Library

the shipment to Moiese and saw the unloading and the reaction of the buffalo to their new home. The reaction must have been good, since some three to four hundred splendid buffalo roam that range today.

The crating and shipping were not the only thrills that the buffalo provided for the Conrads. Alicia Conrad recalled the migratory habits of the buffalo herd, which moved, seemingly by instinct, three times each year. The Smith Valley Ranch was fenced but, when spring migration time came, the female leader of the herd would start to break down the fence. Then the buffalo hands would drop the fence and allow the herd to roam. On their initial migration, the herd stopped on the southerly exposed hill north of Kalispell, and there they settled down. During their first stay here, Conrad bought the land.

After some months, the herd was on the move again, this time in the summer, stopping in the Creston area, where Conrad also bought the land on which they had located. This seemed to establish the migratory pattern of the herd, for, when they left the Creston land in the fall, they returned to their Smith Valley home, which had a southwest exposure, springs, and lush grass that attracted the animals.

198

Kalispell Chief, the Conrad herd bull Courtesy University of Montana Library

Alicia recalled that the moves would be made about the same time each year. When the cry went out, "The buffalo are coming," the buffalo hands would drop everything and tend the herd. Tending did not mean herding or driving. It required quietly following the herd to see where it was going and perhaps trying to drift them to one of their three stopping places, after these had been established — established, as Alicia noted, not by the men but by the buffalo.

For several years, the leader of the herd was a magnificent cow called "Frizzle Top," so named because of the bright henna thatch on top of her head. "Frizzle Top" seemed to make most of the decisions for the herd, even for "Kalispell Chief," its dominant bull. It was "Frizzle Top" who led the way and chose the stopping places. She did let the bulls do the fighting.

Alicia recalled one battle of the bulls that she watched. She said a new bull had challenged the dominant male, and it started a fight to the finish. As the fight began, the cows encircled the antagonists and watched with avid interest. When the defeated male lay on the ground exhausted, the winner withdrew. Then the cows moved in with lowered heads, and they horned, pawed, and stomped the vanquished bull, until he was almost literally ground into the earth in little pieces.

With the profits from the sale of the buffalo, Lettie Conrad constructed a building in Kalispell, located at the northwest corner of the intersection of Main and Third Streets. It was a large, two-story building of brick construction. At the time of its completion, this was the finest building in Kalispell. In acknowledgement of the contribution of her shaggy friends, Lettie named her fine new building "The Buffalo Block." It was a familiar and historic Kalispell landmark until 1976, when it was destroyed by fire, set by an arsonist.

The buffalo left other appelative monuments in the Kalispell area. The Smith Valley Ranch, which was their original home, is still referred to as the Buffalo Ranch. The beautiful residential area on the hill to the north of Kalispell, which the buffalo chose as one of their ranges, still is called Buffalo Hill. And the nearby golf couse, where once the buffalo roamed, is called the Buffalo Hills Golf Course.

The fate of Walking Coyote was not as happy as that of the four little calves that trailed his pony from the Milk River Country, through the rugged Rockies, to St. Ignatius. Walking Coyote insisted that the payment for his buffalo be in cash. He received the $2,500 in paper money, which he took to Missoula. With red-eye whiskey at fifteen cents a shot, Walking Coyote lived a life of dissipation in the Herculean proportions of his dominant buffalo bull. His life ended under a bridge in Missoula. Yet his bull went on to a life of great achievement — fathering the magnificent herds of buffalo that still survive, thanks in part to Walking Coyote and Charles E. Conrad.

CHAPTER 43
Charles E. Conrad, Empire Builder

I. The New Beginning

A study of Charles Conrad's life indicates that, when he left Fort Benton, it was with the half-formed intent to become less active in the business world. The fortune that he had acquired would enable the Conrads to lead any type of life they might desire. They loved to travel, and both seemed to want a quiet, contemplative life given to the search of knowledge and things cultural that had been denied Conrad when the Civil War interrupted his education.

Yet Conrad entered into the development of interests in the Flathead Valley with the same gusto and ability that characterized his life in Fort Benton. The Kalispell Townsite Company was organized in 1891, in anticipation of the arrival of the Great Northern Railway. It was a most successful venture. Soon The Conrad National Bank, well-housed and under good management, was thriving.

Conrad also bought up extensive farm, ranch, and timber holdings in western Montana. Again it appeared that he was preparing for a less active business life, for the enjoyment of his family, and the new home, and for the semi-retirement that seemed to be his goal after the I. G. Baker Company was dismantled.

However, about 1895 — the year the construction of the new home commenced, and a very considerable local empire had been brought together — Conrad caught an empire-building fever that kept him wandering the United States and Canada in search of new businsses and involved in the expansion of his existing businesses. That fever burned within him until his death.

The fever started during the same year Conrad learned he had a fatal disease that would destroy him within ten years. Local doctors could find nothing, but Conrad knew that something was wrong with his health. He seemed to lose weight for no reason, suffered an unaccustomed thirst, and just could not maintain the robust health that always had enabled him to live a rigorous life.

In 1892 Johns Hopkins University in Baltimore, Maryland, was the outstanding medical center in the nation, and Conrad decided to go there for examination. Dr. William Osler, then the most authoritative specialist on diabetes, was on the staff of the University Hospital. Dr. Osler had diabetes himself and was able to diagnose Conrad's trouble almost immediately. Insulin had not yet been discovered, so there was no treatment for the dreaded disease. He told Conrad,

> You have diabetes just as I have. There is no cure and it is merely a question of how long we will live. You have been active all of your life and because of your splendid physical condition you will likely live longer than I. But your days are numbered. By a proper diet, taking care of yourself, and not overdoing, you could live 10 years, but that is the most that you can hope for.

This was grim news for a man who believed that his financial future was assured, and the good life was just beginning.

The knowledge of death is ever-present in the mind of man but can be kept submerged until nearness forces it to the surface. A life expectancy of ten years allows some time for acceptance, planning, and maneuvering. To a man of the demonstrated bravery and fearlessness of Conrad, fright would not be a factor, but planning and preparation would be. His approach was: "I have ten years to live. How do I want to spend these years?"

Empire-building was as much in Conrad's blood as red and white corpuscles. It was the joy of his living. With ten years to live, the life of quiet contemplation and culture-seeking seemed pallid and unsatisfying when measured against the known thrills, pleasure, and satisfaction of winning the world. Conrad decided that he did not want to live out his days in the comfort of home, family, and friends. For he embarked upon a course of empire-building that made impossible the vision of life that lay partially formulated in the minds of the Conrads when they first moved to the Flathead Valley.

The feverish pursuit of added wealth and expanded empire seemed to possess Conrad. This focus is best revealed in his letters written to Lettie during the period from 1894 to 1901 when, at last, broken health stopped the restless wanderings that had kept him away from home for long periods. These absences separated him from a family he truly loved and made impossible any meaningful father-son relationship with Charles D. Conrad. He doted on his son and hoped, in him, for a projection of himself into the future. While he was traveling, it was difficult for him to do any fruitful planning for the preservation and useful employment of the wealth he was creating with single minded devotion. The letters reveal a man who hungered for home and a more meaningful relationship with his family, but who deliberately chose a life which essentially would deny him these things.

The first extant letter was written on November 25, 1894. Construction activity on the new home was at its height. Conrad was in St. Paul and he wrote:

> My darling wife. Your message received saying fur cap was in trunk where I found it all right. Kindly mail Bardwell, Robinson and Co., Minneapolis, Minn., a copy of the revised specifications. Not necessary to send the one for the heating. The drawings and blue prints came through all right and I gave them to Bardwell yesterday. I am feeling ever so much better. Will leave here tomorrow night and expect to be in Chicago two or three days. Will write you from New York, and if I have time, from Chicago. I found White away in Moorhead but he will be back today. The weather is lovely here and I presume it is in Kalispell as our bad weather seems to start from Minnesota, North Dakota, and Manitoba. Love and kisses for yourself and the children. Your devoted husband, C. E. Conrad.

The White referred to in Conrad's letter is A. A. White, one of the men chosen by Jim Hill as an incorporator of the Kalispell Townsite Company. This reference would indicate that part of Conrad's business concerned the townsite. He probably went to Chicago in connection with government contracts. The federal government was buying huge quantities of beef to supply the many Army units stationed in the West and to supply treaty obligations with the Indians. These were lucrative contracts, and Conrad had substantial interests in the cattle business in central Montana, where huge herds could be cared for with minimum effort. These cattle were shipped live to fulfill the contracts for beef on-the-hoof. Refrigeration in transit was little used, and a live critter could be delivered without fear of spoilage.

In 1894 St. Paul was perhaps the nearest place of supply for the plumbing and heating systems that were to be installed in the new house in Kalispell. Wood stoves and the materials for outhouses could be supplied without difficulty by the merchants of Kalispell. Indoor toilets and central-heating plants had to be sought in more sophisticated markets.

On February 25, 1895, Conrad was in Seattle and evidently had been away from home for some time. He had expected to be home on the 25th and had wired his wife to expect him. As with most of his letters, the one written at this time explained that he was detained by business and that he was uncertain when he could return home. Most of Conrad's letters were written from the East. The letter written in Seattle is the only extant one indicating any business interests to the West. Conrad was acquainted with and admired Dexter Horton, a Seattle banker and businessman. Horton played an important role in the development of Seattle. Conrad consulted with him in connection with Horton's role in the development of that city and regarding matters pertaining to the growing Conrad Bank in Kalispell.

In this letter Conrad writes: "Tell Ashby (C. E.'s brother) I received his message, it will not be necessary for me to go to Helena March 7th. It is simply a matter of change of venue in the Bookwalter case." The case referred to was a suit brought by J. Bookwalter against Conrad over a real-estate transaction in which Bookwalter believed himself aggrieved.

Bookwalter, a Great Falls businessman in 1890, had sent his agent, D. R. McGinnis, to buy land in Kalispell. Bookwalter, too, wanted to buy the land on which the Great Northern division point would be located. McGinnis contacted Clifford and Stannard, local real-estate agents, who secured an option on a likely tract of land from the Reverend George McVey Fisher, the first minister in the Flathead Valley. Later McGinnis cancelled the option, and Fisher returned the money he had received. Shortly thereafter Fisher sold the land to Conrad, and it became part of the Townsite of Kalispell.

Bookwalter learned of the profits he had missed. He wanted some money from someone and chose Conrad and the Kalispell Townsite Company as the most likely prospects. He alleged in his complaint that Conrad had conspired with Fisher and McGinnis to prevent him from acquiring the land. He wanted the court to set the whole thing aside and to give him the land for the agreed $6,000, in all probability a sum less than the Reverend Fisher had received from Conrad.

The case had been filed when Missoula County extended to the Canadian border, and Missoula was the county seat. After the lawsuit was filed, the Legislature split off the northern end of Missoula County to create the new county of Flathead. Conrad's attorneys filed a motion for a change of venue to have the action removed to the new county, in which the land lay. Bookwalter resisted the motion, preferring to have the case tried in Missoula, where the litigants were not so well-known. Bookwalter evidently believed that he would fare better in a place where he was not known, while Conrad wanted the trial among people who knew him.

The venue of the action was changed by the lower court in Missoula, and Bookwalter, persistent in his hope for a trial in less familiar surroundings, appealed. The Supreme Court of Montana in its opinion said, "The labor and zeal of counsel in preparing briefs in the case seems to us to be disproportionate to the gravity of the legal proposition involved, which, indeed, occurs to us to be a very simple one." The Court decided that, by the act of creating Flathead County, the suit was picked up in its entirety, taking all its parts and attributes, and transplanted to the newly created county.

Bookwalter's fear of holding the trial in Kalispell must have been strong. He filed a petition telling the Supreme Court that it had erred and asking for a rehearing of the decision which was granted. No argument of Bookwalter convinced the Court of any error, and Bookwalter and his lawsuit were sent back to Kalispell for trial, Kalispell having been named the county seat of the new County of Flathead. However, no trial was held. Once the venue of the action was established in Kalispell, Bookwalter's zeal greatly diminished. The lawsuit then was dismissed by the local court for failure to prosecute. It lay buried in the dusty files of the Flathead County Courthouse until Conrad's reference to it in his letter caused it to be dug out.

Sunday, August 18, 1895, found Conrad in Kipp, Montana, with the Blackfeet Indians and possibly with some Crows. Kipp was not a town but a trading post established by Joseph Kipp, who was a well-known hunter, guide, and trader with whom Conrad had close associations during his Fort Benton days. He wrote to his wife of this visit:

> Dear Lettie. The Indians are very anxious that the agent Geo. Stull and myself accompany them to St. Mary's Lake or to where some mineral has been discovered near there. We have agreed to go and will leave here Tuesday morning. Stull estimates that it will take a week to make the trip. You need not look for us before about Monday a week. (Son) Charley is delighted with the idea of going to St. Mary's Lake. Yesterday he was driving over to the agency with Kipp and a group in a spring wagon and they raised a covey of chickens. Charley killed three, two of which were on the wing. The others had guns and one or two of them fired but Charley was the only one who killed a chicken.

> We have arranged for gentle horses, also a dog, and I think Snooks (the dog) will have a good time. Joe Kipp and Al Hamilton accompany us with an escort of about twelve Indian police and some of their chiefs. Don't worry about us if we should be a day or so behind time. I succeeded in borrowing an overcoat; Mr. Stull will rig Charley out tomorrow with an Indian overcoat and wool hat. He will take Indian blankets from the agency for bedding. I think we will be comparatively comfortable. Kiss Kate and Alicia for me. Love to Mother, Alice, Caroline, Mrs. Stanford and Ashby. A big hug and kiss for you darling. Your devoted husband C. E. Conrad. N. P. Will (William G.) and party returned to Gt. Falls last night. Tell Mother Will looks well and says the children have all recovered.

At the time of the letter, white prospectors were invading the western edge of the Blackfeet Indian Reservation, looking for precious minerals, especially gold. They were interested in the mountainous area east of the Continental Divide, which was of little economic value to the Indians, for it was not suitable for grazing or farming. Yet the region was important to the Indians as a summer camping ground, and it held some religious significance to them. The prospectors ignored all protests, dug lakes, and made clearings at hallowed spots. They killed game, usurped campgrounds, and, in general, were a nuisance and bother to the Indians. In 1893 George Stull, the Indian Agent at Browning, recommended that the land be sold and that the revenue be placed in a trust fund for the maintenance of the Indians.

Conrad's single-handed raid on Chief Black Weasel's camp, in 1882, to arrest the chief's son had made a great impression on the Indians. They admired bravery and Conrad's feat inspired respect and an awe that they remembered. This event, together with his fairness in all of his dealings with them, made Conrad one of the few white men that the Indians trusted. The prospectors presented a problem for which the Indians had no solution. A dead prospector with an arrow or bullet in him brought in the United States Army. The Indians needed strong medicine, the kind that, in their eyes, Conrad possessed. So when trouble came, they called on him.

The trip referred to in the letter was to explore the area that Stull had recommended be sold, and to check on a mineral deposit reported to have been discovered in the area near St. Mary's Lake. They sought Conrad's advice and help. The trip thus was made to survey the area and to decide which, if any, of the lands the Indians might sell.

The mineral find referred to was probably the copper deposit discovered near Cracker Lake, about seven miles from the current site of the Many Glacier Hotel in Glacier National Park. Travelers in the Park today hike or ride horseback to Cracker Lake, where the derelict mining equipment remains one of the attractions. As one ascends, traces of the original road to the mine are discernible. The mind is baffled by the manner in which such heavy machinery could have been transported over the crude roads to the mine site. One wonders if the Indians were not secretly delighted when the mining venture did not prove feasible, and St. Marys did not become another Butte. Their delight perhaps balanced the disappointment of the miners.

Conrad's letter also tells with pride of his son's marksmanship. To believe that a 13-year-old boy could outshoot Joe Kipp and the other frontiersmen named by Conrad indicates a most indulgent attitude by father toward son. The son in his most formative years longed for the attention and companionship of an important and respected father, but the father's time was spent primarily in a dream and in a search for an empire. The dream might sometimes be interrupted by his feeling of guilt at the possible neglect of his wife and children, but there was no interruption of the search.

C. E. Conrad was not home in a week, as he had anticipated, but he evidently sent his son home after returning from St. Mary's. On August 31, 1895, Conrad was at the Blackfeet Indian Agency at Browning, Montana. He wrote that the U.S. Commissioners had arrived, but no council would be held until the next day. The letter mentions the Crow Indians, for whom Conrad must have been negotiating, as well as for the

Blackfeet. Conrad related that, after the council, the Crows would go to St. Mary's Lake for ten days and then return to complete negotiations. He had not intended to stay, but the Indians must have persuaded him to wait until their return.

Conrad had a close relationship with the Indians, and they placed a high degree of trust in him. He was willing to spend almost any amount of time on Indian matters, even though it took him away from his family and business. Contemporaries indicated that Conrad possessed a unique power that enabled him to exert great influence upon the Indians. Indian calls to Conrad for help were frequent, and it appears that he always responded, resolving the conflict in favor of the Indians.

On September 19, 1895, Conrad was still not home. He had remained at the Indian Agency at Browning conferring with the Indians. On that day he wrote to his wife.

> My Darling Lettie. The Indians decided today in council that I should act as their attorney. I presume I shall be here all of next week. It commenced snowing here this morning and there is now four inches of snow and quite cold. I fear you have the same conditions or the cold rain. Hope you will move down to the West Hotel if you have. I do hope you will not get colds before moving. Love and kisses to the children. Your devoted husband C. E. Conrad.

Three U.S. Commissioners had arrived at Browning on August 30, 1895 to negotiate the sale of the land, but the first session was not held until three weeks later. The letter indicates that the Indians, on September 18, had asked Conrad to represent them, for they had learned not to match wits against the white men without help. Conrad was not an attorney, but a staunch and trusted friend.

The first session found Conrad asking $3,000,000 for the land to be ceded and the commissioners offering $1,250,000. A compromise was reached, whereby the Indians received $1,500,000, but in addition they were given the right to hunt, fish, and cut timber in the area, as long as it remained public lands of the United States. Conrad considered these rights most important, and he was pleased with the result of the negotiations. Had he lived longer, his pleasure would have increased. Later it was learned that there were no minerals of commercial value on the area ceded and, in 1910, it became a part of the newly established Glacier National Park.

II. The Continuing Quest

On July 8, 1896, Conrad again was on the move, this time looking for silver and gold in the Neihart area, south and east of Great Falls. He wrote:

> It was raining very hard at Shelby Junction (where he had changed trains going from Kalispell to Great Falls). I hope it reached the Flathead. Have you had any rain since I left? We go to Neihart Friday. I left two pieces of ore on the Hall mantle. Kindly send them to me by mail, one piece will do. There is also a small sack in back office of bank. Have Ashby send a sample of that and mark from Flathead Lake. We have no mosquitos at Butte and very few here. I do not suppose they have all vanished at Kalispell as yet. Love to all. Your devoted husband C. E. Conrad.

Conrad found no gold or other precious metals in the Neihart area. But this does not seem to have been any great disappointment to him. It was the quest that excited him and appeased the restlessness that dug into him like spurs to urge him on.

The reference to mosquitos may seem a strange topic for correspondence. Yet, at that time, having no mosquitos was newsworthy. The Flathead Valley was filled with mosquitos. They came in huge, black droves and attacked anything with warm blood. The spring mosquito season made life miserable. Families moved to higher ground for respite. A favorite spot was the flat area northwest of Kalispell, where the east wind from Bad Rock Canyon held the mosquitos at bay. People camped here during the worst of the season, moving home as the mosquito crop dwindled.

On August 7, 1896, Conrad wrote again from St. Paul.

> I arrived last night, had a very comfortable trip, although it is very warm. I leave for New York tomorrow morning via the Lakes with Mr. (Jim) Hill. He thinks he can get (then Secretary of War D. S.) Lamont and (President Grover) Cleveland to make Jake Smith approve my Indian contract, now that they are second and want some help. I go as his guest by steamer from Duluth. My address in New York will be the Albemarle Hotel, as he stops there. Very likely I will go down to Washington, if so, will stop at Cochran

Hotel. Love to the Mothers and kisses for yourself and the children. Your devoted husband. C. E. Conrad.

The contract referred to in this letter could be for beef that Conrad had contracted to sell to the Indians, or for services rendered in acting as their attorney. He had a penchant for getting things done that often led him to deliver first and to wrangle for payment later. Conrad was a Democrat and a powerful figure in the West. This would have given him an edge in dealing with the Cleveland administration which, as the letter indicates, was in political difficulties. The Populist spirit was riding high in the Democratic Party and the sound-money policies of President Cleveland were not widely supported. He was second and had lost the Democratic nomination for the Presidency to William Jennings Bryan, a free-silver advocate from Nebraska. Bryan captured the Democratic Convention at Chicago in July, 1896, with his "Cross of Gold" speech, and then won the nomination, but lost the election to William McKinley.

Conrad's next letter, from New York and dated August 12, 1896, reveals a sense of sadness and guilt that he was so seldom with his son. He realized that he had reneged on a promised hunting trip and seemed frantic to find for his son other companions, even hired ones.

> My darling wife. I arrived here last night and found yours of the 4th inst. which was forwarded from St. Paul. I am glad to hear Charley went fishing. I promised him to go hunting with him, as his school commenced Sept. 1st. You must let him go. (A. W. Merrifield, friend of Teddy Roosevelt) Merrifield at Pleasant Valley would take good care of him. If necessary, have Ashby hire a good man to go with him and let him select where he would rather go. I cannot tell just when I will be home. Hill wanted me to come on here with him. Said it would be a good time to see Lamont, Sec. of War, and get my Indian contract approved. I will write you often, and keep you posted. It is very warm here but I do not expose myself to the heat much. Love to the Mothers and hugs and kisses for yourself and the children. Your devoted husband C. E. Conrad.

On December 12, 1896, Conrad was in Great Falls in connection with the sale of the bank that the new owners had milked and put into such a financial condition that it was placed in receivership. He wrote:

> Dear Lettie. We have sold the bank here and will get through tonight. We will go down to Benton tonight and spend Sunday. I will then go as far as St. Paul with W. G. and will return from there home which will be next Saturday or Sunday morning. He wants to see Hill on some Kalispell Townsite business. Show this to Ashby and Howard (C. E.'s brothers), as I am too busy to write them. I got Charley a type writing machine and will bring it home with me. I suppose I better get toys in St. Paul for the children. Your devoted husband C. E. Conrad.

On March 29, 1897, Conrad was back in Great Falls, settling the affairs of the bank that the brothers had sold in December and paying off the depositors of the defunct bank. He wrote again:

> My darling wife. I expect to go to Washington Thursday morning. I wrote you yesterday that I expected to be home tomorrow or next day but Capt. Couch came in this morning and W. G., Capt. Couch, and myself will go to Washington. I hardly think we will reopen the bank again, rather think we will liquidate it but have not fully decided. I am feeling all right again. I wish you would send my light overcoat and new shoes to Havre. I can get them there. Kiss Alicia for me. Tell her to write me at Washington telling me what to bring for her. Love to all. Your devoted husband, C. E. Conrad.

On November 8, 1897, Conrad was in Helena. His letter reveals another interest:

> Dear Lettie. I arrived here from Butte and Anaconda today noon, and leave for Great Falls tonight. I shall go via Havre as the other way is too severe. I have had one of my bad spells, suppose too much excitement, but I am feeling better now. This is the reason I have not written before, felt nervous. I saw "Keoma," the (Charles M.) Russell painting in Butte, the owner wanted $150.00 for it. Think I can get it cheaper. Howard is to see him after I left and tell him I am gone and that he missed a chance to sell it. If he talks trade, told Howard to let him ship it for 75 or 100$. Love to all. Tell Kate I have not received the promised message. Kiss Alicia for me. Your devoted husband, C. E. Conrad.

Conrad's strategy for acquiring "Kee-Oh-Mee" must have worked. The painting was owned by Conrad at the time of his death and was included in the inventory of his estate. In its March 29, 1925 issue, the *Great Falls Tribune* carried a story concerning four Russell paintings loaned by the C. E. Conrad estate for an exhibition at the Rainbow Hotel in Great Falls that evening. This date is almost five years after the death of Lettie Conrad. The story states that this was the first time that the paintings had been removed from the palatial mansion of the Conrad Estate. It gave the estimated value of the four oils at $20,000.

The four Russell oils were: "Indian Couch," "Indian Scouts," "Running Buffalo," and "Kee-Oh-Mee," the painting mentioned in Conrad's letter. Of the last work, the article said:

> One of the group will undoubtedly be of special interest to the intimate followers of Russell as well to those whose appreciation of art in general brings them to the exhibit. It is a different type and were it not for its color technique and the intimate knowledge of the Indian life displayed might not be recognized as a work of Russell's.

> Kee-Oh-Mee is an Indian Princess. She is reclining inside of a large lodge with her head resting on a Hudson's Bay blanket on a decorative woven willow head rest, at the top of which rests a beaver skin. Back of that is a painted buffalo shield decorated with five arrows. Suspended behind her is a painted buffalo robe which bears in hieroglyphics a story of the life of her chief, whose pipe and medicine pouch are resting on the floor near

her right arm.

She is dressed in her finest red Hudson's Bay robe adorned with porcupine quills and entirely covered with quills and she wears about her neck and arms the best adornments it was possible to bestow upon a Princess. With her left hand she is fanning herself with an elaborate fan of eagle feathers. It is possible that she has just finished eating for directly before her is an empty earthen vessel save for a carved spoon.

The current location of this painting was learned from Frederick G. Renner, an outstanding authority on the works of Charles Russell. The painting is now owned by the Amon Carter Museum of Western Art, in Fort Worth, Texas. Dr. Van Kirke Nelson, another knowledgeable Russell expert, remembers that all four paintings once were in the possession of Agnes Conrad, the widow of Charles D. Conrad. Nelson tried to buy the paintings, but they were sold by Agnes Conrad for $5,000 to Leonard Lopp, a landscape painter of Kalispell. Lopp immediately sold the four paintings to the David Findlay Galleries of New York City for $6,000, and the Findlay Galleries sold the four paintings to the late Amon G. Carter for an undisclosed sum.

In the judgment of Renner, "Kee-Oh-Mee" alone would bring between $125,000 and $150,000 on today's art market. On the basis of these four paintings — which were disposed of in much the same manner as was the rest of Conrad's estate — had his widow and children been able to retain the estate, today it would be worth considerably in excess of one billion dollars.

In March, 1895, Conrad was in Hot Springs, Arkansas, where he had gone hoping that the famous hot baths would improve his health. On the 15th, he wrote from the Arlington Hotel.

Dear Lettie. Yours of the 6th inst. addressed to St. Paul forwarded here and received Sunday. Have had three baths and am feeling well. The hotels are crowded but no Montana people except three Butte men, only one of whom I have met before, Wilson, manager of the Butte Hotel. You will soon rob Mrs. (Nat) Collins of her title (The "Cattle Queen of Montana") if your herd of cattle keeps increasing. I will not forget the candle shades. I ordered from Vasberg some 32 candle electric globes that will fit in the cut glass globes in the hall. Love to all. Your devoted husband, C. E. Conrad.

Lettie Conrad was not interested in cattle, but it pleased C. E. to designate one of his herds as belonging to her. Like Jacob's Biblical herd, that of Lettie Conrad seemed to increase faster than the normal expectation. But unlike Laban, who was displeased at Jacob's good fortune and suspected treachery, Conrad was always grateful for any beneficial or pleasing thing that came to his wife.

In this letter Conrad referred to Elizabeth Collins, whose title was the "Montana Cattle Queen." The "Queen" referred to the number of cattle she owned, rather than to her physical beauty. Born Elizabeth Smith in 1859, she crossed the plains by wagon train to Denver, Colorado Territory. In 1862 her parents again hitched the mules to the wagon and, bringing Elizabeth, they came to Montana. In 1874 she married Nat Collins in Helena, and they moved to a ranch at Hay Coulee, 26 miles north of Choteau. Having found her niche, Elizabeth Collins took charge of the ranch. She roped, branded, and rode the range for 20 years. Under her watchful eyes, her cows dropped healthy calves with great regularity, even extending themselves to twins more often than was normal. As the number of her cattle grew, so did her reputation.

Conrad, in his search for health, must have taken the baths at Hot Springs several times. Alicia remembered being there with her parents. A highlight of one of these trips was Alicia's meeting with her half-brother, Charles E. Conrad, Jr., C. E.'s son by his marriage to an Indian princess. Alicia recalled him as tall, dark, and very handsome. She was delighted when he perched her on his shoulders and walked around the lobby of the Arlington Hotel. The handsome mixed-blood and the dainty little blonde girl attracted the attention of all of the guests, and Alicia assumed an importance sitting on his tall shoulders that she could not manage from the floor.

Alicia was captivated by her half-brother. This was the first she had known of his existence. He had a courtly and solicitous manner that stood in stark contrast to the treatment she received from her full brother, Charley — who was seldom at home and, when there, either ignored, or teased or belittled her. Alicia would have traded brothers gladly but was to see her half-brother only twice more. She attended his wedding in Montreal and visited with him at the time of their father's death.

On April 21, 1898, Conrad wrote from Chicago, where he was staying at the Auditorium Hotel, an imposing structure shown on the letterhead:

My Darling. Yours of the 14th inst. received. I arrived here Sunday and will leave for New York and Washington via Montreal tomorrow. I may not be back for four weeks, but rest assured I will come as soon as I can for I am very homesick. I attended an auction at Urhlands yesterday and bought some very handsome things very cheap. I was in St. Louis Saturday. Took dinner with Mr. I. G. Baker, later called on the Geo. Bakers, they are all well and wished to be remembered. I am feeling fine. Mr. Comstock of Macleod told me of one Dr. Mitchell here in Chicago who had cured three gentlemen of same trouble that I have. I have been to see Mitchell, he seems very sanguine that he can cure me. He wants 300$ in advance. I have concluded to take a ticket and try him. He does not want me to commence treatment until I get home. I think there is a good deal of a starving process in the treatment. On my return I will get full information. I think I have got everything you gave me a memorandum of except the knives, which I will bring with me. With much love to you all and kisses for Alicia. Your devoted husband, C. E. Conrad.

The demand for $300 in advance smacks of the quack, but a starvation diet would produce signs of temporary improvement in a diabetic. A curtailment of the sugar that the diabetic's body cannot process would relieve some of the symptoms. However, the starvation diet also would create a shortage of protein and vitamins that would weaken the body and make it susceptible to other diseases. Mitchell was on the right track but going in the wrong direction. Diabetes in sixty percent of those persons afflicted currently can be controlled by a restricted diet, but a starvation diet might compound the problem, while indicating a cure temporarily. Fortunately for Conrad, the treatment was to be taken at home. He was there too seldom for sustained treatment and was too intelligent to be long deceived. Since there exists no further mention of Mitchell, Conrad may not have "taken a ticket," and he probably stuck with Dr. Osler.

On May 10, 1898, Conrad was staying in Ottawa, Canada, still looking for more business. He wrote:

My Darling Wife. I wired you this morning saying that I would be in New York tomorrow and Washington the following day. The bids for Canadian Indian beef are to be opened at 12 A.M. today, it is now 10 A.M. If I am unsuccessful, which I expect to be, I will leave here on the 3 P.M. train. The reason I expect to be unsuccessful is that I am bidding 8 cents per lb. Last year it went at 6 cents and I think Cochrane and McEchnan will bid about 7 cents, as the Canadians cannot seem to see that the Spanish American War will have the effect to raise prices on all food products. I cannot say, sweetheart, just how long I will be in Washington. I want to try to get the Indian agreement approved. Rest assured I will not remain a moment longer than is necessary, for if there was ever a homesick boy I am one. Love and kisses to all. Your devoted husband, C. E. Conrad

The Canadian government also held treaty obligations to supply Indians with beef. With the extermination of the buffalo, the Indians were deprived of their meat supply. They were not yet tied sufficiently to the land to engage in cattle-raising, so were dependent on the meat supplied by the government. This situation may not have been beneficial either for the government or for the Indians, but it created a lucrative business for cattle dealers and provided Conrad with a market for his extensive cattle herds that then grazed on the prairies in place of the buffalo.

The Spanish-American War entered into the family life of Conrad as well as into his business. On April 22, 1898, Conrad wrote to the Governor of Montana.

Hon. Robt. Smith, Gov. of Montana. Dear Sir: I have a son, a member of the Militia Company at Kalispell. He will be sixteen-years-old next September, but large for his age. In a letter from his mother received recently,

213

she says that he informed her that, if his company was ordered out to fight the Spaniards, he intended to go. If this should occur, I will ask that you, as a personal favor, to commission him a second lieutenant and arrange with the commanding officer of the regiment to have him attached to his staff. He is a dignified lad with no bad habits and I am certain the commanding officer will never regret taking him. Please write me care of Arlington Hotel, Washington, D.C. Yours very truly, C. E. Conrad.

At the outbreak of the Civil War, Charles Conrad had been even younger than was his son in 1898. C. E. had asked for and received no special treatment, and he came out of the war with a reputation for bravery and resourcefulness that followed him the rest of his life. He also developed a self-reliance that enabled him to handle any situation with confidence and success and that gained him the respect and admiration of all who knew and dealt with him. Like many fathers, C. E. Conrad wanted to spare his son. Yet, in sparing him, he denied him the very experiences and hardships that had molded his own life and made him the person who he was. Though he desired his son to follow in his footsteps, Conrad would erase those footsteps and would leave his son nothing to follow. There is no record of any reply from Governor Smith but, as young Charles did not serve in the Spanish-American War, Governor Smith was probably spared a decision regarding whether to comply with the request made by Conrad in his letter.

III. Detour Into Politics

In 1898, Conrad's brother William G. decided that a term in the United States Senate would be a most suitable climax to his successful business career. Although he was spending most of his time in Virginia, he still had extensive business interests and personal ties in Montana. He believed that he held enough influence on which to base an attempt to win the seat — at that time not an elective office. Senators then were chosen by the members of the Montana Legislature, which next convened in January of 1899. As he did in most things, William called upon his younger brother Charles for help in the undertaking and, as he did in all things, Charles responded to the call.

Prior to the convening of the Legislature, the two brothers traveled the state to visit legislators and to present the candidacy of William. By the time the session began, they had done much groundwork and were hopeful that they could turn the trick. The only serious contenders were Conrad and William A. Clark, one of the "Copper Kings" from Butte. Yet Clark was to fight for prestige as viciously as he did for wealth.

The Legislature was heavily Democratic and both contenders were members of that party. A majority of 48 votes was needed to win. It would be a hard-fought battle in which wealth, prestige, and raw power would win. Both of the Conrads were accustomed to the weapons, but the arena was not familiar.

On January 5, 1899, Conrad wrote from Helena.

> Dear Lettie. Today is Sunday and I have been here for more than two weeks. The prospect for an early termination is not as favorable now as when I wrote you last. W. G. has 38 votes, it requires 48 to elect and it is hard to get them. We are not discouraged. We hold the balance of power and in time they will have to come to us, unless the Republicans go to Clark.

Conrad had not been home for Christmas and must have expected that he would not be. For his letter of December 11, 1898, stated that he had ordered a selection of watches to be sent to Lettie, so she could select one for her Christmas present. His wife would be able to carry on the traditional Christmas celebration, but Conrad would miss the vacation visits of Kate and Charley, and he would be holed up in what he called "a second-class hotel" in Helena. He indicated his dislike at being away from his home and from his family during the holiday season, which had become such an important event in the lives of the Conrads. Neither Lettie Conrad nor the children were fond of William. This was due in part to the demands he made on Charles, knowing that he would respond. It was due to William's request for assistance that C. E. Conrad would be away at this time.

Had the contest remained between Conrad and Clark, it would have been decided in early January. However, Marcus Daly, another "Copper King" and a bitter enemy of Clark, was determined to deny Clark the Senate seat he so coveted. Using Conrad as his best instrument to defeat Clark, Daly threw all of his power and wealth into the battle to defeat his hated rival.

Vote after vote was taken without either contender gaining the necessary majority. By this time, C. E. Conrad was completely out of his element. The nervous strain of excitement and a poor diet were just what he did not need, but loyalty to his brother made him stay in the fight, regardless of health or family.

The newspapers of the day carried lurid stories of the bribes being paid for votes, in some cases as much as $10,000 apiece. It is unlikely that the Conrads indulged in the bribery business. They did not have to, for Daly and Clark were the real protagonists, and they were financing the battle.

In late January it was thought that Clark had his ducks in line. The members of the Senate came to the House Chamber to vote for the seventeenth time. The ballot came as a shocker: Clark still could not gain the 48 votes. But enough was enough. The Republican members of the Legislature, much in the minority, caucused and decided to end the dismal affair. Charles Conrad had predicted that they could hold, unless the Republicans went to Clark. In caucus the Republicans decided to give Clark enough votes to elect him and to get on with the business of the state.

Clark won the nomination, but the corruption that attended his victory was so rampant that it gained national notoriety. As was predicted from the floor of the Legislature, the U.S. Senate did not seat him. He resigned when the Senate threatened an investigation of his election. Then, in 1901, Clark was duly elected and served his full term as a United States Senator. His honor, if not unsullied, at least had some of the stain removed.

216

In 1899 the Conrad brothers left Helena the day after the last vote, with the battle lost and William's hopes of a political career in the U.S. Senate forever dashed. This confrontation must have had an adverse effect on Charles Conrad's health, for it was such situations that made him excited and nervous, bringing on what he termed his "bad spells."

Yet Conrad made a good recovery from his ordeal in Helena, for, on February 11, 1900, he wrote his son — who then was enrolled in St. John's Military Academy in New York — that he had just bought 5,000 head of young cattle in southern Oregon. He planned to place 3,500 head at the ranches near Dupuyer, Montana, and the balance at the ranch near Chinook. All were to be shipped between May 10 and June 10 by rail, and they would go through Kalispell. Buying 5,000 head of cattle at one time is some indication of the carrying capacity of the ranches that the Conrads owned in eastern Montana and of the far-flung efforts of Conrad to market them. He must have sold them on contracts to the governments of Canada and the United States, to feed the Army and the Indians, for there are no extant records of shipments to Chicago, then the largest cattle market in the world.

On May 30, 1900, Conrad was aggressively searching for new business. He wrote from Great Falls.

> Dear Lettie. We have just come back from the stockyards, where we went to see the cattle for the Dupuyer Ranch. They looked in fine condition and are an extra fine lot, they are high-grade Herefords. We leave tomorrow for the East. W. G. expects to return with his family about July 1st. Address me care Windsor Hotel, Montreal. Love to Mother and Mrs. Stanford. Hug and kiss Alicia for me. Tell her to write me a letter saying what she wants for a birthday present. Your devoted husband, C. E. Conrad.

On June 4, 1900, Conrad was in Montreal. The letterhead on which he wrote was from the Place Viger Hotel, not the Windsor. The stationery shows a huge, turreted, French-style hotel, beautifully located. Under the picture, the letterhead reads: "European Plan Only. Rooms $1.00 and upward. Rooms with bath $2.00 and $2.50." Conrad wrote.

> Dear Lettie. I arrived this morning and found yours of the 27th enclosing the one from Charley saying school will be out on the 14th. I will arrange to be there not later than the 13th, perhaps before. If the boys are not in too big a hurry about coming home, I will return by way of Washington and take them with me, as I want to see about my claim with the Blackfeet Indians. However, if they do not want to go, I will come direct home with them. I will wire you when I see them. I parted with W. G. at St. Paul, coming direct here on the Soo Line. We were only in St. Paul four hours. Love to all. Your devoted husband, C. E. Conrad.

There is a gap in the correspondence but on February 23, 1901, Conrad wrote from Helena.

217

My darling wife. This is the first chance I could find to write you. I am feeling well, my leg is better, I have not walked on it but very little. This is Saturday. I think something will be done next week. I will wire you as I shall start home as soon as it is over. I am taking good care of myself. As careful on the diet as it is possible to be at a second-class Hotel. Give my love to Mother and Mrs. Stanford. Hugs and kisses for Alicia. Your devoted husband, C. E. Conrad.

Leg trouble is not uncommon in persons afflicted with diabetes. Conrad had subscribed to a regime which indicates that his doctors had prescribed dieting and that his diabetes was becoming more destructive. As Charles indicated, it would be difficult to follow a diet at the hotel in Helena where he was staying, or at any other hotel of that day, for hungry men and big appetites for heavy food were then in vogue.

Conrad continued on the move. On April 20, 1901, he wrote from Great Falls.

Dear Lettie. Just arrived from Malta. I traveled from Havre to Malta with Mr. Jim Hill. I am in hopes to leave for home Monday morning and will write you when I start. I want to go to the Flathead convention (Democratic) Wednesday. Stinger writes that they commence to round up the buffalo Monday. I wish to go down and see them divided. Love to all. Hug and kiss Alicia for me. Your devoted husband, C. E. Conrad.

Conrad referred to his other associates and friends by their first names, but it was always "Mr. Hill" when he mentioned the railroad builder, James J. Hill. Hill was one of the great movers and shakers of his day. His accomplishments had earned him a respect that did not lend itself to familiarity or first names. Conrad, on the other hand — although highly respected and admired — retained a quality of humility that earned him both respect and endearment. Thus he could be addressed as "Charley," with no loss of respect or admiration.

The "Flathead Convention" was the county convention of the local Democratic Party. Conrad was a staunch, unreconstructed Democrat. That is, he was content to fight the Civil War only once. He was finished with the Old South as a place to live or even to visit. It was that war and the subsequent Reconstruction policies that catapulted him and the Democratic Party into power, and he never strayed from its tenets.

Conrad spent most of the autumn of 1901 at his ranches in eastern Montana. On October 13 he was in Dupuyer, where he had traveled to see Chamberlain of the Conrad-Chamberlain Cattle Company. He wrote to his wife that Chamberlain was away and would not return for two days. So many times Conrad seems to have traveled to confer with someone, only to find him gone. This pattern indicates that he did not make advanced appointments; but, if the person he wanted to see were away, Conrad settled back and waited for his return. Not chafing at a delay of several days seems out-of-character for a man of such wide and consuming business interests. In this letter to Lettie, however, he indicates that he had sent to Dupuyer for a gun and hoped to enjoy some productive duck and goose hunting in the interim.

In this October 13, 1901 letter Charles also asked Lettie to look in the pocket of his light pants, which he last wore with his dark coat, to see if she could find his "pass over the Great Northern" and to send it to Great Falls. A permanent pass over the Great Northern would be unusual. A shipment of cattle, say to Chicago, normally would entitle the shipper to a free ride to the market on the caboose of the cattle train and a pass on the passenger train to return home. Conrad's pass, however, would indicate that he either was a valued friend of Jim Hill or was a heavy shipper on the Great Northern, and it was perhaps the former.

The ten years of remaining life that Dr. William Osler had predicted for Conrad in 1892 were growing to a close. The treatment by Dr. Mitchell, the baths at Hot Springs, the annoying diet, and the care and ministration of a devoted wife all had failed to slow the deterioration of his health. Still, Conrad made little if any concession to health, as he continued to superintend and to build his fortune.

Just 13 months before his death, on October 28, 1901, Charles wrote to his family from Great Falls.

> Here it is Monday, and I cannot tell when I can start home. It may be a week or it may be sooner. You used to laugh at me for trading cattle and horses. Now it is sheep. I have tonight so far 7,000 head and am trying to buy more. I wish you were with me, to learn a new business. How do you think you would like it around sheep corrals? I will wire you when I can see my way clear to start.

Conrad seemed a little surprised at finding himself in the sheep business. From no sheep to 7,000 head would be quite a jump for most men, but Conrad, once in the business, was looking for more. It would seem that a man in his position would attempt to bring some order to his extensive holdings, rather than to explore into another venture about which he knew nothing. However, Conrad was cast in another mold. He saw an opportunity to make a profit in sheep, and he could not pass it up.

Yet Conrad must have found a place for his sheep. In the inventory of his estate, the Chamberlain Land and Sheep Company is wedged among a number of cattle companies. When listed, Conrad's name appears as an owner in the cattle companies, but not in the sheep company. Perhaps his cattle interest was too strong to admit to any interest in sheep.

Conrad did not return home at the time he predicted. Again opportunity knocked and he responded. This time it was cattle in North Dakota. On November 5, 1901, he wrote that he was trying to buy more cattle but that he could not see them until the following day. He did not know when he would be home, for he did not know if he could purchase the cattle.

Then he got the cattle. Four days later he wrote from Cut Bank that his men had just finished the branding. He was scheduled to leave for Great Falls the following morning and planned to be home on Sunday, "unless something comes up unbeknown." But something unknown did come up. This time it was not business but one of Conrad's few ventures with public life. He wrote on the next day, from Great Falls, that Governor Joseph K. Toole had appointed him one of the Commissioners to the Louisiana Purchase Exposition to be held in St. Louis in 1904. The Commissioners were to meet in Helena on Wednesday, and it was essential that he be present. He wrote to Lettie:

> If I should go home Sunday, I would have to leave home Monday night, so as to be on time for the meeting. I presume the best thing to do is stay here and go up on Tuesday, although I dislike it very much. I wish he had not appointed me to be one.

The purpose of the Commission was to secure funds for a Montana exhibit at the St. Louis World's Fair. Conrad despised being connected with a failure of any kind, but despite his efforts, the Legislature failed to appropriate any money for the Montana exhibit. This was certainly frustrating to a man so geared to success.

By this time, Conrad's health was declining visibly. His diabetes was entering its final stage of destruction. Its manifestations made it increasingly difficult for his once-strong body to respond to the iron will that had driven him since he began his career in Fort Benton during the 1860s. So the failure of the World's Fair Commission disturbed Conrad, especially when he remembered the prodigious energy that he had been able to give to the Montana Constitutional Convention, which had met in 1889.

That Convention introduced Conrad to the full political power of the "Copper Kings," who exerted considerable influence upon the writing of the proposed state constitution. Conrad and his group were able to exercise some restraint upon the appetites for power of the copper interests. Yet, in spite of all efforts, the final constitution contained clauses protecting what these companies conceived to be their interests. One stipulation required that all metals be taxed only on their value in place in the ground. Another provided that cities in Montana should have only the powers given to them by specific act of the Legislature. By these provisions, metals could be taxed only in their least valuable state. Further, the companies could control the action of all Montana cities and towns at one central point, the state legislature, which met only every two years for 60 days. Cities and towns in Montana still are hampered in their exercise of legislative power by the vestiges of those provisions in which the copper interests sought to control the state's legislative power in 1889.

IV. The Quest Ends

Beginning during the Spring of 1902, Conrad spent almost all of his time at home. The circulatory problems caused by diabetes had made the use of his legs more and more difficult. He tired easily and required frequent rest. But, in spite of the declining health of her father and the knowledge of his impending death, Alicia — then eight years old and unaware of both — recalled that it did not seem to be an unhappy time for the Conrads. She remembered that her mother and father spent many happy hours in the library, doing those things of which they had dreamed when they first came to the Flathead Valley.

Conrad had always loved to have people in his home. During the last months of his life, Grandmother Conrad was in Great Falls, too ill to return to Kalispell. His son, Charles D., and his daughter, Kate, were at school in the East. So the Conrads, Grandmother Stanford, and Alicia were the only members of the family at home. They were seldom alone, however. Old friends from across the nation came for short visits. Alicia remembered Charlie Russell coming to the Mansion. Russell was a particular friend of her Uncle Hal Stanford, Lettie Conrad's brother. Hal, a world recognized taxidermist and naturalist, had much in common with Russell, and the two of them would discuss with Conrad the "olden times," which had been so much a part of all their lives.

Alicia related that Russell seemed particularly fond of the painting, "Kee-Oh-Mee." Each time that Russell visited the Conrad home, upon leaving he would stop before the painting, which was hanging in the Great Hall. He would look at it, in obvious pleasure, for several moments. Then he would break his silent reverie, bid goodbye to all, and amble out the front door. On the occasion of his final visit, some weeks before Conrad's death, Russell again stopped in front of the painting. But this time Russell broke his silent communion with his painting, and he said softly, "Goodby, Old Girl." He did not look at or say goodbye to anyone; he hurried out the door much faster than his usual ambling gait took him.

Gazebo at Conrad Mansion Courtesy University of Montana Library

Charles Conrad's need for rest became more frequent, as did his need to be alone when pain struck. Lettie had prepared a room on the third floor of the Mansion which she called his "Sky Parlor." The walls were decorated with the colorful shawls from India which Conrad had bought for her. There was a comfortable couch, almost as big as a double-bed, covered with gay pillows. When Conrad retired to this room, it was a signal of his need for rest and for privacy, and Lettie was adamant that he be left undisturbed.

For the warm days of summer she hung a comfortable hammock in the gazebo, where he could rest and enjoy the beautiful grounds and the ever-changing Flathead Mountain Range to the east, the view of which had become an important part of their lives. When the weather was fair, Conrad spent many hours in his outside retreat, where his need for privacy was also respected.

Then the chill of autumn ended the days of resting in the gazebo. The weather, however severe, had never been an obstacle to anything Conrad wanted to do, but now it dictated his activities. When his strength permitted, he would climb to the third floor where, surrounded by mementoes, he spent time in solitary thoughts. Most of his time, however, was spent with Lettie. Both knew that his health was failing so rapidly that he did not have long to live. It was difficult for them to discuss a future which did not include them both. Nor was it easy to make plans for the care and supervision of the empire he had built. Conrad not only was its architect but also was its foundation. With the foundation gone, on what would the empire stand?

Charles E. Conrad, circa 1901 Courtesy Conrad Mansion Directors

William G. Conrad was a partner in most of the varied businesses and was capable of taking the full responsibility. However, he wanted to remain in Virginia and Lettie Conrad did not want to leave her future entirely in his hands. Her brother, James Stanford, held a financial interest in some of the business, but Lettie did not want to be dominated by her brother either.

Little time had been spent in planning, and time was slipping rapidly away. Not until a few days before his death did Conrad start to plan. He wished to be buried on the promontory where he and Lettie had last ridden. He directed the purchase of the point and of ten acres surrounding it. He drew a sketch of a mausoleum to be erected at a place on the point where it sloped steeply to the Whitefish River. This spot commanded a sweeping view of the Valley. The sketch and design he drew gave the dimensions of, and the materials from which, the mausoleum was to be built. It was to contain enough burial crypts for the entire family, perhaps allowing for a greater family proximity in death than in life.

This task completed, he turned his attention to his estate. Conrad's final will gives the appearance that it was planned and drafted in haste. It is handwritten, not typed, on a cheap grade of lined paper, and it was signed only five days before his death. The estate, which it had taken over thirty years to accumulate, was disposed of in five handwritten pages. It was not in Conrad's handwriting, but probably that of his attorney, George Grubb.

Family records preserved at the University of Montana Archives indicate that, from time to time, Conrad thought about the disposition of his estate but did no real planning. Among these records is a will, in Conrad's handwriting, which he prepared himself. In this document, Conrad acknowledges his mixed-blood son but leaves him only $10. He also left his mother $50 per month, while she lived, but no such provision was made for his mother-in-law. One-half of the remainder of the estate was left outright to his wife and one-half to the other three children. It appears that Conrad at this time had not consulted an attorney, for at the end of the will he wrote: "This form was drawn up and given to me by the late Justice Horace R. Buck and I used the same in making my will on Jan. 18th, 1898. C. E. Conrad."

This will appointed Lettie Conrad, William G. Conrad, and James T. Stanford the coexecutors. Lettie, however, did not want to be burdened by coexecutors and, in the final will, she alone was appointed executrix. In this last will Conrad also changed his attitude toward his first-born son and treated him the same as he did the other children.

The final will made no provision for Conrad's mother. At times during C. E.'s life, he had placed property in the name of his mother, but never in that of his mother-in-law. Conrad's preferential treatment of his mother seems to have been a cause of irritation to Lettie. That irritation must have been evident for, in the final will, no provision was included for Grandmother Conrad. After Charles' death, his mother spent more and more time with her daughter, Alice, in Great Falls, and she was living there when she died in 1904. In the University of Montana Archives, there are many pictures of the Conrad family, including several of

Catherine Stanford. There is none of Maria Conrad.

By his final will, Conrad granted outright one-half of his estate to his wife. The other half he divided equally among the four children. Any monies that the first-born son owed his father were to be deducted from his share.

The will directed that all of the estate be held in trust for a period of eleven years from the date that it was signed, on November 22, 1902. This provision was probably made because Alicia would be of legal age at the date the trust would be terminated. Lettie Conrad was appointed trustee, without liability for any losses suffered by the estate. She was to receive $2,000 per month, and each of the four children $150 per month, from the estate as long as the trust continued.

Lettie Conrad, circa 1920 Courtesy University of Montana Library

The provision for the 11-year trust was distasteful to everyone except Lettie Conrad, for it gave her control over the estate with no liability for its losses. Any of the children — except the first-born son, who died without children before the 11-year period of the trust had expired — could have forced a distribution of the estate at any time after November 22, 1913. However the strength of Lettie's personality and determination prevented her children from taking any such action. None of the heirs sought a distribution, hungry for money though each was. In any event, Lettie Conrad did not terminate the trust in 1913, as directed by the will, but continued to control the entire estate until her death in 1923.

Conrad's signature on the will gives no indication of his infirmities and approaching death. It is as clear and bold as were the letters he signed when he was in prime health, although death was only five days away. With satisfactory arrangements having been made for the disposition of his body, and Lettie installed to care for his empire, Conrad faced death with the same courage and stoicism with which he had faced the dangers of the frontier.

Alicia was kept home from school during Charles' final days, to help her mother, who remained at her husband's bedside every hour of the day. In the only conversation Alicia remembered from this time, her father said, "Letty, if only we could have been together longer." Her mother answered, "But darling, I was only 18 when we were married, so you have had the best years of my life."

Death did not come easily to Charles E. Conrad. He fought it as he had welcomed life, with every ounce of his strength and will. But both strength and will ultimately failed. The final cause of death was congestive heart failure. Excessive leg pains and an inability to breathe while lying down prevented Conrad from resting prone. He sat up in bed, with Lettie and Alicia holding his legs in an elevated position for hours on end to make him more comfortable.

On November 27, 1902, Alicia was resting in the Great Hall, when she became aware that silence had fallen upon the Mansion. The sound of heavy breathing from the upstairs bedroom had stopped. She ran to her parents' bedroom and found her father lying back on the bed, still and silent. Her mother was lying beside him, exhausted and crying silently. Lettie Conrad looked up and said, "Dear, your father is gone. Please leave me alone with him for awhile and then I will come to you."

Alicia went to the third-floor "Sky Parlor," where she always felt close to her father. Her mind refused to accept her father's death. When her mother came to her, the two sat silently, holding each other, until Lettie said, "There is much to be done and you are the only one to help me." So mother and daughter plunged into the work of notifying the children in the East and all the friends and relatives.

Conrad died at 11:29 a.m., and news of his death spread rapidly throughout Montana. The story of his death was carried in all of the newspapers. These accounts include a common theme of admiration and respect. Typical was the story in the *Great Falls Tribune* of November 28, 1902.

> He leaves an estate that is very conservatively valued at over one million dollars, his investments being in almost every branch of industry that exists in Montana, with great interests in the Canadian Northwest.

> The foundation of Mr. Conrad's great fortune was an act of kindness, and throughout his life he was ever doing good. One of his most intimate friends, in speaking of him last night, said, 'Although he had become wealthy, Charlie Conrad was almost unassuming and modest. He was always doing good and was ashamed to have it become known. Often when he wanted to help someone, he feared that it might become known that he had done the act he contemplated, and he would get some friend to act for him in order that it might not be known that he was concerned. He was a most kindly, good and modest man, and there are many who have him to thank for aid, the source of which they did not know or had wrongly located.'

> Throughout Montana Mr. Conrad had many warm friends, some of whom had known him for 34 years, and the news that his life is ended will be saddening to all. He was an agreeable companion, a faithful friend, kind and true. He loved Montana, and for his state and the city where was his home he had done much.

The funeral was held on Sunday, November 30, which gave time for the children in the East, and for friends and relatives from all over the state and the nation to attend. The rites were held in the Mansion, which had become such a symbol of his life. The service was simple, in keeping with Conrad's request — it included Kate singing for her father for the last time.

The long funeral cortege stretched for blocks behind the black, horse-drawn hearse. Alicia said that, during the last days of her father's illness, his horse, "Champ," refused to eat or drink. The horse was tied to the hearse and followed it to the place of burial. But, as had happened so often during his life, Conrad was not yet home. The construction of the mausoleum, though started, would not be fully completed until 1908. So his body was placed in a temporary vault, located on the promontory which the Conrads loved. In the fall of 1908 it was moved to one of the crypts of the mausoleum that he had designed. Then Charles E. Conrad would be home to stay.

CHAPTER 44
Lettie Conrad's Memorial to Her Husband

Charles Conrad still had been able to ride early in the autumn of 1902. When the weather and his health permitted, he and Lettie took horseback trips throughout the Valley. On one sunny, Indian summer afternoon, they went to the beautiful promontory to the east of Kalispell for a better view of the Flathead Valley, then resplendent in the colors of fall.

The easternmost point of this promontory was their destination. When they reached it, Charles seemed more tired than usual, so they dismounted to rest. Both were silent for some time, engrossed in their own thoughts and in the quiet beauty that surrounded them. The silence was broken by Charles, who said, somewhat to himself, "I can think of no more peaceful and lovely spot for a place of final rest." As the sun set, the Conrads returned home to the bustle of the Mansion. Lettie was troubled that the ride had tired her husband and that he had spoken of a burial spot, a thought so foreign to his mind.

Lettie had known that her husband suffered from diabetes, but they did not speak of his ailment or speculate on how long he might live. Charles knew that the end of the time predicted by Dr. Osler was fast approaching. Four days before his death he told Lettie that he wanted to be buried on the promontory to which they had ridden earlier in the fall. Mr. Grubb, the family attorney, was instructed to purchase the site, which he accomplished without any trouble, so great was the esteem in which C. E. Conrad was held by the people of Kalispell.

Charles had drawn plans for a mausoleum to be erected on the site. The *Great Falls Tribune* story of his death, in the issue of November 28, 1902, states:

> Mr. Conrad's mind was clear to the last and only a few days ago, realizing that his death must soon come, he gave directions concerning the disposition that he desired made of his remains. He bought 10 acres of land, lying northeast of Kalispell, overlooking the town of which he

229

deserved to be called the founder, and directed that a mausoleum be erected in that plot, in which his body should be placed at rest. He outlined the plans and design of the mausoleum and gave orders for its construction, and work on it will begin right away. The funeral will be held at Kalispell Sunday and the body will be placed in a temporary vault from which it will be transferred to the mausoleum when that shall have been completed.

Conrad Mausoleum Courtesy the author

Following the death of her husband, Lettie Conrad resolved to create a lovely cemetery in the area that had been so dear to them both and to dedicate it as a perpetual memorial to her husband. She met with attorney Grubb, told him of her plan, and instructed him to purchase the entire promontory, consisting of about 87 acres. At this meeting Lettie learned that there might be obstacles. The desired land existed as several different parcels, in diverse ownership, and some of the owners might be hesitant to sell. She learned also that the lawmakers of the young state of Montana had not contemplated such an act of generosity. No legislative authorization existed for a memorial cemetery to continue in perpetuity, an oversight that could not be remedied until the next session of the Legislature convened.

Lettie Conrad's resolve would recognize no obstacles to the accomplishment of her desire to honor her husband. She instructed Mr. Grubb to take any measures necessary to complete what had become the most important project in her life. Lettie also left with Attorney Grubb the task of acquiring the balance of the land and securing the enactment of the necessary legislative authority. Lettie and her daughter Alicia then made an extensive tour of other cemeteries, to compare them and to gather ideas on how to make this memorial the most beautiful in the world.

On this journey they inspected cemeteries all over the United States, Canada, and Mexico, learning and absorbing. In St. Paul, Minnesota, they met a landscape architect who was a kindred spirit. He came to Kalispell to look at the site and to advise on landscaping. After walking around the promontory and studying its setting for several hours, he told Lettie, "I cannot improve upon God's architecture. My advice is to disturb as little as possible. Do not move a shovelful of earth that is not necessary. You already have one of the most beautiful cemetery sites in the world."

Happy to have her opinion confirmed by an expert, Lettie was eager to complete her cherished project, but progress was torturously slow. Not until April 27, 1904, was the last piece of land acquired from the Kalispell Townsite Company.

On February 16, 1905, the Ninth Legislative Assembly of the State of Montana passed *Senate Bill 3*, entitled "An Act to Provide for the Formation of Cemetery Associations, To Define Their Powers and Duties and Provide for Their Management and Control." This enactment created the legislative authority to proceed.

On April 8, 1905, the Certificate of Incorporation was filed for the C. E. Conrad Memorial Cemetery Association of Kalispell, Montana. At long last the legal entity had been formed to carry forward the dream that had consumed Lettie Conrad after her husband's death.

On April 17, 1905, Lettie signed a deed giving to the Cemetery Association the original 87 acres of land. This tract comprised the current entrance, the hillside on which the approach roads are located, and the entire raised promontory that thrusts from the level valley floor as a foretaste of the majestic mountains that rise to the east. In the early 1930s and again in 1951, by separate purchases, the Cemetery Association acquired the flatlands lying to the west of the original cemetery site. There probably will be no further expansion, since no more contiguous land seems available.

In 1981 there were about 12,000 bodies buried in the original cemetery site, with additional space remaining for about 23,000 more burials. The subsequent land additions provided space for about 9,000 more graves.

Clifford O. Miller and Donald Buckingham, who have sat on the Cemetery Board for many years, estimate that the current site will be able to meet the needs of the community for about 150 years. With burials to date approximating the current population of Kalispell, such estimates are difficult to make. However, even when the capacity of the entire cemetery site is reached, and there exists no further income from the sale of lots, the perpetual care of the cemetery is assured, due to the foresight of Lettie Conrad.

Lettie insisted upon the creation of a Perpetual Care and Improvement Fund, one that could be used for no other purposes. She was adamant that the memorial she was creating for her husband would remain a place of beauty and solace. This aim she accomplished by insisting that the cemetery association's bylaws include a requirement that no less than 15 percent of all revenue from lot sales be placed in the trust fund, to be used only for perpetual care. At present there is more than $450,000 in this special trust fund. The Cemetery Board each year places an additional 15 percent of the lot-sales monies, plus additional sums when available, in the trust fund — and still charges less for burial lots than any comparable cemetery in the state and very likely in the nation.

The final touch was the completion, in 1908, of the mausoleum, situated on the easternmost point of the promontory. This structure was placed at the resting place where Charles Conrad had spoken musingly of the beauty and peace of the spot as a place of final rest. Lettie's daughter Alicia recalled that the reddish stone of the mausoleum is Grinnell Argillite, obtained from a quarry site near Essex. Lettie had samples of the stone tested and used it only after being assured of its superior qualities of durability.

In the mausoleum are 11 burial crypts. Charles Conrad was placed in one upon the mausoleum's completion. Lettie Conrad lies at his side. Son Charles D. and daughter Kate each occupy two crypts. Billy, son of Charles D., who died as a young man, in a hunting accident, was placed beside his father, and four crypts are not occupied.

The Conrads are surrounded by the beauty that Alicia Stanford Conrad created and preserved in the memory of her husband. Her rest must be the more peaceful in knowing that his memorial will continue as long as the promontory stands.

CHAPTER 45
Christmas for Captain Winter's Children

Through the duration of their marriage, which lasted only 21 years, Charles and Lettie Conrad remained extremely close. Their greatest joy resulted from being together, either in the home which they both loved, or in their travels. They intended that each trip would be a broadening and educational experience, and they made it so. Following her husband's death, Lettie Conrad would not experience again the happiness she had known during the marriage, but she was determined to fill her days with worthwhile actions and to dedicate herself to the enrichment of the lives of others.

The Salvation Army was one of the organizations that received her strong support. At that time, Captain A. O. Winter was the head of the local Army. Lettie Conrad believed that he was a true man of God and that he tended and fed his flock with the love and understanding that Jesus asked of all his shepherds.

In the autumn of 1918, Lettie was talking with Captain Winter of the coming Christmas. She asked, "What of the children of the families you help? What kind of a Christmas Day will they have?" Captain Winter told her that the Salvation Army would try to make it as much like Christmas as possible, but that there would not be the festive table or the joyous Christian Spirit of Christmas. The Army would provide a plain, nourishing meal and perhaps a toy for each child, but many of the homes would be cold and cheerless.

Lettie reflected for a few moments, her heart heavy with the thoughts of the children and of the Christmas that had been described by Captain Winter. Groping for something she could do, she asked, "Could you arrange for the children to come to our house for dinner on Christmas Day?" Captain Winter, after a few minutes of thought, said, "That might be arranged." When Lettie asked how many children there might be, Captain Winter answered that there could be almost any number. She then inquired what the age group might be, and Captain Winter estimated they would range from babes in arms to any age limitation they might decide upon. Lettie Conrad said, "Bring them all."

Good shepherd that he was, Captain Winter knew that even kindness and generosity sometimes must be tempered to meet the exigencies of a situation. He said, "How would you want them to eat, at the table or scattered everywhere around the house?" Spontaneously, Lettie replied, "Oh, around the table. Otherwise the whole spirit would be lost." So they measured the table and decided that, if small chairs were used, more could be seated. Lettie then added, "We must include some babies. That would make it even better." Sure enough, they indeed could handle a few babies by placing highchairs behind the other chairs at the table.

It was settled that Captain Winter would issue the invitations, and that he would explain to the parents why grownups could not be invited and how the number of children had been determined. Dinner would be in mid-afternoon, so the children would have time to enjoy the meal, and the tree and to share in the spirit of Christmas. This arrangement would leave time to clear the table, to clean the house, and to make ready for the Christmas dinner for the Conrads and their guests.

Captain Winter thought it would be better if the mothers brought the children to the door of the Mansion. Both he and Lettie dearly would have loved to gather them all up in the big sleigh, with the black horses steaming and the Christmas bells ringing, but the timing just did not permit this touch.

Lettie insisted that the children enjoy the same dinner menu that would be served to the family later in the day and that the main course be turkey. She assembled a number of highchairs and asked the ladies, who were to attend the subsequent dinner, to come early and to help with the party. From the F. A. O. Swartz toy catalog, she happily chose scores of little toys. She ordered more than enough for the number of children they expected, for in her mind it would be unforgivable on Christmas for any child not to get a gift. She sent the order by wire, fearful that a letter might be delayed.

F. A. O. Swartz entered into the festive spirit and, with the company's boxes covered with "Urgent, Do Not Delay" and "Rush" stickers, the toys arrived well in time for the party.

The kitchen staff also caught the spirit. No grumbling resulted because two dinners had to be prepared, and on Christmas Day all was ready. The mothers had been told to bring the children to the side entrance of the dining room, so that they would not see the tree until the dinner was over and the big moment had arrived. It seemed that the children arrived all at once. As they appeared, the mothers handed their little ones to the ladies who were helping. Daughter Kate took one of the babies and put its head on her shoulder and held it. Kate wore a low-cut evening dress and, as she was rather fat and soft, the baby snuggled down into the warm, smooth skin and promptly went to sleep. As Alicia remembered, Kate held the baby throughout the party. Kate never did have children of her own, although she loved them, and for this Christmas afternoon the baby was hers. Alicia said that she never could understand how they got all of the wraps off the children, where the clothing was stored, or, even more puzzling, how they returned the correct clothes to each child when all was finished.

The first sight that met the children's eyes was the long table that seemed to stretch to the horizon. White damask tablecloths covered the table and shimmered from the light of the candles reflected from the cut-glass goblets, with the prisms of the glass sometimes suggesting the colors of the spectrum. The highly polished silver seemed to shine in welcome.

Lettie Conrad had used her best china, which glistened in the flickering light, and she had decorated the table lavishly with freshly cut flowers. The children gazed awe-stricken, and each seemed to sense that, had Lettie been entertaining a reigning monarch, the table would not have been set in a manner more elegant.

Somehow everyone was seated. Captain Winter asked God's blessing, and with the "amen" arrived the turkey. All eyes followed the progress of the majestic bird as it was carried to the far end of the table. As the bird was placed on the carving board, one little girl could contain her amazement no longer and exclaimed loudly, "Wow, it's a real turkey!"

The turkey was carved by Captain Winter. He then handed the plate to Lettie, who added piles of dressing, mashed potatoes, candied yams, and green beans. As each youngster received a plate, the eating began immediately, and some children were asking for seconds before others had received their plates. Eventually everyone was served. The vegetable dishes required replenishment, but the big turkey sufficed, even though the accumulated appetites threatened to destroy it. It was fortunate that the Conrad dairy herd had not failed, for many pitchers of milk were required to keep the goblets filled.

As the dinner progressed, the children grew more relaxed, and the quiet that initially had pervaded the dining room was replaced by happy voices and childhood banter. The youngsters seemed to sense that, more than anything, Lettie Conrad wanted them to know that they were true guests and that all of the hospitality which could be extended was theirs.

With this relaxation came the diminution of propriety. Milk was spilled, and overfilled forks dropped food on child, table, and floor.

235

Lettie and her helpers appeared immediately to clean up all spills and to assure the embarrassed child that the fork was crooked, or that the spoon had a hole in it, and that such things happened all the time to all their guests. When little girls spilled on their dresses, the dress was whisked off, rinsed, dried, and returned — the child being wrapped in a shawl during the process. The excitement also caused many trips to the bathroom. These forays produced recurring amazement that no trip to the outhouse was necessary and that a little room really did exist, right in the house, where this sort of activity could be accommodated.

Even the heartiest appetite will sometime be filled, and that moment finally arrived. When Lettie Conrad asked who wanted Christmas Pudding and who desired ice cream, an unanimous shout rose for ice cream. The young guests were not sure what the pudding might taste like, but they knew about ice cream, and it came so infrequently that no one could miss such an opportunity.

Just before the children finished eating, the beeswax candles on the tree were lighted. When the tree was shining in all of its Christmas glory, the doors into the Great Hall were opened. The children were silent for a moment, as the beauty of the tree held them enthralled. They followed Lettie through the Library and into the Great Hall, where the huge tree with the candles ablaze and its ornaments glowing extended to the second floor.

The children were seated on the floor around the tree, with their backs to the fireplace, where flames leaped up the chimney and crackled as though with joy at the sight of the happy children.

When Lettie Conrad called for quiet, there was not a sound from the children. It was time for the Christmas Story to be told. During the years, the Story was related by different people. Alicia remembered best a local teacher, Elnora Tinsley, who told the tale in such a way that the children listened with rapt attention. The telling of the Story usually took fifteen minutes and, during all that time, the children sat without a movement or a sound. There was no scrambling around, no wanting to change seats, and no squirming. They were awed by being in a strange place with a great, big forest tree standing in the middle of the house, all decorated, and with soft music drifting in from the Music Room.

When the beautiful Story of Christmas ended, the background music stopped also. From the second floor then floated the sound of a violin playing "Silent Night." Descending the stairway came the Christmas Fairy, dressed in a white costume with flaired skirt, stars, and bangles, and wearing a sparkling crown. The Fairy seemed to glide down the stairs, continuing to play the sweet strains of the violin until she reached the seated children. She then started playing the familiar Christmas carols. The grownups began singing softly and, one by one, the children joined them, until a full chorus of voices filled the house with the beautiful songs of Christmas.

During the singing, two stablemen carried in a huge box and placed it on one side of the fireplace. All eyes followed the progress of the men and continued to rest on the box as it sat there, its contents unknown. But each child had a suspicion of what the box might contain. Lettie Conrad then approached the box and started removing gaily wrapped packages, each marked "Boy" or "Girl." These parcels she handed to the grown-ups, who then distributed them to the children. Even during this excitement, the children stayed in their places and, slowly and with much wonderment, began to unwrap the gifts. Slowly, because it seemed that they almost feared to have the unwrapping completed and to come face-to-face with what was in the package.

The squeals of delight, from those youngsters who first unwrapped their packages, hastened the unwrapping by the others. Soon the paper was flying, as excitement and delight caused all care to be abandoned completely. Quickly the floor was filled with paper and the room with laughter and with cried of happiness.

Then Lettie asked for quiet, and quiet replaced pandemonium almost immediately. She told the children that their mothers had come for them and that she was sorry they had to go. She thanked them for coming and said that she had never before entertained guests that she enjoyed so much as the children who had shared this day. She hoped that they would remember the Christmas Story, which had been told to them so beautifully, and that they would let it be a guide for their lives. Finally Lettie Conrad said, "I wish I could hug and kiss you all goodbye, but here is a goodbye kiss for each of you," and she blew them a kiss.

Then the mothers and the ladies who had helped with the party managed to get the right clothes on each child, and the young guests departed, clutching their gifts and calling back "thank yous" and "goodbyes." When Kate returned the baby to the waiting arms of his mother, her reluctance could be sensed by all, and the mother held the child more tenderly, seeing the tears glisten in Kate's eyes.

Thus occurred the first of the Christmas parties for Captain Winter's children, but it would not be the last. Another tradition had begun in the Conrad home. Lettie Conrad would continue it, bringing the true spirit of Christmas to hundreds of children, who would treasure it for the rest of their lives.

For many years afterward, Alicia said, some lady or man would stop her on the street or in a store and say, "I was one of the children who had Christmas dinner at your home, and I cherish the memory more than anything that happened in my childhood." When asked why they did not include a Santa Claus, Alicia said, "Mother did not like the idea of a dressed-up Santa Claus. I agreed with her and still do. She would say to me as a little child, 'Now, I never saw Santa Claus, and I never knew anybody that had ever seen him. The people on the street that say they are Santa Claus are just playing Santa and they never are.' I think Mother's way is better. I just cringe at the Santa Claus-people who are asked to hold little children and ask 'Now what do you want for Christmas?' That's the market place and the market place shouldn't have a place in Christmas."

Although the market place may be present, the spirit of Lettie Conrad and Captain Winter will forever be in the hearts of untold millions as they celebrate the birth of Christ in all the years to come.

CHAPTER 46
Lettie Conrad

When Charles E. Conrad died, his empire lost the genius that had created and managed it. His brother, William G., continued to manage the businesses owned by the Conrad Brothers Company in which Charles had held one-half interest, but the management of his personal affairs and the business interests owned by C. E. alone fell entirely upon Lettie Conrad. The inventory of Charles Conrad's estate property covered 40 legal-size sheets. It consisted of land, cattle, mining claims, sheep, banking, and other corporate interests scattered throughout Montana, Idaho, and Canada. In 1902, millionaires were not plentiful, and Conrad had been one of this highly exclusive group.

Lettie Conrad had not been prepared for the management of an estate so huge and diverse. Her role had included providing a pleasant, comfortable, well-run home for her husband and giving him cheerful and congenial companionship. These tasks she had accomplished most successfully. With Conrad away from home so much of the time, in the management of his many businesses, the responsibility for the care and training of the children also had fallen upon Lettie almost entirely. In 1902, the year of Conrad's death, Charles D. was 20, Kate 17, and Alicia 10 years of age.

Yet Lettie's service as a wife had been far more successful than her service as a mother. Charles and Kate, although older, were not much more mature than 10-year-old Alicia. The two older children had been placed in boarding schools when they finished the eighth grade in Kalispell. Transportation remained such that they returned home only during the summer vacations. But summers were too busy for much companionship between mother and children. Lettie felt guilty and frustrated about her relationship with her two older children. As a result, she became indulgent, and indulgence replaced the discipline that they might have been given had they lived at home. Charles had provided a background of firmness and authority, but then that too was gone. Before her husband's death, Lettie Conrad had been responsible for the home and family. Thereafter she assumed the management of the family fortune as well.

From the time that they came to Fort Benton, Charles and William Conrad had functioned in business as partners, first under the name of I. G. Baker and Company, and then as Conrad Brothers. The Kalispell Mansion, stables, and surrounding land were in Lettie Conrad's name. The 486 shares of Conrad National Bank stock were held in C. E. Conrad's name alone. The rest of the property was owned by the Conrad Brothers' partnership, only one-half of which was owned by Charles Conrad. Lettie neither liked nor fully trusted her brother-in-law, William, but Montana law gave him the right, as surviving partner, to conclude the partnership's businesses. William possessed great self-assurance and was confident of his managerial ability. However, Charles, during his lifetime, had provided much of the direction and management of the affairs of the partnership. William would miss sorely his brother's business acumen and supervising ability.

William assumed complete charge of the many business enterprises which continued under his management during his lifetime. He also remained a substantial stockholder in the Conrad National Bank, but Charles had owned a majority of this stock, which gave Lettie the controlling interest. The Bank seemed a beacon of security to her. She believed strongly that the family always must retain a majority interest in the Bank. Almost as strong was her determination that her son, Charles D., would be installed as president of the Bank, as soon as that could be accomplished.

Following the death of C. E. Conrad, most of the money that came to his family derived from Conrad Brothers' activities, and this income resulted largely from the liquidation of its holdings rather than from its continued operation and expansion. No indication exists that William was unfair, but the results of his management suggest that the success of the partnership had depended heavily upon C. E. Conrad.

William continued to manage Conrad Brothers until his death in February of 1914. Then the assets of the partnership were placed in the hands of James T. Stanford, Lettie Conrad's brother, and George H. Stanton, a Great Falls businessman. They remained in control until the liquidation of the partnership in 1920. Upon the dissolution of this partnership, the remaining assets were divided between the estates of the two brothers. There remained only town lots in dying settlements, timber lands, and stocks and bonds for worthless corporations. In the final accounting, the once proud and prosperous cattle, sheep, mining, and banking interests are listed with the notation: "No further value."

Written off also in this accounting was the "Indian Treaty Account." Charles Conrad's correspondence indicates that he spent much time and money acting as the agent of the Blackfeet Indian Tribe in the treaty negotiations with the United States government, when its reservation was established. All of his efforts to collect this debt from the federal government failed. Yet Conrad never tried to collect the debt from the Blackfeet and, when Conrad Brothers passed from the scene, this debt passed with it.

Conrad signed his will on November 22, 1902, five days before his death. His handwriting is firm and clear. His witnesses included: Hector E. Clowes, pastor of the Episcopal Church, which the Conrads attended; Leland Tansel, cashier of the Conrad Bank; James Swaney, a longtime friend; J. Harrington Edwards, a vice-president of the Conrad Bank. All of the estate was to be held in trust until November 22, 1913. At that time it was to be distributed — one-half to Lettie Conrad and the other half, in equal shares, to the four children. In the will, the children are identified:

> Charles Davenport Conrad, Catherine Conrad, and Alicia Conrad, the issue of the marriage between myself and Alicia D. Conrad; and also that certain half-breed Indian known as Charles E. Conrad, Junior, who has been educated by me in Canada and who now resides in the City of Montreal. Out of the share of said Charles E. Conrad, Junior, there shall be deducted any and all notes due or owing to me by said Charles E. Conrad, Junior, at the time of my death.

During his life, Conrad had acknowledged this Indian son as his own. He had advanced the son large sums of money — $26,000 during the period from May 29, 1899, to July 2, 1902. He had met this son on business trips, but he had never allowed him to visit the family home in Kalispell. At the solemn moment of his last will and testament Conrad did not acknowledge this son or even refer to him as such. He called him "that half-breed Indian who has been educated by me."

The will provided that Lettie Conrad would be both the executrix of the estate and the trustee of the trust. For her services she was to be paid $2,000 per month, and she was not to be responsible for any losses that might result from her management. Each of the four children was to receive $150 per month, with these payments to continue for the period of the trust. On December 20, 1902, the court authorized the payment of these amounts. With the exception of Charles E. Conrad, Jr., who died in 1904, these sums were paid until Lettie Conrad's death in 1923.

Following the funeral of C. E. Conrad, both Charley and Kate returned to school, but neither remained there long. The hope of Charles and Lettie Conrad that their son would attend Yale was not fulfilled. Further, C. E.'s restraining influence on Charley had disappeared. Charley knew that the strong will his mother exhibited in most things would not be directed toward him. When he completed prep school at Exeter, in the spring of 1903, Charley had finished school. Over the protests of his mother and the known wishes of his father, Charley came home to stay. The suggestion of his uncle, Hal Stanford, that Lettie needed help in the management of the estate provided the excuse Charley needed to forego any further education. Lettie Conrad did need help, but not the kind that Charley would give her.

Kate simultaneously suffered a disappointment in her never-too-deeply-seated desire for a career in music. She had neither the temperament, nor the ambition, nor the self-discipline for a career of any type, especially one involving music. Kate loved the easy life of the family home and the active social life that was available to her in Kalispell. She returned home eagerly, knowing that she could overcome any objections that might be voiced by her mother.

Alicia had never been spoiled or indulged. She was deeply devoted to her mother and became her constant attendant. After her graduation from the eighth grade, she had no further formal schooling. Alicia was eager for knowledge, but she received no encouragement to continue school. She was pleasant, loving, and easily bent to the wishes of her mother. Knowingly or not, Lettie Conrad made Alicia her nurse and companion, a quiet harbor for the stormy times that lay ahead.

Lettie tried to keep life at home running in the same pattern that had been established prior to her husband's death, but that life was not the same. The summer home at Foy's Lake became a vacation haven for family, relatives, and friends, from its opening in the spring to its closing in the fall. The guest rooms in the Mansion developed a high rate of occupancy for an amazing variety of visitors. Botanists studying the flora of Glacier Park were guests, as were biologists studying the area's animals and fish. Artists, musicians, writers, and scientists, who learned of Lettie's hospitality, came for varying periods of time in pursuit of their interests.

The Salvation Army and the Red Cross received Lettie Conrad's special attention. During the years of World War I (1914-1918), Lettie was named Regional Director of the Red Cross. The Mansion was closed as she travelled much of the time, overseeing the activities of the Red Cross in the western United States. In 1918, she directed the nursing for the local victims of the national influenza epidemic. She spared neither herself nor any able-bodied person she could commandeer. When the schools closed, she enlisted the teachers. Any who refused were hauled before the local school board, which told them to work or be fired.

Lettie Conrad's religious convictions also deepened with the passing years. She maintained an active and ever-expanding interest in the

242

Charles D., Alicia, and Catherine Conrad, circa 1893
Courtesy University of Montana Library.

affairs of Kalispell's·Christ Episcopal Church and especially in its charitable activities. The community developed a deep respect for Lettie, which was evidenced by its universal reference to her as "Madame Conrad."

Alicia remembered that her mother lived as though Charles Conrad were only absent on one of his trips and soon would be returning. He had been interested in the preservation of the buffalo. The herd that Conrad had acquired numbered 47 when he died. No one was very knowledgeable about the preservation of buffalo at that time, for extinction techniques had dominated to that point. Lettie Conrad assumed the management of the buffalo herd, and it became her chief interest. She gradually learned as much about the buffalo in captivity as anyone in the United States. It pleased her to be consulted about their care and management and to feel that she had played a major role in the survival of the species.

Time did not weaken Lettie's feeling of the presence of her husband. Kenneth Adams, who grew up in Kalispell, remembered that, when his brother, Frank, worked for Lettie Conrad, one of his duties was to harness the horses to the carriage each evening, when the weather permitted. Lettie would be waiting, and Frank then drove her to the cemetery. The carriage stopped in the drive west of the mausoleum, and

243

from that point she would walk to her husband's burial place. After spending some moments there, she would return to the carriage, seemingly refreshed, to be driven home.

The Conrads had intended to travel to the Orient, but business always interfered with any specific plans which they made. Lettie Conrad finally decided to take this trip, with Alicia as her companion. No travel agencies existed to make arrangements, so Lettie planned the trip. This preparation included having the Conrad Bank arrange with the Bank of Tokyo to give them personal and financial assistance during their stay in Japan. They left the Mansion on the day after Christmas, 1909, and sailed from San Francisco to Hawaii. Following a rest stop in Honolulu, they sailed aboard the S.S. *Manchuria* on what Alicia recalled as a one-month trip to Japan.

They landed at Yokohama, the treaty port and the only one open to American ships. Alicia noted that they necessarily stayed in that city two weeks, waiting for their luggage. Lettie Conrad had packed, in that luggage, several containers of Postum, a popular cereal drink. The Japanese custom officials held their baggage and restrained the Conrads until the Postum had been analyzed, to insure that they were not smuggling drugs.

From Yokohama they traveled to Tokyo. This trip was made by rickshaw, a distance of some 15 miles, and took what seemed to Alicia a rather short time. She recalled that the men worked in relays. The rickshaw was weighted so that it lifted the runner almost off the ground, and thus he could run without carrying the full weight of the rickshaw. At Tokyo, they contacted the Bank of Tokyo. The officials there had arranged for their finances and for a guide who would accompany them at all times.

Alicia remembered that their travel was made by rickshaw or by chairs with handles that were carried by four men. As the two women toured, they stayed at Japanese inns chosen by their guide. After leaving Tokyo, they did not see an American until their return. Except in Yokohama — the treaty port where Americans clustered and were hated — the Conrads were treated well by the Japanese people. Their guide arranged for them to visit a beautiful and remote Japanese shrine. As they moved from room to room, Alicia felt an unseen presence that seemed to follow her. She said,

> Mother was in the lead and I became aware of somebody being awfully close to my shoulder, so I would turn and never saw anybody. But I felt somebody there, and I got kind of worried, and I went faster to keep closer to Mother. But somehow or other that presence was there, and I thought, well, I'm just imagining it because there isn't anybody there. But when we left that day, the person that had been there stepped forward, made a low

244

bow to me and said in Pidgin English, 'Peace, ssssss (said as though the 'C' were many 'S's), what kind of bird are that a tail to in your hat?" I had a brown beaver hat I had bought in San Francisco, a very dressy hat. It had a cascade of orange and brown ostrich feathers. Imagine him saying, 'What kind of a bird are that a tail to!'

The Conrads arrived in Japan in January, 1910, and left in April. When their guide injured his foot, he arranged with an aristocratic Japanese man, about 75 years old, to guide them. He spoke no English, but showed them the traditional Japan that they so wanted to see. He was somehow able to communicate it to them, although they shared no common language. Alicia recalled that "He wore the gray silks of the very rich, the Samurai sword, and head dress. He commanded respect wherever we went and arranged for us to see things that otherwise would not have been possible."

Alicia said that, at that time, Americans were supposed to register with the Japanese government upon arrival. But Lettie said, "No, we are not registering, because then we'd just be thrown in with the other tourists and not see the real Japan." They did see the real Japan. They did not travel by plan. They carried no travelers' checks. They did not speak Japanese and, in 1910, few Japanese spoke English. But, through the Conrad Bank, they had the Bank of Tokyo behind them. That power proved sufficient for them to roam Japan for three months and see things that few Americans were allowed to see.

On their return trip, the Conrads stayed in Hawaii for three months. They arrived again in Kalispell during the latter part of July. Thereafter Alicia was convinced that the way to see the world was to travel with her mother.

CHAPTER 47
Halloween at the Conrad Mansion

In late October, 1910 — the year that Lettie and Alicia Conrad toured Japan — fate prepared the Conrad Mansion for a gala Halloween party. Yet, in the preparation the Mansion was almost destroyed.

On that autumn night, Lettie and Alicia, who then was 18 years old, had returned from a dinner party. Still in their evening dresses, they sat in the Library, discussing the party. About 10:30, Lettie started upstairs to bed. Alicia was extinguishing the downstairs lights, when there came a beating on the front door, and a man's voice shouting, "Your house is on fire!" Alicia ran to the door, and the man pointed to the north end of the house which was in flames.

Alicia told her mother to call the fire department and said that she would get the hose from the second floor and try to get out on the roof and fight the fire. Moving around on the Mansion roof was no problem for Alicia. For years, unknown to her mother, she had reconnoitered the roof area of the house, partly from curiosity and partly for the thrill she felt when exploring high places in her stocking feet. But traversing the roof with a hose writhing under full water pressure was a different matter entirely.

Since there was no one to help her, Alicia had to unroll the hose to the Mansion's second-story, west-side door, run back in and turn on the water, and then try to drag the wriggling hose up the roof to the ridge line to play water on the blazing fire on the north side of the house. By the time Alicia had struggled with the hose to the ridge, she was soaked. Her sheer party dress was plastered to her body and, as the light of the flames played upon her, she appeared from the ground to be a naked nymph battling the flames of an inferno.

Alicia fought the fire alone for what seemed an eternity. From her high, precarious perch, she first heard and then saw the Kalispell Fire Department galloping down Third Street, with bells sounding and people trailing. And gallop it did, for in 1910 Kalispell offered only horse-drawn fire equipment. Alicia's daring and determination effectively had delayed the spread of the flames. With the help of the Fire Department and the townspeople, the blaze finally was brought under control and then extinguished, but not before the Mansion had suffered extensive damage from fire and water.

The fire had started when sparks from the fireplace ignited the dry leaves of the Virginia Creeper that covered a portion of the house's north wall. On this night, there was a high wind that spread and whipped the flames. The man who gave the warning was driving by almost by accident. He was returning home from nearby Bigfork, after having damaged his wagon along the way. This problem delayed him for more than two hours, but placed him outside the Mansion as the fire started. Moreover, had Alicia not been accustomed to scaling the roof of the house, the fire likely would have destroyed the Mansion.

After the flames were controlled, a small army comprised of almost every able-bodied person in town worked to minimize the water damage. All of the Conrads' blankets, bedding, and camping gear were used to mop up the water on the third floor, to prevent it from seeping to the downstairs rooms. The water was sopped up in the blankets and bedding and passed, by a human chain, to the laundry room, where they were wrung out and passed back for another load of water. Much of the camping bedding sported colorful hues of red, green, and yellow. These colors quickly faded and stained everything and everyone they touched.

By the early hours of the morning, the volunteers had finished their work. After expressing their sorrow to Lettie and Alicia, the neighbors, friends, and strangers who had toiled so long to save the Mansion from even more extensive water damage went home wet, bedraggled, and stained in varying shades of yellow, green, and red.

Alicia and her mother surveyed the damage. Part of the north roof was burned off, and the sky was visible through the void. The third floor and everything in it was soaked and stained. The plaster had fallen in the master bedroom, in Kate's old bedroom to its left, and in Alicia's bedroom to its right. All of the beautiful beds, the floors, and the furniture were covered by a gray mass of cold, soggy plaster. Some water had seeped through to the rooms on the main floor but, because of the efforts of the water-sopping brigade, this damage was not extensive.

Alicia had watched her mother through the ordeal, fearful of the effect that the dreadful evening might produce. She had seen her mother everywhere, helping, directing, giving strength to everyone. She had heard her mother say: "Don't move the furniture out of the house. Move it back from the drip and let it stay." Alicia asked her mother why she did not allow the furniture to be removed, and she replied: "Had it been taken out it would have been damaged or perhaps stolen. If the Mansion went, I wanted the furniture to go with it, so we could make a clean start on everything."

Alicia knew that her mother was worried about business affairs. It was becoming more and more difficult to manage the many interests that had been left by Charles. Greedy people existed who gladly would wrest from her anything that they could. Under these pressures, Alicia feared that the Mansion fire and the extensive damage might be so discouraging to her mother that she would surrender and would lose the things she was trying so courageously to save.

In despair, Alicia said to her mother: "Everything is destroyed. What will we do now?" Lettie took Alicia in her arms, and she who needed comfort became the comforter.

Alicia, we have lost nothing that cannot be repaired or replaced. Life brings adversity and we must be prepared for it. Anyone can crumple and despair when trouble strikes, and that is what certain people expect and hope that we will do. Alicia, you and I have always loved Halloween more than any other season, partly, I suspect, because there is a good bit of the devil in both of us. Each year as Halloween approaches, I long to be able to get on a broom and give vent to all the mischievousness that collects during the year. This year we'll do it. We'll give the greatest Halloween party that ever was. Fate has prepared the house. We will take advantage of our fate and what a party it will be. For some it will give entertainment, and for others it will be a demonstration that we know how to deal with adversity.

Leaving the house to be watched by the faithful men from the stables, Alicia and her mother made their way to the home of Kate. By this time, Kate had become the wife of Charles Van Duzer, and their home was only a short distance away. Here they would live until they could return to the Mansion. During the walk, Lettie was quiet, deep in thought. She slept little, her mind full of plans for the party.

During her fitful night, Lettie Conrad conceived a party theme suitable to the Halloween season, to her mood of despair caused by the fire, and to the courage and hope that the Conrads would recover from the disaster: The Inferno of Alighieri Dante's *Divine Comedy* would be the motif. It would encompass the "Hell" of the fire, the "Purgatory" of the struggle to recover, and the "Paradise" awaiting at the finish of the perilous journey.

Early next morning, Lettie was on the telephone, engaging carpenters, electricians, and workmen. When they had assembled at the Mansion, she started them to work and directed the whole operation as though it were a stage production. No attempt was made to repair the roof, which was left open to the sky. Nor was the fallen plaster removed. For it was to become a stage prop, both on the floor and on the beds and furniture. As Dante reserved the lower regions for hell, so did Lettie. "Hell" would be in the basement. The second floor would be "Purgatory," and the third floor would be "Paradise."

The electricians began to restore the wiring and to install the additional lines and fixtures needed for the lighting effects. The carpenters built a circular stairway in the elevator shaft from the second floor to the basement. Stairs also were constructed from the basement, up through the coal chute, to the outside. Workmen carried and piled furniture, boxes, and crates to create corridors. Seamstresses made shrouds and decorations. Lettie's brother, Hal Stanford, the taxidermist, was caught up in the excitement. He made bats of all size, with cotton-stuffed bodies and cardboard wings, with the veins eerily sketched with white ink.

Each doorway was covered with wet, clammy canvas, then a beaded curtain was wired to give a slight electrical shock as one passed through. The main floor was hung with shrouds and Spanish Moss. The bats were suspended on wires from the ceiling of both the main floor and the second floor.

The mirror at the top of the stairway to the second floor was shrouded. On it was written, in large white letters: "All hope abandon, ye who enter here" — the words from Canto III of "Hell" in the *Divine Comedy*. At the south end of the hallway on the second floor was placed a large, iron witch's cauldron, with lighting effects to simulate a roaring fire beneath it.

The circular stairway within the elevator shaft was dark, with fluttering strings and threads to resemble cobwebs. The doorway from the elevator shaft in the basement was covered with wet, cold, clammy canvas, which enveloped the frightened pilgrim as he pushed his way through — only to be met by a beaded curtain that gave him a shock when he parted it to enter the basement and get into "Hell." The exit from the basement was the steep stairway in the coal chute, again complete with twisting bats and the cobweb effect.

The north bedrooms were open to the sky, and the wet, gray plaster was used in their decorations, to create volcanic mounds and cones. In these rooms, lighted only by the licking flames of the volcanoes, the plaster on the floor was covered with canvas and burlap. This effect produced a wet, uneven, and treacherous trail for the poor pilgrim struggling through purgatory with his feet in the mire and his head among the bats and cobwebs. Meanwhile the wails of lost souls rang in his ears.

The furniture on the third floor, together with packing boxes, crates, and whatever else could be used, created a series of corridors. This route led the way to the three rooms of "Paradise" and to an exterior porch, onto which the pilgrim could step and see a quarter moon, fleeing through a ghostly, clouded sky. The three rooms in "Paradise" included the "Sweetheart's Room," filled with flowers and beautiful scents. Here a beautiful girl swung languidly in a hammock. The second room was the "Hunter's Paradise," draped as a sylvan bower. It contained trophies of the hunt and beautiful birds, prepared by Hal Stanford. The third room was the "Music Room," decorated to present the Euterpe, the Muse of music, and designed to waft beautiful music to the pilgrim, as he climbed from "Purgatory" and into the beautiful, ethereal light of "Paradise."

By Halloween everyone was exhausted, but all was ready. The guest list included anyone who wanted to come. The invitation had been extended by word-of-mouth, by public ads, and by any other manner that could be used to inform the people of the area that they would be welcome at this gathering. For the party was to be the Conrads' way of publicly saying "thank you" to all the people of Kalispell, who had volunteered to save the Mansion from the fire and the water damage.

The party was scheduled for midnight. By 11:30, a throng of people had gathered on the Mansion lawn, each dressed in costume, thereby fulfilling the only condition for entry into the festivities. Precisely at 12:00, the front door was opened, and guests in all manner of costume filed into the Great Hall, into the Music Room, into the Library, into the Dining Room, and into any first-floor space that could accommodate a human body. In the dim light, the bats flew overhead, wafted by strategically placed electric fans. The ghostly shrouds and Spanish Moss, dangling menacingly from the chandeliers, ceilings, and walls, subdued the bravest spirits and produced an eerie quiet.

Suddenly a satanic figure stepped onto the little balcony, extending from Lettie Conrad's bedroom. The ghostly light revealed a demon dressed in shimmering black tights, a black cape, and a horned mask. Slowly he unrolled a scroll and, in a deep, sepulchral voice, intoned.

'Tis now the witching hour of night, when church-yards yawn and graves give up their dead. Here it behooves to leave every fear; it behooves that all cowardice should here be dead. Only those of highest courage and brave heart are destined to find Paradise. Paradise is here tonight but will only be found by those courageous souls who can taste the horrors of Hell and the terrors of Purgatory.

Those souls brave enough to start this dangerous journey should pray for the fortitude and courage to face the perils without succumbing, hopefully then to reach the gates of Paradise.

Be on your way ere perils here enforce your stay! Follow yonder guide and start to pray.

The demon pointed to a guide, dressed as a wayfarer, and then he withdrew. The guide beckoned and slowly led the assembled throng up the stairs, through the flying bats and cobwebs. First to greet the pilgrims' view was the shrouded mirror, with the whited words inscribed, "All hope abandon, ye who enter here."

Then slowly down the hall the silent group wended, to the iron cauldron, with fire blazing. Three crones, dressed as witches, slowly stirred the contents of the huge pot, while they cackled and muttered incantations. Back then the line wound, to the elevator shaft and the tortuous climb down the narrow, darkened stairway to the basement, with every step creaking and the air filled with bats and cobwebs. Finally the group slipped through the clammy curtains to the beaded portiers, which shocked the hands that groped to part them, and gained entrance into Hell.

Once through, the pilgrims stepped onto a wooden platform, laid on ten-gallon kerosene cans, that rolled and swayed like an ocean wave as they made their way to the furnace room. Here the flames of the furnace lighted the glistening torsos of two blackened giants who fed the furnace and cried in broken voices, "More bodies, more bodies."

From this inferno of "Hell," the guide led them up the steep, narrow steps within the coal chute to the outside, then to the northwest corner of the porch, and back into the Mansion by the front door. Here again they fought their way through the clammy opening and the beaded curtains, with their stinging shocks.

Slowly the procession wound up the stairs once more, but this time into "Purgatory" — into the northwest bedroom, walking over the sickenly wet and slick floor and into the inferno of shooting volcanoes. The lighting effects made it appear that flames were shooting and licking from the cones that had been built on the beds and floors. All this presentation was accompanied by cries of anguish, apparently coming from the volcanic cones in which some poor sinner might be burning. The inferno continued into the rooms of Lettie and Alicia, until the pilgrims finally emerged into the hall, where they caught the first glimpse of "Paradise."

Down from the third floor, a shaft of light partially illuminated the stairway. Slowly the guide led them to the stairway and up, up into the ethereal light of "Paradise." Here soft strains of beautiful music replaced the unearthly screams, screeches, and incantations of "Hell" and "Purgatory."

No more bats or cobwebs. No more clammy and shocking curtains. No more wet and rolling walkways. In "Paradise" the paths between the corridors were carpeted with soft, green, grass-like materials. The walks were garlanded with flowers, embedded in the netting that had been used to cover the furniture, crates, and boxes, from which the corridors had been constructed.

In the "Sweetheart Room," the lovely girl in a party dress swayed in her hammock in time with the music. The birds and animals in the "Hunter's Paradise" seemed serene and relaxed, as though they would not be stalked. On the west porch, the clouds were fleecy lambs, gamboling with the quarter moon. All was well in "Paradise," and there was no hint of the trials through which the pilgrims had been led to reach it.

The guide then announced that the pilgrims had withstood the perilous journey so well that they were entitled to join the merriment of the evening. When they returned down the stairs to the first floor, they found that the Great Hall, the Library, and the Dining Room had been converted into a ballroom. In the normal light, the bats, shrouds, and Spanish Moss became festive Halloween decorations. In the Music Room, an orchestra was seated and ready to play, and the fernery was decorated and lighted in the motif of Halloween.

Lettie Conrad greeted her guests and explained that the party was in their honor, as an expression of the deep gratitude she felt for all their help in saving the Mansion on the night of the fire. She told them the party would last until dawn, and there would be food and refreshments all through the night. They were free to unmask or remain masked as they pleased. Thanking them again, Lettie signaled to the orchestra, and the party commenced.

Food, punch, and other light drinks loaded tables, which were placed in the arched areas under the stairs and which were kept filled for the rest of the night. Some of the visitors began to slip away as the night wore on. When the orchestra stopped playing, at the appointed hour, many guests still remained. But they too departed with the arrival of dawn.

When there remained in the house only Lettie Conrad and Alicia, they sat by the fireplace and relived the evening. Both were still exhilerated by the number of guests and their evident enjoyment of the party. Moreover, they delighted in the knowledge that their home had been preserved and that they had shared it with anyone in Kalispell who had wanted to come. Could there be a better gesture of appreciation?

As they walked through the dawn to Kate's house, where they still were staying, both were silent. When they reached the steps Lettie stopped, her face lighted with a smile, and she said, "That was a real Halloween party. There will never be another one like it. But the best part of all is that it ridded my life of a whole bunch of goblins."

CHAPTER 48
Charles Edward Conrad, Jr.

Charles Edward Conrad, Jr., was born in Fort Benton, Montana Territory, in 1876. C. E. Conrad, his father, had arrived in Fort Benton in 1868, so he had been there eight years before the birth of his first child. That the boy's mother was an Indian, there is no doubt, although no record of the birth exists. By Conrad family lore, however — recalled by the youngest daughter, Alicia — the young Indian maiden was a princess, the daughter of a Blackfeet chief. Yet even family lore did not give her a name.

It can be conjectured, with some certainty, that she was beautiful, based upon the known fastidious and discriminating taste of C. E. Conrad, and upon the handsomeness of the son, as recalled by Alicia from the few times she saw him. The first time was at the Arlington Hotel in Hot Springs, Arkansas. The second encounter occurred in Montreal, at the wedding of the young Charles and Marie Blanche Lionais, an attractive French-Canadian girl, which was attended by Charles and Lettie Conrad and Alicia. The third and last meeting of young Charles and Alicia followed her father's funeral in Kalispell, on November 28, 1902, when the first-born son came to learn about his share of his father's estate.

The Indian mother had been converted to Catholicism. She elicited from Charles Conrad the promise that their son would be raised as a Catholic and would be given the same education that a white father normally would provide a white son. Thus Charles E., Jr. received an education that would be considered adequate for that time. He received his education in Montreal, and there he lived from the age of about two.

Charles Conrad and the Blackfeet girl had been married by a Catholic priest, and both considered it a solemn marriage, blessed by the Church, which was intended to last until death parted them. But the deep need of the Indian maiden to remain with her people proved stronger than her marriage vow: she left with her father's band when it moved to Canada to

Charles E. Conrad, Jr. in 1898 Courtesy University of Montana Library

escape the influence of the white man.

The relationships between white men and native women varied on the Montana frontier. Some of the so-called "squaw men" took Indian women often to satisfy a physical need. However, when a white man of higher morals took an Indian wife, it was usually by means of a true marriage, performed by a priest. If the marriage were terminated, it

254

frequently was because the native woman refused to move to the East and to live in the world of the white man. Many white men, such as the fur entrepreneur Alexander Culbertson, remained in the West rather than to forsake their Indian wives and families. That the relationship between Conrad and his Blackfeet wife was of the latter type is indicated by the fact that Conrad gave his name to the mixed-blood son, naming him Charles Edward Conrad, Jr.

How long young Edward Conrad remained in Fort Benton is unknown, but he was not in residence when Alicia Stanford arrived there in 1879. Since he would have been only two years old at that time, and since he did not go with his mother, Conrad apparently placed him in some Catholic school in Montreal, since there was no place in Fort Benton for the adequate care and education of a child. Charles Conrad then was overseeing the Canadian business operations of the I. G. Baker Company, and he could not have cared for a small son himself.

All knowledge of the life of this first-born son has been obliterated, except for those few traces that can be gleaned from the public record. From his signature on the only correspondence that is extant, it is apparent that he used the name Edward. The year of his birth can be established as 1876, by the information contained in the petition for the probate of his father's will. This petition was filed in the Flathead County Courthouse in Kalispell on December 3, 1902. It states that, on that date, Charles E. Conrad, Jr. was 26 years old and a resident of Montreal, Quebec, Canada.

The record also shows that Charles Conrad maintained an interest in his son, even though that son never visited the Conrad home except following the funeral. The inventory of the elder Conrad's estate reveals that, by reason of several promissory notes, the son was indebted to his father for almost $40,000, a sizeable sum in 1902. The same inventory reveals that Edward operated some kind of an import business in Montreal, since it includes promissory notes due from the Conrad Importing Company and from the Porter-Conrad Importing Company, both of Montreal.

In 1900 Edward still was living in Montreal, engaged in a business partnership with a man named Porter. He was contemplating marriage, but believed that he needed financial help for such a venture. He had written to his father for help, but evidently had not received the response he sought. He then wrote to Lettie Conrad, hoping to secure her as an advocate for his cause. This letter was written on March 14, 1900, from Montreal.

My dear Mrs. Conrad: I do not know whether my father tells you of my letters; I hope he does, you could be such a good help to him, for there are subjects that the quick natural conception of woman is more true, unselfish & lenient; the latter I want, especially, I want an advocate; I need it. I have been a black sheep, and like the prodigal, returns, after spending his wealth — that of the Scripture has been a costly payment for experience — whilst, mine is on a very small scale, and not so wicked, in fact, it has been honorable, only with too many friends and too much heart — that I have spent my money and more. Now I see the fatality of such living. If it was not for the bright prospects of my business, my love for a good woman (with your consent, she could be such a good helpmate — my better half) my duty towards you and yours, and, also my partner, I would not stop a minute in this place, but start anew, without the aid of anyone, in another country.

I saw Father Lacombe, Rev. Bro. Jerome, the most clever and worldly man of the Christian Brotherhood, and St. Dominic, a Franciscan, a noted theologist. They urge me to get married. That was my opinion before I saw them, but the importance of such subject cannot be limited to one man's opinion. Mr. Porter is one of the strongest advocates for my settlement, among my friends.

You must not be afraid of my age, or an idea of mine, rather premature. It is a true conviction, I have thought it over a great deal — My candid opinion, it is my salvation. Of course, I am alluding and comparing to my means. I figured the other night my annual expenses, which were shocking, and asked my little sweetheart, how much she could live on comfortably and she came just the half of my amount. From all sides it is the best I can do. It is always better for a business man, he has more interest & interests, steadier and better respect, draws more interest in general. I would like very much to see you down with father, on his next trip, so you can see everything for yourself. I hope I have not taken too much of your time. I think I owe this letter. If I did not I would send it anyway; for the short time I have known you, my greatest respects and admiration have been won without resistence; and I feel proud when some of my friends permit you to be called my mother; I hope I do not offend. It is so nice, it is a world in itself — the word, "mother." When I see the exchange of affection between child & mother, it often makes my eyes water. Give my love to Alicia & tell her my sweetheart is making a doll for her and hope father is well,

Believe, I remain,

Yours very sincerely,

Edward

Lettie Conrad must have been an effective advocate, for the records of Conrad's estate show that, on June 11, 1900, Edward received $11,136.86 from the Conrads. Subsequently he received additional money: August 12, 1901, $1,300.00; November 1, 1901, $7,052.06; October 14, 1901, $3,776.14; April 17, 1902, $1,536.67; July 2, 1902, $1,632.24.

The wedding did occur. The invitations, in French, announced the wedding of Marie Blanche Lionais, daughter of Monsieur and Madame Alfred Lionais, to Charles Edward Conrad, son of Monsieur C. E. Conrad, to be held at Montreal's Catholic Cathedral, on June 27, 1900. The Conrads attended the wedding, as did Alicia. Alicia did not remember the wedding. She did recall the beautiful girl who became the bride of her half-brother. She remembered that this girl played with her on the steep, red-carpeted steps of an elegant house, which was narrow and several stories high.

The marriage apparently did not stabilize Edward and was of short duration, for Edward and Marie were not living together at the time of his death, in 1904.

Edward was almost certainly improvident. Shortly after the probate of his father's estate was commenced, he began his effort to obtain a share of the estate. For this purpose, he engaged the New York City law firm of Steele and Otis.

The will provided that the estate of C. E. Conrad would be held in trust for a period of 11 years, commencing on November 22, 1902 — the date on which the will was signed and only five days before Conrad's death. During this 11-year period, each of the children, including the first-born son, would receive $150 per month from the estate. In 1902, $150 represented a rather substantial amount, more than the monthly salary for the president of an ordinary small bank. But this sum was not sufficient for Edward. The will also provided that, if any of the children of C. E. Conrad died childless before the termination of the trust (November 22, 1913), then the deceased child's share of the estate would be forfeited, and that share would be divided among the surviving Conrad children.

Charles E. Conrad, Jr. did not like either of these provisions. First, he wanted to receive his full share of the estate immediately, but the will's provision for the 11-year trust prevented this aim. Second, if he could not receive all of his money immediately, he wanted to be able to borrow money and apply his share of the estate as collateral to the loan. But the will's forfeiture provision prevented this intention. For no substantial sums could be borrowed against an interest subject to forfeiture, should he die without issue.

In February, 1904, Edward's New York City attorneys, acting through Kalispell attorney, W. B. Rhodes, filed suit in the estate probate proceedings to have these two provisions of the will declared invalid. To finance this effort, Edward assigned to Steele and Otis a one-tenth share of his interest in the estate. Young Conrad also managed somehow to borrow $10,000 from the Guaranty Trust Company of New York City, for he had assigned to that bank his remaining interest in his father's estate as collateral for this loan.

The trial of the petition to invalidate the repugnant provisions of the will occurred in October, 1904. Attorney Otis arrived from New York for the trial, representing not only Edward Conrad but also his own law firm, Steele and Otis, and the Guaranty Trust Company of New York. All of young Conrad's hopes to obtain any immediate money from the estate were dashed when Judge D. F. Smith, on October 31, 1904, ruled that the provisions of the will were valid. This ruling confirmed that Charles, Jr. could receive nothing from his father's estate, except the $150 each month, unless he were living on November 22, 1913.

The trial, however, did produce some beneficial results for Edward. During its course, all of the persons involved in the deceased's estate signed a stipulation acknowledging that Charles Edward Conrad, Jr. was, in fact, the legitimate son of Charles E. Conrad. Also at this time Lettie Conrad must have made some type of financial settlement with Edward. Alicia, who then was 14 years old, remembered Lettie saying that she had given Edward the proceeds of one of his father's life-insurance policies, in the amount of $50,000. Some confirmation of this settlement is indicated by Lettie's final account, filed at the close of her administration of the estate, on June 1, 1923. This account states that, on October 31, 1904,

> Charles Edward Conrad, for a valuable consideration, conveyed all of his title and interest in said estate and said allowance (of $150 per month) to James T. Stanford and that thereafter the said James T. Stanford conveyed the same interest to Charles Davenport Conrad and Catherine Conrad, who in turn conveyed one-third of said interest to Alicia Conrad McCutcheon.

The date of October 31, 1904 was an ominous one in the lives of Charles Edward Conrad, Jr. and his creditors. On this day, Judge Smith ruled that all of the provisions of Charles E. Conrad's will were valid. This determination destroyed the hopes of Edward and his creditors that he might immediately receive his share of the estate against the provisions of the trust. On this day also, Edward assigned to Lettie Conrad's brother all interest in and rights to his father's estate. The Halloween of 1904 was a witches' day for Edward, and his future did not appear bright.

Edward returned to Montreal, having sold all interest in his father's estate and knowing that this source of income was depleted, including the monthly payments of $150. Whatever compensation he received did not last long. On September 13, 1905, his father-in-law, A. Lyonaise, wrote to Lettie Conrad.

> It has been my painful duty to appraise you, on the first of September, of the sudden death of Mr. C. E. Conrad, son of your late husband. Charlie died suddenly on the morning of the 1st of September. Both my daughter and myself understand that certain transactions have taken place between the estate of your late husband and Charlie, but what the nature of these transactions were are (sic) unknown to us. We would certainly be grateful to you to let us know what those transactions were. The situation as it now

stands shows that Charlie left his wife penniless, having mortgaged and disposed of, long ago for his own use, the house and household furnishings given to my daughter by your late husband. The creditors of Charlie are not numerous and do not seek very large amounts, but they are restless and are trying to dispossess my daughter of even the few household effects left. This is the situation that I thought it my duty to bring to your knowledge. Respectfully yours, A. Lyonaise.

If Lettie Conrad answered this letter, her response was not satisfactory. Either Lettie asked her brother-in-law, William G. Conrad, to answer Lyonaise or, failing to hear from Lettie, Lyonaise solicited help directly from William. For, on October 10, 1905, he wrote again to William.

Dear Sir: I acknowledge receipt of yours of the 3rd inst., for which I thank you.

I have now all the information which I was seeking. It stands on record that my late son-in-law sold to the brother of his step-mother his whole interest, then present and future, for the sum of $88,000, less $38,000 of indebtedness to the said estate.

According to the best American commercial agencies, at the time of the death of the late C. E. Conrad, Sr., his estate was worth in the neighborhood of two-and-a-half million dollars. The commercial agencies then reporting that, if carefully carried on, the estate would net, when opened at the time of the youngest child becoming of age (1913), in the neighborhood of three-and-a-half to four million dollars.

My son-in-law was heir to one-eighth of the estate of his father; in other words, some $300,000, with a possibility of this amount being increased to $500,000 eleven years hence.

By the transaction entered into with my son-in-law, Mrs. C. E. Conrad, Sr. becomes heir to my son-in-law's share of the estate of his father (sic). Deducting the amount paid Charlie, she stands to make a profit of $262,000, and a probability and possibility of making a profit of $462,000.

Since the death of my son-in-law, I have paid each and every one of the creditors who had claims against my son-in-law and my daughter jointly. I have also paid all funeral expenses, etc., and have taken my daughter back with me. I have thus relieved the name of Conrad in our part of this world, of any indebtedness with which the name of my daughter could be coupled. I have not paid Charlie Conrad's old debts nor his personal debts at the time of his death, and I do not intend paying them either.

You are aware that the late C. E. Conrad, Sr. had given a $10,000 house to my daughter, which house my son-in-law succeeded in mortgaging and finally selling for his own benefit.

Considering the enormous amount of money which reverts back to Mrs. C. E. Conrad, Sr. by the death of my son-in-law, I submit to you that, as a simple matter of justice, Mrs. Conrad, Sr. should relieve the name of Conrad from any indebtedness in our country.

At the present moment, the known debts do not amount to more than a couple of thousand dollars. Several creditors (owed) the amount of several hundred dollars — about $1,200 — have seized the horse and carriages which my daughter is unable to defend, although they were supposed to be her property.

No indication exists that the widow of Edward received anything further from the Conrad estates or the family. In his letter to William, Lyonaise said that the commercial agencies estimated that the Conrad estate, "if carefully carried on, should be worth in the neighborhood of three-and-a-half to four million dollars." The key words here are "if carefully carried on," for, by 1913, the estate had shrunk considerably.

During his life, Charles Edward Conrad, Jr. received generous financial help from his father, far more than might have been expected. Yet he sought more than just financial help. His only extant letter, quoted in this chapter, shows a longing for a mother and for family ties. The handwriting in this letter is similar to the script of his father and indicates a background of some culture. What he did from the time his mother left Fort Benton, about 1878, until the first trace of him appears in the records (1897) is not known. But he never became a true part of the Conrad family. To Alicia, he was a handsome apparition, which sometimes appeared when she traveled with her father and mother, and a shadowy bridegroom in a wedding ceremony she did not remember.

No record remains of Marie Lionais Conrad, the little wife whom Edward had hoped would bring order and stability to his life. However, this task proved to be beyond her capability. She did not bear him any children. Lettie Conrad's final account in her husband's estate recites that Edward died without issue.

Edward's death perhaps was timely, for his life span was coextensive with the period during which he was able to receive money either from his father or from his father's estate, upon which he had become almost totally dependent. His life must not have been easy. He belonged nowhere, nor to anyone. His single extant letter, written to Lettie, reveals the depth of his longing for family ties. He never knew a mother, but made Lettie Conrad a mother image. Yet this projected relationship was so remote and unreciprocated that it could produce in Edward only feelings of hurt and rejection.

Charles Conrad believed himself responsible for his elder son, at least financially. But there developed no indication of fatherly warmth, love, or even acceptance. In his will, Charles referred to Edward not as his son but as "that certain half-breed Indian known as Charles E. Conrad, Junior, who has been educated by me in Canada."

Edward's Blackfeet mother thought that her son would be rejected by the native community and would fare better being raised by his white father. But rejection was the fate in store for Charles Edward Conrad, Jr. Circumstances shaped his life, and perhaps he managed it about as well as might have been expected.

CHAPTER 49
Charles Davenport Conrad
I. The Early Years

Charles Davenport Conrad was born at Fort Benton on September 29, 1882, the year that business activity in the little town was at its height. Davenport was a highly regarded name in Lettie Conrad's family, and it was her middle name. The Conrads would have named this son after his father, but the name already had been given to his Blackfeet son, the first-born. When the Conrads left Fort Benton to reestablish their home in Kalispell, Charley was eight years old. He had grown up during the years when Fort Benton was at its peak, and he saw its decline. Until 1888, when the Conrads' Canadian business was sold to the Hudson's Bay Company, C. E. spent most of his time in Canada, overseeing the lucrative trade north of the border. During these years, Lettie was the dominant influence in the life of young Charley.

At this time, school in Fort Benton was held for periods varying from four to six months. Thus Charley had plenty of time to spend at the docks, experiencing the excitement of the arrivals and departures of the Missouri River steamboats. He became a strong, brave lad, for Mollie Sedgwick, who grew up in Fort Benton, recalled the Charley once saved her life by diving in and pulling her from the Missouri River when she tumbled off the dock. The boy was fascinated by the new people who arrived at the levee. He looked anxiously for new boys his age. The ox teams also held his interest, and he followed them through town and up the steep embankment out of the river bottom. On this tough pull, the bullwhackers used their most colorful language, which could increase considerably the vocabulary of a young boy.

Life in the raw village of Kalispell would have seemed a bit dull to a boy accustomed to the excitement of Fort Benton. But in the Flathead Valley Charley became interested in hunting and fishing and remained an ardent follower of these sports for all of his life. His younger sister, Alicia, said that Charles was at his best in the out-of-doors: "He hunted and fished a lot and was good at them both. He was happy doing something he was good at, and he was only good at athletics and out-of-doors things." She noted that business bored Charley, and that he made no effort to learn business or to excel in commercial activities.

The boy's love of sports came from, and was fostered by, his father. Several letters from father to son tell of efforts to enhance the hunting and fishing in the area. On January 30, 1900, C. E. wrote,

> Yesterday I received four dozen quail from Wichita, Kansas. We put them in the wire cages where we kept the pheasants, about fifteen got through the wire netting before we had it properly fixed with a mosquito bar over the wires. Perhaps it is just as well to have some in the woods near the barn. The balance I will turn loose on the Cornish Ranch about April 15th.

On May 6, 1900, Conrad wrote again:

> Yesterday your mother and I were in the garden and a quail sang out in the woods, "bob-white, bob-white." We shipped in over twenty dozen this spring. In a few years we will have fine shooting.

The quail were one of Charles Conrad's few failures. Mild weather permitted their survival for one winter, but they died in the cold and snow the following winter. The fine shooting predicted by Conrad did not materialize. The sportsman decided that, for quail hunting, it would be necessary to travel to where quail were established, not to try to stock the Flathead Valley, where the weather was inhospitable to them. The soft call of "bob-white, bob-white" was heard no more in the Conrad garden.

As early as 1900, C. E. Conrad talked of stocking the Flathead Valley's waters with fish. He wrote to Charley:

> We have been trying lately to have the lakes in Flathead County stocked with Lake Superior Whitefish. We had the President of our board of trade write to (Montana) Senator (Thomas H.) Carter to urge the Fish Commissioner in Washington to send out some for that purpose.

But, even in 1900, bureaucracy, if not rampant, was casting its eye toward a newly developing part of the nation to engulf in its tentacles. The Fish Commissioner, from his lofty post in Washington, D.C., wrote that the whitefish found in St. Mary's Lake — just east of the Continental Divide, which separates the Columbia River watershed from that of the Missouri River — were the same as those whitefish found in the headwaters of the Columbia River.

Conrad, in his letter to Charley, continued.

> Is it not strange that our government is so lacking in information. We

intend to send our Commissioner, as soon as they can be obtained, a Whitefish from both lakes. Evidently he has not taken the trouble to look up the maps to see that St. Mary's Lake, while in the United States, outlets into Lake Winnipeg, where Whitefish abound. The balance of the waters of Eastern Montana flow into the Missouri River, and no Whitefish have ever been in that stream or its tributaries.

In the same letter, C. E. told his son, "We expect to stock Foy's Lake with bass this coming spring." This planting, in a small lake near Kalispell, could be made without permission from the Fish Commissioner in Washington. Conrad's death, in 1902, deprived him of an intimate knowledge of the bureaucracy that has become such an unwelcome part of modern business life and private life.

Charles D. Conrad at St. John's Military Academy, circa 1900 Courtesy University of Montana Library

During his first years in Kalispell, Charley shared in the excitement of the construction of the new Conrad home, which was completed in the autumn of 1895. Lettie continued to be his predominant parent, as the business activities of C. E. became ever more distant and demanding. Charley finished grade school in Kalispell and would have preferred to attend high school there, but both parents wanted better things for their son. They especially wanted him to attend Yale College in Connecticut. So they enrolled him in St. John's Military Academy at Manlius, New York. The school was a long way from home for a small boy, and he was very lonesome. However, he soon became interested in football and played well. Thus Charley visited his family only when the school vacations could permit the long train trip in each direction.

From St. John's, Charles enrolled at Phillips Exeter Academy in Andover, Massachusetts, a preparatory school for Yale. Here again, football was his main interest, with academics a very distant second. Letters from the Conrads to their son refer to almost constant supplemental tutoring in many of his subjects.

Charley did not like school, and he held no desire to attend Yale. On December 31, 1900, Norman L. Bassett, one of the instructors at Exeter, wrote to Charles Conrad. The purpose of the letter was to suggest that Conrad urge his son to attend college. Bassett wrote that he had talked with Charley about Yale: "He told me that he would like to go to college and that you are very willing. But he fears that a preparation at this stage of the game is too difficult for him and not within the range of possibility." However, Bassett wrote, "I assure you, as I have already assured him, that it is not only possible, but is a comparatively easy matter."

On February 7, 1901, C. E. Conrad replied to Bassett.

I have been absent for over a month and on my return find yours of Dec. 31st. I am very much obliged for the interest you take in my son; nothing would please me more than for him to go to Yale. As you have been helping him with his Latin, if there is any other branch in which he needs coaching, I will be only too glad to pay extra to any one of the faculty who will help him along.

As I said, your letter came during my absence. Charles was at home at that time. His mother showed him your letter and he expressed himself as being quite willing to go to Yale, if it did not take too long for him to prepare for that college.

On the same day C. E. wrote his son.

Nothing would make mother and I (sic) happier than to have you go through Yale, and if you do go through it will be a source of great satisfaction to yourself. If you need coaches in other branches of your studies, employ them. I will not mind the expense as long as you are being benefited by the expenditure. Owing to so little snow this winter, the quail have done well. Farmers report seeing them in numbers every day.

Conrad did not spare any expense for his son's education. Each summer a tutor from Exeter arrived to spend the vacation and to help Charley with his studies. Alicia remembered that her brother instructed the tutor in summer activites in the Flathead Valley, and that the tutor often learned as much as did the student.

Charles Conrad was more than willing to spend whatever money was needed to benefit Charley's progress — he also was willing to use his considerable influence for that purpose. However, nothing seemed to arouse in Charley any desire for education. He traveled to Kalispell from the East for his father's funeral in November, 1902. He then returned to Massachusetts to finish the year at Exeter. When he came home in the summer, he was home to stay, through with education. He had attained the equivalent of a high-school diploma. Had Charley graduated from Yale, this accomplishment probably would not have produced for him what the parents hoped. For he already had received far more education than his father. The fact that Charley would not follow his father in the management of the Conrad business empire was not the result of his lack of education.

Lettie Conrad made an unsuccessful attempt to persuade her son to return to school the following fall. Charley was abetted in his determination to avoid education by his uncle, Hal Stanford, who urged him to stay and help Lettie with the management of the extensive Conrad business holdings. Charley's assistance was unnecessary, though, since William G. Conrad was the surviving partner in all of the Conrad businesses. W. G. continued as the managing partner until his death in 1914. However, Stanford's counsel was the advice that young Charley wanted to hear.

A place was created for Charley in the Conrad National Bank of Kalispell, but his uncle, William G., assumed the Bank's presidency. At the time of C. E. Conrad's death, his estate became the owner of a majority of the stock of the Bank. The prerogatives of this majority ownership devolved upon Lettie Conrad, as the executrix of the estate and as sole trustee of the trust created by Conrad's will.

An uneasy relationship existed between W. G. and Lettie Conrad during the interval between the deaths of the two brothers (1902-1914). W. G. remained president of the Bank from 1902 until his death, even though he knew that Lettie wanted her son to serve in that capacity. However, a financially interested uncle could make a more dispassionate evaluation of the business abilities of a nephew than an overindulgent mother could make of a son. Lettie Conrad wisely avoided a fight with a brother-in-law who controlled the partnership that owned most of the assets of C. E.'s estate. Whatever her reasons, William continued as president of the Bank until his death left the office vacant.

The death of William G. Conrad in 1914, removed the only obstacle between Charles Davenport Conrad and the presidency of the Conrad National Bank. He was installed as the Bank president following the death of his uncle and thus began the career that would help to dissipate the fortune amassed by his father.

The Conrad National Bank of Kalispell provided Charley with the only formal employment that he attempted during his life. While Lettie lived and could assert control, his position at the Bank was secure, and he was free from any real degree of responsibility. Alicia remembered that Charley enjoyed his bachelorhood. He maintained an apartment in downtown Kalispell. Parties held there became well-known for their frequency and boisterousness, and for the questionable character of the women attending. Alicia said that, if her mother were aware of the parties, she chose to ignore them. Yet Alicia knew that her mother worried about Charley. Lettie hoped that he would marry and that marriage would bring stability to his life, give him a sense of responsibility, and cause him to settle down.

Charley was considered the most eligible bachelor in Kalispell, a distinction he was not anxious to relinquish. However, one of Kalispell's most attractive and ambitious girls determined to marry Charley. Alicia recalled that Kokoa Baldwin came to Lettie Conrad and announced that she had decided to wed Charley. Lettie, perplexed, asked how long they had been going together. Kokoa replied that they had not yet dated, for she had just recently decided to marry Charley.

Kokoa was the daughter of one of Kalispell's most prominent families, headed by M. D. Baldwin. She was spoiled, headstrong, spirited, and stimulating. She also was accustomed to having her own way and getting what she wanted. In this case she wanted Charley, and she began a courtship that was lively, tempestuous, and successful.

Kokoa's announcement to Lettie Conrad was prophetic. On March 12, 1907, Charles Davenport Conrad and Kokoa Baldwin were married in Kalispell's Christ Church Episcopal. The marriage of the children of these two prominent families produced the most lavish social event in Kalispell's short history.

The bride was the daughter of Major D. Baldwin, a former Indian agent on the Blackfeet Indian Reservation, who had established a law practice in Kalispell. His beloved daughter had been christened Kokoa, the Blackfeet word for "little girl." She was a high-spirited, attractive, intelligent, and rather willful young lady, and she was doted upon by her father as was Charley by his mother.

Dressed in a princess gown of chiffon and in a veil decorated with orange blossoms, the bride walked down the aisle of the Conrad family church at "half after six" that Friday evening to solemnize an apparently fairy-tale wedding. But the proximity to the Ides of March cast its shadow on the future of the match: a bitter divorce, some eight years later, left a son and a daughter to spend much of their childhood with their grandparents.

Kokoa Baldwin, circa 1907 Courtesy Joan Baldwin Zalewski

Divorce seemed inconceivable, based upon the Kalispell *Inter Lake's* frothy account of the wedding festivities, published on March 15.

The church was beautifully embowered with southern semilax and in front of the altar hung the wedding bell of semilax interwoven with white flowers. The music of Mendolsohn measured the approach of Miss Catherine Conrad, the bridesmaid, Miss Lucille Whiteside, the flower girl, and the bride, accompanied by her father. The bride carried a shower bouquet of white roses and lilies of the valley, as she walked to meet her bridegroom at the altar.

A wreath of semilax, white carnations, and roses decorated the Baldwin family home the scene of a reception given by the bride's parents following the wedding. Little misses acted as attendants for the guests, and young lady friends of the bride served them in the dining room.

Charley and Kokoa Conrad left on the evening train, the newspaper said, for a stay of several weeks in Ohio and New York, before returning to Kalispell to live. When asked who paid for the honeymoon, Alicia answered, "Why, Mother, of course. Charley had no money of his own."

II. Marriage and Later Life

Upon the newlyweds' return to Kalispell, they found that Lettie Conrad had created an apartment for them in the Mansion from the first-floor suite of rooms that had been occupied by the grandmothers during their lives. For a long period, both Kokoa and Charles were quite satisfied with this arrangement. Kokoa was a lady of leisure. All of her needs and wants, as well as those desires of her new husband, were supplied by Lettie's staff of domestic help. Kokoa could ride, hunt, fish, or spend her time as she chose. Lettie Conrad then purchased one of the first automobiles in Kalispell, and her daughter-in-law was enthralled. The car quickly became hers, and thus the scope of her daily wanderings was enlarged proportionately.

The couple lived at the Conrad family home for almost two years, enjoying a rather extended-honeymoon mode of living. Yet this arrangement eventually palled, and Lettie purchased and furnished for them a home of their own, one block from the Mansion. Soon after the move into the new home, Charley and Kokoa's first child was born. Still, Kokoa was loath to relinquish her gypsy-like outdoor life. So Lettie hired two Hungarian women to care for the child and for Kokoa's home. In addition she paid for remodeling the third floor of the new home, to provide living quarters for the live-in help. Kokoa was free again.

During the first years of their marriage, Charley and Kokoa's mutual love of the out-of-doors created a bond that united them. Kokoa had grown up with a love of sports, instilled by her father. M. D. Baldwin and his daughter had spent countless hours hunting and fishing during her childhood. Thus the happiest times during an unhappy marriage were those hours that Kokoa and Charley spent in the pursuit of these out-of-doors activities, in which both excelled and were competent.

Charley and Kokoa had two children. A girl, born on April 17, 1908, was named Catherine. But, like her mother, she was called Kokoa. A boy, born on May 14, 1909, was named after his grandfather, Charles Edward Conrad. This son, although named for his grandfather, was called William, or "Billy," after his uncle, William G. Conrad.

The young boy was beloved by his parents and received more attention than did his sister. In his twenty-first year, Billy was killed in a tragic hunting accident. He had asked his father to go bird hunting with him, but Charley declined, for business reasons. So Billy went alone to hunt geese and ducks on a slough east of Kalispell. He tired and sat on a log to rest and, in some manner, his shotgun discharged, the load striking him in the chest. He was killed instantly.

The newspaper account of Billy's death notes that he was not missed until the following morning, because both his parents and his grandparents thought that he had spent the night in another's home. Billy was found by his father the next morning. Charley was grief-stricken by the death of his son. For the rest of his life he was haunted by the thought that, had he accompanied his son when asked, the terrible accident might not have happened.

Billy Conrad Courtesy Joan Baldwin Zalewski

The daughter, Kokoa, never received the affection that was given to Billy. She was a lonely child, never enjoying a real home after the separation of her parents. She did experience a happy marriage and seemed to sense the historical significance of the Conrad family. It was she who found, among her father's effects, the letters that C. E. and Lettie had written to Charley when he was in school in the East. This correspondence she saved and donated to the Montana Historical Society before her death. The preserved letters are a rich source of the history of the Conrad family and of the times in which they lived. These communications, and the letters that C. E. Conrad wrote to his wife, comprise the only correspondence that has been preserved. That no extant letters exist from Charley, while he was attending school, would indicate that much of the family correspondence was lost through neglect or vandalism, since the letters from C. E. and Lettie to their son note that he wrote to them regularly.

Kokoa Conrad Courtesy Joan Baldwin Zalewski

The children born to Charley and Kokoa did nothing to stabilize their marriage. The indulgence that both parents had known since infancy made it impossible for them to spread their love beyond themselves. With Kokoa able to shift to others the responsibilities for homemaking and child raising, a real home never was created for either parents or children.

The marriage became progressively acrimonious. Kokoa suspected that Charley was entertaining other women in the downtown apartment, which he had maintained since his bachelor years. Kokoa's suspicions probably were well-founded. Alicia said of her brother,

> He got into an awful lot of trouble with women, girls, and older women that I remember. Mother used my $150 (monthly estate payments) which had been deposited until I would need them. But she used that all up on Charley, to fish him out of scrapes and to pay off the parents of the girls.

The morning after one of Charley's outings, Kokoa rode her horse to the Bank, flung the reins to the janitor, and entered. The Bank was filled with people. Charley was seated at his desk, visible to customers in the lobby. Kokoa approached the desk in a normal manner, but, when she came close, she screamed, "I'll teach you not to go whoring around with other women." Then she started to horsewhip Charley with her riding crop. She beat him until the stunned crowd recovered and responded. Some of the patrons subdued Kokoa and spared Charley any further humiliation.

On May 14, 1915, Kokoa filed for divorce, alleging mental cruelty. She charged that her husband nagged her constantly about financial matters, that he refused to take her to social events, that he stayed away from home for nights on end, and that he choked and struck her "without just provocation." The divorce was granted. The decree provided that Kokoa would receive the family home and its furnishings, as well as the sum of $12,000 and that each parent would be entitled to the children one-half of the time.

Following the divorce, Kokoa went to Hollywood, California, lured by the hope of starring in motion pictures, a dream shared by many young women of the time. Testimony in subsequent court records indicates that Kokoa held sufficient money to establish herself and the children in an apartment and to hire a housekeeper. Stardom eluded her, but she did enter the fringes of the movies, playing bit parts and acting as a stand-in for female western-film stars, who could swoon and flutter their eyes at Tom Mix and William S. Hart, but who could not ride horses or fall off cliffs in the convincing manner dictated by the script.

As the Conrad family fortunes ebbed in Kalispell, so did the money

Kokoa had been receiving. On August 13, 1919, Kokoa returned to court, asking for help in the support of the children, who had resided with her since the divorce. The hearing concerning Kokoa's request for child support sparked additional acrimony and accusations. In a written statement, Margaret Wallace Neilson described what she had observed, while employed as a housekeeper for Kokoa in Hollywood. Kokoa, according to Neilson, neglected her children, smoked and drank too much, and entertained men in her home at hours which implied more than mere sociability. Neilson also alleged:

> On the date of August 11, 1918, on which the said Kokoa Baldwin shot herself in the left breast in the den of her residence on El Centro Street, Hollywood, it so happened that I was in Santa Monica on this particular day, it being my day off. However, she stated to me afterwards that she had premeditated the shooting and had planned the same, a week before committing the deed, giving as a reason for shooting herself that it would bring money from her former husband, Charles Conrad, for the benefit of the children.

The presiding judge in the case granted little credence to Neilson's statement, saying that the sworn statement was "intermixed with facts and conclusions and irrelevant matter" and was "of little or no value," particularly because it was taken without an opportunity for cross-examination.

The judge submitted written findings in the case, two of which are particularly relevant.

1. That the defendant, Charles D. Conrad, is a man of integrity, morality, and good standing in the community in which he lives, and that his home surroundings are of the best; that since the rendition of the decree of divorce between him and the plaintiff, up to November 1, 1918, he has failed to contribute to the support of said children any sum whatever, except a few bills of small amounts paid in the City of Los Angeles. That notwithstanding the fact that the decree of divorce entitled him to the custody of said children one-half of the time, he, at no time from May 14, 1915, up to the commencement of this hearing, demanded of the plaintiff said children or their possession or custody; that his attitude towards the said children has apparently been one of indifference to their welfare. That he has recently been married to a woman other than the plaintiff and is now living with her.

2. That the plaintiff, Kokoa B. Conrad, the mother of the children, is a woman of good moral character and has shown herself to be an exceptionally good mother to the children; she, however, seems to be over-emotional and tempermental, and has, since the rendition of said decree, been married and divorced, and has taken up the motion-picture business and intends to follow this as a means of livelihood, and in order to do so, intends residing on the Pacific Coast and outside the jurisdiction of this court. That the child, Kokoa Baldwin, is nearing the age of twelve years,

and Billy Conrad is nearing the age of eleven years, and they are both children of more than ordinary intelligence for their ages, and show by their demeanor that they have been well and properly reared, and have had school advantages commensurate with their ages. Both of said children express a wish to live with their mother rather than their father. Since July, 1919, the said children have been residing with the plaintiff's mother and father, Mr. and Mrs. Major Baldwin, in the City of Kalispell. That the defendant, C. D. Conrad and his present wife are residing with his mother, Mrs. A. D. Conrad, his sister and her husband, Mr. and Mrs. Van Duser, and another sister in the City of Kalispell. That the defendant, Charles D. Conrad, has not demanded the custody of said children, but has rather shown by his conduct that he did not want them with him between May 4, 1915, and November 1, 1918, and that the plaintiff has been required to pay for their maintenance, education, and support during all of this time.

Kokoa Baldwin Conrad in Hollywood costume Courtesy Joan Baldwin Zalewski

Major Baldwin, Charles D. Conrad and Billy Conrad, circa
1911 Courtesy Joan Baldwin Zalewski

The judge concluded not to change the provisions of the original
decree regarding the custody of the children, and thereby continued to
give each parent the right to have the children one-half of the time. But
he also stipulated that the children should not be removed from Montana without the consent of the court and that, during the time they were
in the custody of Kokoa, they remain with her father and mother, the
Baldwins.

Following the court hearing in 1919, Kokoa returned to California,
leaving the children with her parents. Sometime in 1916, possibly in a
spirit of revenge toward Charley, she had married Royal A. Beall, who
maintained some minor involvement with the movie industry. This
marriage was short-lived since, at the court hearing in 1919, she reverted
to the name of Kokoa Baldwin Conrad. After 1917, she abandoned any
further attempt at a movie career and settled in San Diego. Here she
apparently drifted for some time. In 1922 the Kalispell judge gave her

permission to take the children with her to live in San Diego. After this time, the children were shuffled back and forth among Kokoa, Charley, and Kokoa's parents.

Kokoa returned to Kalispell, following the death of her son in 1930. She opened a small shop, which she called "The Farmer's Market." She continued to pursue her outdoor activities, but her grief at the death of her son was heavy, for she had loved him deeply, as a favorite child.

Kokoa's life did not include the happy ending that might have been portended by the elaborate Kalispell wedding at which the belle of the town married its most eligible bachelor. Her life was filled with turmoil, bitterness, strife, and grief, none of which did her upbringing equip her to handle.

Kokoa Baldwin Conrad died on January 3, 1932. The *Daily Inter Lake* account of her death listed the cause as a cerebral hemorrhage, "which it was believed resulted from the violent exercise (engaged in) while skiing on New Year's Day." Locally rumors of suicide gained some credence, probably because of her attempt at suicide in California some years earlier.

Kokoa was buried in the Baldwin family plot in the Conrad Memorial Cemetery. Her gravestone gives her name as "Kokoa Baldwin." She returned in death not only to the family name, but also to the family burial ground. Her son, Billy, is buried in the Conrad family mausoleum, which stands at the east end of the cemetery. Her daughter, Kokoa, is buried at Libby, Montana, with her husband, Henry Hammer.

Perhaps it is fitting that, in death, Kokoa rejoined her father, with whom she spent the most truly happy years of her life. It may be fitting also that they lie buried near a spot where the two Baldwins had spent many contented hours hunting for birds and game and fishing in the stream that glides by the foot of the hill.

On July 14, 1919, Charles D. Conrad married Agnes Hannaman, who recently had moved to the Flathead Valley to live with her brother, the contractor for a new post office in Kalispell. A month after this marriage, motivated somewhat by pique, Kokoa filed the suit asking more money for herself and for the children. The new bride honeymooned on the acrimony and bitterness produced at that court proceeding.

Charley's second marriage developed more smoothly than the first. The change was due less to any transformation in Charley, than to the fact Agnes was more complacent and tolerant than was Kokoa. Charley remained a heavy drinker. Even though Prohibition was in effect, liquor was plentiful, supplied by "rum runners" who secreted liquor across the Canadian border, only about 70 miles to the north.

Mrs. Charles (Agnes) Conrad in music room and front hall of
Conrad Mansion, circa 1919 Courtesy Montana Historical Society

With Lettie, Charley continued to direct the Conrad Bank and the
family property, and neither the Bank nor the Conrad holdings prospered under his management. While Lettie lived, the family property
remained in the name of the estate. As executrix and trustee, she was
able to exercise control over its disposition. However, the estate property
always was available to Lettie to extricate her son from any of the
predicaments brought on by his bad judgment and frequent peccadillos.

Charles did not possess the ability, the temperament, the integrity, or
the character of his father. During his tenure as president of the Conrad
Bank, many loans were approved on the basis of friendship, sympathy,
and self-interest. Alicia loved her brother. For a time she, like her
mother, was blind to his faults. To Alicia, Charley was "a very handsome
boy. I thought he was beautiful. He was tall, broad-shouldered, strongly
built, with fine hands and feet, and bowlegs, and he was a very, very
handsome young man." As the property left by C. E. Conrad dissipated,
though, Alicia saw her brother more clearly. She said of him: "As bank
president, he was a failure. He was loaning money to his friends and
getting a kickback on every loan he made." Still the Conrad Bank
sustained no losses. For Lettie Conrad bought the bad loans from the
Bank. To this end she used the dwindling resources of the family, and
thereby she concealed the mistakes and misadventures of her son. Always she tried to exculpate him for the consequences of his acts. For this
purpose a corporation was formed, named the Montana-Idaho Investment Company. With money supplied by Lettie, this corporation bought
the bad loans from the Conrad National Bank. Thus the Bank sustained
no loss, and Charley was spared any trouble with bank examiners.

Despite the growing evidence of her son's inability to manage the affairs of the Bank and of his general lack of personal responsibility, Lettie could not bring herself to replace him. For, as long as Lettie lived, the family continued to own the majority interest in the Bank, and Charley was retained as its president. During her lifetime, Lettie could exercise some restraint on her son — for she, as executrix and trustee, had to sign all of the documents relating to the family property. Yet, the knowledge of her impending death spurred Lettie to plan for the protection of the family property. By the action she took, she unwittingly granted Charley almost complete control of the remaining property.

Conrad National Bank of Kalispell, early 1950s, now First Interstate Bank of Kalispell Courtesy First Interstate Bank of Kalispell

CHAPTER 50
Catherine Conrad

Catherine Conrad inherited from her grandmother, Catherine Coggin Stanford, a great musical talent, but her self-indulgence and love of a good time were acquired traits, not previously evidenced in any of the older Conrads or the Stanfords.

Kate, as she was called from childhood, was born in Fort Benton on June 12, 1885, and was five years old when the family moved to the Flathead Valley. Alicia included a description of Kate in a discourse on hair coloring.

> She had a lovely peaches-and-cream skin during her early life and during the time she spent in school in the East. It was a lovely color and, of course, people didn't use makeup or artificial anything then, except a particular class of women that did. But that was taboo — no lipstick, not even powder.
>
> During her early years and when she was in the East, Kate was a blond. Like everyone else who came west, her blond hair darkened, and it was a rich brown — not a red brown, but a rich sort of chestnut. This happened to Aunt Carolyn, Ashby's wife, too. She had been a blond, and there were hardly any natural blonds, and no artificial blonds, so though they might come from the East with golden hair, and did, in a short time it was brown. I don't know why that would be, but it was consistently true.

Kate attended grade school in Kalispell. She was then sent to the Hills Academy, a girls' school in Spokane, Washington, where she received the equivalent of a high-school education. From Hills she enrolled in the Delafield-Colvin Finishing School, in Boston, Massachusetts, a very exclusive girls' school, where young women from wealthy families were taught the social graces.

Kate developed a beautiful soprano voice. While at school in Boston, she took voice training at the Boston Conservatory, where her voice so impressed one Dr. Whitney that he wanted Kate to travel to Italy for more training. Whitney told C. E. and Lettie Conrad that Kate possessed great

Catherine (Kate) Conrad as a young matron Courtesy University of Montana Library

talent and a beautiful voice. He was sure that, if Kate took voice training at the school at La Scala, Italy, the prestige of that school, combined with her lovely voice, would insure a successful career in the opera houses of North America and perhaps of the world. He believed that Kate's talent was one that should be shared and enjoyed by people all over the world. Whitney himself planned to spend a year at the La Scala Opera, and he offered to take Kate with him, to watch after her, and to supervise the training that she would receive.

Much to the disappointment of both Kate and Dr. Whitney, the Conrads did not consent to the plan. They thought that sheltered young women whose parents could afford to support them should be subjected neither to the rigors of such a course of training, nor to the temptations and the public exposure that are a part of life on the stage.

Alicia believed that, at 18 years old, Kate must not have harbored any deep-seated desire for an opera career. Otherwise, accustomed as Kate was to getting her own way, her parents would have capitulated in the face of the force that Kate was able to muster to secure what she really wanted.

After this hope for a career in opera was smothered, Kate finished the course at Delafield-Colvin and ended her education and voice training. The social graces she acquired at the school prepared her somewhat for the life she was to lead, but she was probably overtrained for the limited social activities of Kalispell. Delafield-Colvin also was an expensive school. In a letter from Lettie Conrad to Kate, dated April 13, 1904, she was advised that her school expenses for three months totaled $1,782.64 — which, in 1904, was a significant sum for one-quarter year of girl polishing.

Kate returned to Kalispell upon her graduation from the Boston school and settled into a carefree social life that indicated little disappointment at missing a career in the opera, or any concern that a great talent was bottled up within her. The James Talbots, a banking family in Columbia Falls, and the John O'Briens, a Somers family with interests in timber and lumbering, had children contemporary in age with Kate. So life for Kate became essentially a round of parties spread among the three homes, reached by horseback and carriages, with sleighs replacing carriages for the winter months.

Alicia said of Kate:

> She laughed a lot, nice laughter. I mean it was not ridicule of anybody. She enjoyed anything she planned or anything that was planned that she could add her ideas to. She didn't do the work. Other people did the work, but she did have good ideas. She was very knowledgeable about the theatre of that day and had a very valuable collection of pictures and photographs. At the Delafield-Colvin School, which was a finishing school, they made a point of having writers of fame, authors, both men and women, to functions at the school as part of their invited guests, so the young ladies could know who was worth knowing in their different walks of life and how to entertain them. Kate liked to carry that on, as much as this area offered at the time.

According to Alicia, Kate entertained primarily at the Mansion, where she could do the planning and have the Conrads' household help do all the work. This entertainment centered on food and dancing, Kate's favorite pastimes. At times Kate would conceive, cast, costume, and direct a play or skit, relying on the skills learned at finishing school.

Alicia remembered that Kate enjoyed many beaus and that she was especially fond of Scott Lintner. He loved music and realized the quality of Kate's voice. With his encouragement, Kate shared her voice as frequently as the opportunities arose. Many persons in Kalispell assumed that they would marry, but, when Scott was sent to the Philippine Islands to assume an enginering job, their romance ended. He asked Kate to marry him and to accompany him to Manila as his bride, but the thought of living in the Far East chilled Kate's ardor. According to Alicia, Kate told Scott, "No, I don't want to go to Manila, Goodbye."

Alicia would have loved to go with the suitor to Manila or to any place else, but she was too young for anything but fantasy.

On June 12, 1908, Kate would be 23 years old; in that era, she was thought to be approaching spinsterhood. She shuffled through her beaus for a possible husband and chose Egbert James Van Duzer, an employee of the Missoula Mercantile Company, which operated a large department store in Kalispell. Their engagement was announced, and the wedding date was set for February 4, 1908, well before Kate's twenty-third birthday.

The Kalispell stores, in 1908, were incapable of supplying a wedding gown and trousseau befitting the occasion, so Lettie and Kate Conrad traveled to Boston. At the fashionable commercial house of Ballard and Son, a wedding gown was created for Kate. As the two women waited for the gown to be finished, the Boston shops yielded other creations for Kate to wear, when she returned to the East on her honeymoon, for a dizzying round of parties, dinners, luncheons, theatre dates, and other entertainments. This trip would signal her departure from Eastern social life and her acceptance of the life of a small-town matron.

The people of Kalispell long had awaited, with great anticipation, the first wedding in which a Conrad daughter would be married. The weeks before the wedding date were filled with parties for the bride. Frenzied activity characterized the decoration of the Episcopal Church and the Conrad Mansion, where the reception would be held. Invitations were much coveted, for this wedding would be the greatest social event in Kalispell's history. Its lavishness would equal that of high society anywhere.

The Inter Lake reported the event in detail.

> The wedding, with the reception that followed, was the most note-worthy as well as the most elaborate and perfectly appointed event in the social history of Kalispell. For weeks it has been a matter of eager interest by the many friends of the bride and groom, and there has been a succession of gatherings with Miss Conrad as the special guest. They all culminted in the happy and brilliant affair of Tuesday evening.
>
> The church had been beautifully decorated in white and green, with ferns, palms, and semilax, threaded everywhere with carnations. The decorations at the Mansion, as in the church, were in white, pink, and green, with the use of semilax, chrysanthemums, roses, and carnations. The Inter Lake described one of the attendants as "dainty little Helen Dickey, the bride's special flower girl.

In 1978 Helen Dickey Johns remembered the lavishness of the wedding and the reception, but, best of all, she remembered being pulled around the Mansion's polished floors on Kate's wedding train, which equally delighted Helen, Kate, and the guests. The Inter Lake's account continued.

> Dancing followed the reception and was continued to a late hour at the request of the bride, suffering only a short interruption when Mr. and Mrs. Van Duzer bade their friends goodbye to take the train for the East. They will spend a few weeks with friends in Boston and New York and then return to Kalispell.

Alicia said that Lettie Conrad paid for the honeymoon, which became a rather expensive affair. Kate was quite experienced in wiring for money and in overdrawing her account at the Conrad Bank. Kate's husband, Egbert, quickly became acquainted with spending money in the grand style, which his meager salary had never permitted previously. He liked it, and he became skilled in obtaining money from the Conrad estate.

When Kate and Egbert returned from the East, they moved into a house less than one block from the Conrad Mansion. Here they lived out their rather prosaic married life. Van Duzer willingly relinquished the name of Egbert to become "Bertie." As befitted a member of the Conrad family, he traded his job at the Mercantile for a position in the Conrad National Bank.

Marriage did not separate Kate from her family, either physically or financially. The $150 monthly payment from her father's estate, although quite a handsome sum in1908, was insufficient for Kate, even when combined with Bertie's Bank salary. To obliterate the difference between her expenditures and her income, Kate lavishly used her mother's charge accounts. In protest, Lettie tried to break Kate of this habit. Kate then provided her mother with a choice: allow her to continue the unlimited use of the Conrad credit; shut off that credit with the local merchants, an embarrassment Kate knew Lettie did not want to face; prosecute her, an alternative that Kate knew was unthinkable. So Lettie selected the path that she so often had chosen — she let Kate's will dominate. Lillie Adams, C. E. Conrad's youngest sister, once said, "I do hope that Kate never tips back her head and sees the moon. If she saw it, she would want it, and brother Charles will send for ladders and go right up and get it for her."

Alicia loved her sister, although she also was completely dominated by Kate. Until Kate's return from school in the East, Alicia did not really have the opportunity to know her sister, for Kate had spent little time in Kalispell. When Kate returned to the Mansion permanently, however, Alicia very quickly learned the place of the younger sister. Alicia remembered Kate saying, "I am the eldest daughter. You can't play with those paper dolls. They are mine. Get me this; get me that; brush my hair; clean my shoes." This pattern continued, until Alicia believed herself a reincarnation of Cinderella.

Alicia said that she always shampooed Kate's hair and dressed it for her. If Kate were ill with a cold, with the flu, or merely indisposed, she always sent for Alicia to amuse her.

Kate also made generous use of the Conrad Mansion furniture to furnish her new home. Alicia recalled one beautiful desk, part of a set in the Antique Room, that Kate wanted. Lettie said that she did not want the set broken, but Kate insisted: "I want it, and I'm going to have it!" She ordered two stablemen to carry it to her house and, as the men removed the desk, Lettie stood mute — again the loser in a clash of wills with Kate.

In addition, Kate always had admired her mother's jewelry. She loved to borrow it. Kate believed that, since she was the eldest daughter, the jewelry was rightfully hers. Alicia recalled that, at the time of her father's death, Kate was attending school in the East. After the funeral, Kate informed Lettie: "Mother, I'm the eldest daughter and I want you to know that and remember it. Father is dead, and you are 42, so I'll take your jewels now, for they are rightfully mine." When asked what response her mother made, Alicia said, "She didn't say anything. Just turned white."

Kate's personal dominance did not exist in her own home. Bertie maintained a tenacious hold on the proposition, popular in 1908, that a man ruled his home. He firmly believed that the wife was subservient to the husband, even though that wife had been a Conrad. Bertie did not like Kate to sing, so he forbade it and her lovely voice stilled — Alicia believed from jealousy. Alicia remembered Kate singing on only one occasion after her marriage, at Lettie's funeral. At her mother's request, Kate sang three of the hymns Lettie loved best. Alicia remembered that Kate's voice was so beautiful that it produced a sort of musical alchemy, changing sadness and despair into an ethereal hope, and promising that all was well and that death was a reuniting, rather than a simple departure.

During her mother's life, Kate continued to depend on Lettie. If Kate wanted to entertain or to hold a big party, Lettie would arrange it for her, and the function would be held at the Mansion. The Van Duzers also spent summers with Lettie — invariably at Foy's Lake, where the Conrads maintained a large summer home on the big island.

Based upon their relationship, Alicia characterized Kate.

> She was very self-centered, very selfish, not meaning to be, but her wishes were law. She had been indulged to such an extent that she didn't really seem to know there was any other way. But she was generous in a way also. She loved to pick out lovely things to give to people who already had a lot. But many times, if the gift was something that Kate liked particularly, she would get one or two for herself at the same time.

But the people she chose to be awfully generous to, and good to, and interested in, were people that already had a lot. She didn't have the feeling that there were people in need who would have profited more by that. I don't think that seemed to occur to her. I don't think she had any sense of anybody having a hard time or a lean time in any way. It was rather like the French queen who, when told the starving people had no bread, suggested that, if they had no bread, they could eat cake.

During one Christmas season, Kate was ill, and it did not appear that she could leave her home to shop. Thus she asked Carl Hummer to bring the stock of fine handkerchiefs from his store, so she could choose her Christmas gifts. She bought the entire stock! Then she made a miraculous recovery, which enabled her to shop as usual. Kate ultimately used the handkerchiefs as tuck-in presents, sprinkling them liberally among the gift-wrapped Christmas packages.

Kate's childhood tendency to plumpness blossomed into near obesity after her marriage. Whether this craving for food served as an outlet for frustration or simply became another form of self-indulgence, Alicia never determined. Yet, within a few years, Kate grew to 250 pounds, and the rest of her life she weighed between 250 and 260 pounds. This weight carried on a five-foot seven-inch frame, resulted in an enormous woman. Despite her size, however, Kate moved with amazing grace. She loved to dance and excelled in waltzing. Alicia said,

Kate had the same grace as the elephant. Great beasts of bulk though these are, their movements are so beautifully exact. Kate moved with the same surefooted grace as the elephant, picking its way up the narrow boarding plank to enter the circus car.

Kate's weight problem was exacerbated by her love of chocolate candy, particularly Whitman's chocolates. Boxes of these chocolates were kept on stands by each chair and were replenished constantly. Prior to World War I, Ken Adams worked at Chester's Confectionery. One aspect of his job was to ensure that Kate's candy supply remained complete. Almost daily he would deliver a stock of chocolates to the Van Duzer home. The empty boxes would be replaced, and the partially filled boxes would be consolidated. Each place where Kate might sit was supplied with a full box of candy. For Kate ate candy constantly and urged it upon her visitors. Although little boys ordinarily do not care to accompany their mothers when they visit friends, little boys in Kalispell loved to go with their mothers when they called on Kate, for she would urge them to devour as many chocolates as their mothers would permit.

Alicia believed that Kate generally was satisfied with her life. She was a true epicurean. Until the death of Lettie in 1923, Kate was able to indulge herself almost completely. The family fortune, although dwindling, remained sufficient so that no significant restraint in the family spending was exercised by Lettie. But following Lettie's death, the erosion of C. E. Conrad's acquired wealth was rather precipitous, with property being sold to provide income to maintain the highest possible standard of living.

In June of 1935, Kate developed appendicitis, which required surgery. The surgery seemed successful, and she had progressed in her recovery so she soon could leave the hospital. Then, suddenly, an embolism struck. She died instantly, on June 12, 1935, her fiftieth birthday.

Kate's parting assumed the grand style. For one whole day and night her body was displayed in an open casket at her home, so friends could say their last goodbyes. As Kate would have arranged, plenty was provided for the guests to eat and drink. Mahlon Hall, a contemporary of Kate, recalled that friends worked two-hour shifts, supplying the callers with food and drinks, from shortly before noon on the first morning to the early hours of the following morning. Their display would have delighted Kate's epicurean heart.

Kate's funeral was held at the Mansion and she was buried in the Conrad family mausoleum. She joined there her father, her mother, and her nephew, Billy, who had been killed in a hunting accident. Alicia said that, because of the size of Kate's casket, two of the mausoleum's burial crypts were needed.

Kate's life lasted just about as long as did the Conrad fortune, so her death occurred at what was an opportune time. For, without ample supplies of Conrad money, Kate probably would not have known how to cope with life. She never did develop a sense of tradition or history. To preserve the family home and to establish it as a memorial to her parents seemed to her utter nonsense. She perceived the Conrad fortune as a means by which to indulge herself and to supply her wants, which it had accomplished only because of the brevity of her life.

Catherine Conrad Van Duzer was a warm-hearted, lovable woman, who was a product of her time and circumstances. As Alicia said, Kate did not want to be selfish and self-indulgent, nor did she realize that she was. She just never learned that needs other than her own existed in the world. One would not expect her to be significantly different from the way she was.

Kate was no Saturday's child, who "works hard for his living." This role fell to her younger sister, Alicia. Kate was born on Friday. The traditional birthday verse rhymes, "Friday's child is loving and giving." This line did characterize Kate, but the loving and giving sometimes took rather strange directions.

CHAPTER 51
The Family Fortune

Charles E. Conrad died on November 26, 1902. The inventory of his estate was filed on March 2, 1903. The estate was appraised at $743,986.66, which was a low estimate. The true value probably was one-and-one-half million to two million dollars. Lettie Conrad was appointed the estate's sole executrix on December 16, 1902. She retained the administration of her husband's estate until her death in 1923. C. E's will granted Lettie complete authority to manage the estate, and it also provided that she could not be held liable for any losses that the estate might suffer as a result of her administration. The house, stables, surrounding land, and some other properties already were deeded in Lettie's name, so none of these assets was included in her husband's estate.

As executrix, in July, 1903, Lettie Conrad filed her first accounting of the estate, covering the period from November 27, 1902, to June 30, 1903. This account shows that she received income totalling $22,493.11, of which $12,929 derived from the Conrad Brothers operations. The account also indicates that all of this income was expended.

The next accounting covers the period from July 1, 1903, to December 1, 1903. During this time the estate received $26,193.85, of which $18,561 derived from the Conrad Brothers. In this accounting, the disbursements again equal the income.

The account statement for the period of December 1, 1903, through June 30, 1904, shows receipts of $57,168.64, of which Conrad Brothers contributed $51,268.50. The amount received from Conrad Brothers included $35,000 from the estate's sale of its interest in the Conrad Brothers Banking Company, which had been owned by the two brothers. William G. Conrad was the purchaser. This sale was challenged by the mixed-blood son, Edward, who contended that the sale price was inadequate. The objection was overruled, however, and the sale was approved by the judge. Again the statement's disbursements equalled the receipts, leaving no balance to carry forward.

The next accounting covers the period from July 1, 1904, to January 1, 1905. During the period the estate received $18,127.71, of which $7,679.93 derived from Conrad Brothers. No balance remained in the account, as all of the income was expended.

During this 1903-1904 period, Edward Conrad filed various law suits to break the will, to set aside the trust, to secure the distribution of his share of the estate, to prevent the sale of the Conrad Banking Company, and, in general, to object to the manner in which Lettie Conrad was handling the estate. All of these suits were decided against Edward. To remove any question of Lettie's legal authority, the court included a specific provision in its decree entered on October 31, 1904.

> While the said estate shall be held by the said Alicia D. Conrad in trust, she shall have full power to conduct and manage the same, and to that end to sell and dispose of any portion of the same, either real or personal property, without the necessity of applying to or obtaining an order from the court, and to execute all proper instruments of conveyance for transferring to the purchaser the title thereto.

On the same day, Charles E. Conrad, Jr. relinquished his right to inherit from his father. Thus all of his ties with the family were broken, and they could not be renewed.

The next accounting addresses the period from January 1, 1905, to June 1, 1906. Receipts of $48,813.35 accrued to the estate, of which $26,590 was received from Conrad Brothers. Once again the expenditures equalled the receipts.

The years 1906 and 1907 are covered in one account statement. During this period, the Conrad estate received a total of $92,732.07, of which $66,480 was paid by Conrad Brothers. William G. Conrad sold the Bigfork Power and Electric Light Company, and the estate received $17,500 for its interest. This company built, owned, and operated the first hydroelectric power plant in the area. The Conrads built a dam on the Swan River, near Bigfork, and they sold commercially the power generated by the falling water. This dam, currently owned by the Pacific Power and Light Company, is essentially the same structure that was built by the Conrad brothers.

The statement for the period ending December 31, 1907, was the last made by Lettie Conrad until June 13, 1923, when she filed her final accounting.

During the years following the death of her husband, Lettie maintained a rather lavish lifestyle both for herself and for the children. The records show that, if the estate income were not sufficient to satisfy the family's desires, property was sold to provide more money for the luxurious living of the Conrads.

Lettie Conrad enjoyed vigorous good health during the years of her marriage and for some years thereafter. In 1919 she underwent a mastectomy and, for the first time, became concerned about her health. However, she continued those activities which interested her. She also continued to travel, although some trips were associated with her medical treatments. For some years she had been concerned about her children's ability to preserve the family holdings, which she could see dwindling. Despite her anxiety, Lettie had formulated no plans; in fact, she had not confronted the problem. Her only positive actions had been to maintain control of the estate and to refrain from distributing the children's shares of the estate. The trust should have been dissolved in 1913, had the directions of the will been followed, for then Alicia attained her majority. However, Lettie extended the trust, for an additional decade.

In the winter of 1922 Lettie required more medical treatment, for it was feared that her cancer might be spreading. She concluded that finally she must make some plans, find some solution to her problem, for time was expiring. Lettie discussed the matter with her attorney, George Grubb, who was very familiar with the family and its problems. Grubb told her that, if the estate were to continue, undivided, a better chance existed for the preservation of the Conrad holdings. Then a child neither would own specific property nor would be able to dispose of it without the consent of the others. He suggested that Lettie and the three children could transfer the estate property to a corporation, in which all parties would be shareholders and would participate in its management. If all three children were to share the decision-making, each child might be able to exercise some restraint on the others. Grubb also told Lettie that she had filed no accounting of her husband's estate since 1907 and that this omission should be rectified immediately.

Lettie Conrad accepted Grubb's suggestions, knowing that no perfect solution existed. Grubb was instructed to undertake the final accounting for the estate. He also was directed to prepare the papers necessary for forming the corporation and for transferring to it the assets yet remaining in the estate of C. E. Conrad. With this legal work commenced, Lettie and Alicia traveled south for the winter. They established themselves at Pass Christian, Mississippi, then a famous winter resort on the Gulf of Mexico. From there Lettie commuted by train to the Tulane University Hospital, in New Orleans, for her X-ray treatments.

The winter in the South was not pleasant. The treatments were debilitating, and Lettie also developed a bad case of shingles. The radiation treatments finally were completed. Lettie and Alicia then returned to a beautiful spring in the Flathead Valley. Both were delighted to be home.

290

Lettie spent hours in visiting with Kate and in relaxed talking with the neighbors. When rested from the long train trip, Lettie called on George Grubb. Everything was ready. The accounting was completed and was a lengthy document, covering the estate's transactions from 1908 to June, 1923. All the legal instruments necessary to form the corporation also were prepared for Lettie's approval.

On June 12, 1923 Lettie and the three children signed an agreement stating that, as soon as the C. E. Conrad estate was distributed to them, each would transfer his share immediately to the C. E. Conrad Estate, Incorporated. Lettie would receive $250,000 in stock, less $16,067.09, which she owed the estate. Each of the children would receive $83,333.33 in stock, less the amount that he owed the estate: Charley, $2,707.52; Kate, $11,000; Alicia, $7,351.81. The parties also agreed that a note from the Montana-Idaho Investment Company to the estate would be assumed by the Conrad Bank, but would be guaranteed by the estate. The corporation then would advance to each of the parties money to meet his needs, and it would provide perpetual care to the Conrad mausoleum. At this time, the direction of the corporation also was chosen. Lettie Conrad would share with the children the right to manage the family property, a right that heretofore had been hers alone.

The final estate account was filed on June 13, 1923, and the necessary court hearing for it was set for June 30. Since the death of Charles E. Conrad, in 1902, his estate had received $1,186,818.35 in income and spent $1,186,149.25. For the first time a balance existed, but only one of $669.10. During this 20-year period, Lettie Conrad, as executrix, had expended approximately $55,000 annually for herself and the three children, two of whom had married and were not living at home. This annual expenditure was made at a time when $5,000 a year was considered a rather handsome income.

So, on June 30, 1923, the account was to be approved and the property was to be distributed, one half to Lettie Conrad and the other half to the children in three equal shares. Upon distribution, the property then would be transferred to the C. E. Conrad Estate, Inc., and George Grubb's idea would be tested. Lettie Conrad's mind finally was relieved. She had done her best.

CHAPTER 52
The Death of Lettie Conrad

Alicia Davenport Stanford Conrad died on June 24, 1923. She did not live long enough to attend the hearing on her final estate account, which had been set for June 30. Nor did she ever learn how George Grubb's plan to preserve the family property would succeed. Alicia remembered that, on June 23, her mother was feeling well and was exuding that happy sense of returning home after a long, disagreeable winter. With Kate and Alicia, Lettie then went for a visit with a dear friend, Selma Dodge, the wife of Dr. A. A. Dodge. When the women returned to the Mansion, Lettie said that she wanted to lie down and rest, an unusual request for her. A short time later, her breathing became labored and was audible to Alicia, reading on the first floor. Alicia ran to her mother and sensed the seriousness of her condition. She called the family doctors and alerted Kate and the neighbors. She dispatched a messenger to Charley, who was bird hunting on the Flathead Indian Reservation.

As she had for so many years, Alicia served as her mother's nurse, while others slept or took turns sitting with Lettie. Alicia was at her mother's bedside continuously. Both sensed that death might be approaching, and Alicia was desolate. She had spent her life loving and caring for her mother, and she feared that she could not face the void which would be created by her mother's death. When Alicia cried out against this injustice, Lettie said, "Dear, do not grieve. It hurts me deeply to see you unhappy. I am going to join your father. That will make me happy, and I want you to be happy with me." Not consoled, Alicia asked, "What will become of me if you go?" Her mother answered,

> I have tried to provide for you. And I have pleaded with your brother to take care of you and Kate. I can only hope that the pleas of a dying mother will be more effective than the voice of a living mother.

Lettie's heavy breathing continued through the night. About sunrise, a change occurred. Alicia told of her mother's final hours:

Her breathing was labored, terrible and the house just rocked from that, the whole structure of the house. You could stand in the front hall and the balcony doors and the windows were all open. Nothing existed but the building and the breathing. This went on hour after hour. Then suddenly, about sunrise, her breathing became easier. Mother didn't say anything but I'm sure she thought, "Oh, I've passed the crisis." From then on she had no trouble breathing. Kate and Bertie came over and had gone to bed in Kate's old room. Charley was in the Violet Room, and Dr. Brassett was in the Antique Room.

I went down to tell the people in the kitchen and hurried back upstairs, as I knew that relatives and close friends would be wanting to come into the room, and I knew that, as they came in, mother would know them. They came upstairs quietly and stood in a circle close to the wall, with the fireplace and the door on the west side. Mother greeted each one as they came in, just exactly as she would if they had been coming to have dinner with us. She was calm, quiet, peaceful, and alert, keenly alert. She had a little something to say to each one. Uncle Hal (Stanford) and Uncle George (Stanford) had been in the kitchen, and she had a merry little thing to say to each of them. It was very personal and referred to something they understood between them. It seemed a time of joy and relief, and I think it was for her.

Before the crowd came, I sang the "Twenty-third Psalm" to her. She asked me, "Oh, has it come? The birds are singing, but it's dark in here. Can you put the lights on?" Mother's glasses were on the dressing table and Kate put them on her. Mother made a little gesture like, "Take them away, they won't help." Then her breathing became normal. I don't think that Kate realized at all what was happening. The crowd was filing in quietly and was growing larger. I turned to make sure all of the east windows were open wide, and I saw the beautiful bank of orange-red poppies that had just opened, and a great yellow rosebush, a tremendous thing, making a bank of yellow and scarlet, with the sun on the mountains.

She had hardly said the last words to the last visitors, when she suddenly sat up in bed. She was propped up on two pillows, had been throughout the night, of course, to help her in her breathing difficulties. She was still strong and sat up alone, unaided. Almost upon her last breathing of words to someone, she held out her arms toward the east windows. Everybody was tense and so quiet you could hear any sound that ever happened. Then a joyful look came to her face, pure joy. She extended her arms and said, in a voice filled with strength and exultation: "Charlie! You've come!" Then she fell back on the bed, and death came.

Uncle Hal was standing beside me, and he put his hand on my shoulder. He always felt strongly that he was an atheist, and there was no hereafter, just nothing. He had such an incredulous look on his face as he turned to me and whispered. "He really came for her. He was here. I am so glad that could happen." I looked out the window and the poppy stems were bare. There wasn't a speck of scarlet. The golden rosebush was still there with its beautiful yellow flowers. But those great big poppies! There was no wind, there wasn't a breath of wind stirring. It was a beautiful, beautiful twenty-fourth of June morning, and there wasn't one petal on those poppies. They had all dropped off.

When asked, "Did you ever ask anybody about that?" Alicia answered,

I never did. What could they tell me, except that I was mistaken. I was never more keenly aware of everything in my whole life. Everything was so clear and somehow so in place. I've always loved that great style of poppies.

The funeral service for Lettie Conrad was held at the Mansion. Kate had almost ceased singing, but Alicia prevailed upon her to sing at the service. The funeral was attended by people from all over the state, for Lettie was a much-beloved and respected woman. The report of her death in the *Great Falls Tribune* stated: "Her death brings down the final curtain in a life of benevolent deeds, and (marks) the passing of a figure beloved in all Northwestern Montana because of her noble and kindly charitable acts."

The *Daily Inter Lake* of June 25, 1923, also wrote of Lettie.

Mrs. Conrad was one of the most public-spirited and best-known women in Northwest Montana and her death will be a great loss to the community in which she has lived for so many years. There has never been a movement for the public welfare in which she has not taken an active part and her acts of charity and kindness were many. One of these in which she took the greatest pleasure was the Christmas Tree for the poor children of the city, which she gave at her home and was an annual event until very recent years, when, on account of ill health, she was obliged to be away during the winter months.

During the war Mrs. Conrad was very active in all war work and especially the Red Cross. She was Chairman of the Flathead Chapter and, due largely to her untiring efforts, the Chapter was not exceeded in production per capita by any other of the entire northwest district and was equalled by only one, a small district in Southern Minnesota.

The funeral services will be conducted by Bishop Fisher at the home Wednesday afternoon at 3:00, and she will be buried beside her husband in the family mausoleum in Conrad Memorial Cemetery.

CHAPTER 53
The End of the Family Fortune

With the death of Lettie Conrad, the remaining assets of the Conrad fortune became, for the first time, subject to the control of the three children. They were appointed to complete the administration of their father's estate. The final estate accounting filed by Lettie was refiled by the children in September, 1923. In their petition requesting appointment as joint administrators to close the estate of their father, they state that the remaining estate carried a value of $275,000. The resultant decree of distribution, made in October, 1923, shows 1,331 shares of Conrad National Bank stock, 3,200 acres of farm land and timber land in Flathead County, 550 acres in Lincoln County, 320 acres in Bonner County, Idaho, and 250 acres in British Columbia — as well as $5,564.27 in cash, an unusual item in a Conrad accounting. The decree described other property, none of which held significant value. The combined property was distributed in the ratio of one-sixth to each of the three children, and one-half to Lettie's estate.

Alicia D. Conrad's will was dated June 22, 1923, only two days before her death. It reflects little thought or planning. She merely bequeathed all of her estate, in equal shares, to the three children and appointed them coexecutors. The inventory of Lettie's estate was filed on August 15, 1923. It lists property appraised at $261,107.77. Her one-half interest in her husband's estate comprised $168,428.80 of this amount. The property in her own name was appraised at $92,678.91.

On August 15, 1923, each of the Conrad children controlled an estate of $143,650.85. Of this figure, $87,035.92 represented his shares of Lettie's estate, and $56,614.93 represented his shares in the remainder of C. E.'s estate.

On November 10, 1923, the three children filed an agreement which supplemented the document of June 12, 1923 — that arrangement by which they agreed to transfer all the family property to a corporation to be known as the C. E. Conrad Estate, Incorporated. The supplemental agreement provided that, although the mother had died, the children still would transfer all of the property to the corporation.

Another provision of this supplemental document states that Alicia D. Conrad had owed the C. E. Conrad Estate $16,067.09, which would be paid by granting her less stock in the corporation. It stated further that Charles D. Conrad owed his mother $15,923.27, which would be paid by deducting Charley's debt to Lettie from her debt to the estate. This transaction would leave only $154.80 due from the deceased Alicia D. Conrad to the corporation. By what appears to be a rather slick bit of juggling, the new corporation was poorer by $32,000, and Charley's debt of almost $16,000 disappeared like the pea from the carnival shell game. This maneuver provided some indication of how Charley would heed his dying mother's plea to take care of his sisters.

The supplemental agreement also provided that Alicia could, for a time, receive $225 per month. This gesture probably was designed to compensate for the salaries drawn by Charley and Bertie Van Duzer from the Conrad National Bank.

The estate of Lettie Conrad was distributed, in equal shares, to the three children on May 13, 1925. They immediately transferred all of the property remaining from the estates of their father and mother to the C. E. Conrad Estate, Inc. George Grubb's idea for preserving the family fortune finally was to be tested. At this time, the Conrad fortune conservatively was appraised at approximately $430,000. The family property was transferred to the C. E. Conrad Estate, Inc., during mid-May, 1925. The three children then became directors of the corporation. Charley was designated its President and Chief Executive Officer. Kate and Alicia were named to minor offices, but they did not participate in the actual management of the corporation's affairs. Alicia said that they relinquished control to their brother, Charley, because they did not know what else to do. According to Alicia, "Kate did not care what happened to anything, as long as she got money to spend." She also said, "Nobody ever told me that I had any rights. Mother told me that Charley would take care of me, and I thought that I had to do whatever Mother wanted."

The corporate form of ownership and management provided Charley almost complete control over the disposition of its property. He alone signed the transfer instruments as president. The signatures of Kate and Alicia were not required for the sale of property, even though they owned more than two-thirds of the corporation's stock.

The records show that, after 1925, some of the corporation's farm and timber lands were sold to provide income for the voracious appetites of Charles and Kate. Alicia apparently received little from these transactions after a divorce from her first husband, Walter McCutcheon, in 1924.

The three Conrad children, through the corporation, owned 1,331 shares of Conrad National Bank stock, a substantial majority of the issued stock. From 1908 to 1923 the Bank had paid annual dividends on the Conrad-family stock of about $10,000. In addition, Charley and Kate's husband, Bertie Van Duzer, received salaries from the Bank. Lettie Conrad had known the children could live comfortably on the Bank dividends alone, for, at that time, $3,000 a year was more income than most families enjoyed. For this reason, she instructed them to retain the Bank stock, regardless of circumstances.

With Lettie's death, however, even the little restraint that she had exercised over Charley disappeared. Lost too were her ready funds, used to cover his bad loans. Bank examiners were not as understanding of Charley's activities as had been his mother. The Bank's affairs reached such tenuous straits in the 1930s that the family corporation's stock was pledged as collateral to obtain a loan from the Federal Reconstruction Finance Corporation (R. F. C.). This loan merely provided the Bank with operating capital, but was a federal-government precondition for the continued operation of the Bank.

Under Charley's direction, some of the corporation's lands were sold piecemeal after 1935. Then, in 1938 and 1939, more than 1,600 acres of the family's farm and timber lands in Flathead County were sold for the non-payment of taxes. By 1940 all of the property that the children had inherited either was sold, or was lost, or was covered by mortgages — even the Mansion.

No money existed in the corporation for redemption of these lands, so ultimately they all were sold for taxes, and lost.

When the payment fell due on the R. F. C. loan, the Conrad corporation had no money and nothing left to sell or mortgage. So the corporation stock was sold for nonpayment of the debt. All of the Conrad-family stock was acquired by a group of Kalispell businessmen, headed by J. G. Edmiston. The new group immediately assumed control and management of the Bank, the one asset Lettie Conrad had cautioned her children to hold in any event. The new owners allowed Charley to retain the title of president of the Bank, but it was an empty title, and Charley became a figurehead president. He earned a small salary and was allowed to keep a desk at the Bank, because of the respect which the new owners held for his parents.

Kate's death, in 1935, saved her from the corporation's leanest years, but even she left pathetically little of the substantial estate that she had inherited from her parents. The inventory of her estate listed only minimal assets:

New York Life policy	$2,000.00
Household goods and furniture	1,000.00
Equity in home given to her by her mother, subject to a mortgage, decedent's interest at death	500.00
35-acre tract of land	1,000.00
TOTAL ESTATE	$4,500.00

A detailed inventory of Kate's furniture and household goods was not made. Her home had been furnished almost completely with pieces taken from the family Mansion, as had the home of her brother, Charley. After Lettie's death, Kate had insisted that all of the fine linens, silver, china, and glassware be divided in thirds among the children, leaving no child with a full set of anything. Kate's share of these items reverted to her husband, Bertie. He subsequently remarried and, upon his death, all of the lovely pieces from the Conrad Mansion either were sold or were scattered among the relatives of Bertie's second wife.

After losing the Bank, Charles devised one last plan. In partnership with a local bar-owner, he proposed to convert the Conrad Mansion into a bar and casino, with the implication of a bordello on the second and third floors. The wife of the bar-owner told Alicia of the scheme. By this time, Alicia had married George Campbell, who proved an effective advisor to her in family matters. Alicia was resolved to save the family home and especially determined to save it from Charley's threatened disgrace. So Alicia and George conferred with J. G. Edmiston, who managed the Conrad Bank's operations. He listened to Alicia's story and told her,

> Alicia, you have had the most unfair treatment of anyone I have ever known. The Bank is not in the real-estate business. If you want the home, I will arrange for you to buy it with a small down-payment and the lowest rate of interest I can justify.

Thus the sale was arranged, and Alicia saved the Mansion, although it would be a burden to her for many years. Charley was furious with Alicia, but he could not reverse the transaction.

Charles Davenport Conrad died on February 9, 1941. Fifteen months before, he had developed lung cancer. Although he fought the disease gamely, it finally destroyed him. Yet even death did not remove him from the shadow of his father. The *Daily Inter Lake* carried the account of his death under the headline, "Charles D. Conrad, Son of Pioneer." He was buried in the family mausoleum with his father, his mother, his son Billy, and his sister Kate.

Charley's widow, Agnes, filed no probate of his estate. This fact was noted by the Montana State Board of Equalization, which apparently assumed that Charley would have left an estate on which an inheritance tax was due. On December 16, 1941, the Board wrote a letter to the widow, asking why no probate had been filed. On January 9, 1941, Agnes Conrad replied to the Board.

Gentlemen: Sorry to be slow in replying to your letter of December 16th, regarding the estate of Mr. Conrad.

The reason for no probate proceedings for the settlement of this Estate is due to the fact that Mr. Conrad left no estate.

He had been heavily in debt for many years; and a few years ago, in settlement of these debts, he gave up everything he had except ten shares of stock in the Conrad National Bank of Kalispell which it was necessary for him to keep in order to be an Officer and Director in this Bank.

A few years prior to this, he gave me all the furniture, etc. in our home to repay me for money of my own which I had given him and later gave me a deed to the house.

At the time of his death, he had no cash whatsoever, as he had been ill for fifteen months and we had completely used up all available funds. He carried no Life Insurance of his own.

He had coming to him from an Annuity in Mutual Life Insurance Company, left him by his mother, just two more yearly payments of $167.50 each. After that, had he lived, he would have received $500 yearly for life.

I have not filled out the paper you sent me, as I could see nothing that could be put on it, unless it might be the ten shares of Bank Stock, and possibly the two yearly payments of the Annuity. The Bank Stock Mr. Conrad had signed over to me some time previous to his death; but I did not have it transferred to my name until later.

If there are any other questions you would like to ask, I'll be only too glad to answer them and, if you think the above two items should be put in the paper you sent me to fill out, I'll do so. Yours very truly, Agnes M. Conrad.

Charles Davenport Conrad was 58 at the time of his death, and Kate was 50 when she died in 1935. Alicia would live for another 40 years after Charley died, part of that time in poverty. All that was left of the family fortune for Alicia was the family home, which she was determined to save — even though that battle would last for almost 40 years.

CHAPTER 54
Alicia Conrad Campbell
I. Early Life and First Marriage

Alicia Conrad, the youngest of the Conrad children, was born on June 21, 1892. "Tuesday's child is full of grace," according to the familiar rhyme, and Alicia possessed that quality in abundance. Her life made her somewhat of a "Wednesday's child" also, for it was liberally sprinkled with woe. In 1892 the Conrad family recently had arrived from Fort Benton. Housing in Kalispell was scarce. And Charles E. Conrad sought a house to accommodate two grandmothers, two parents, and two children. On the day of Alicia's birth, the most private place to be found in Kalispell was the Kalispell Townsite Company cabin, a crude structure from which that business operated. Lettie gave birth to Alicia on a large table used for spreading out the maps of the townsite company's properties to show prospective buyers the lots available for purchase. The birth of the Kalispell Townsite Company had preceeded that of Alicia by only a few months. The two were practically twins, and a bond was created between the child and the town that will be remembered as long as Kalispell exists.

Alicia was ten years younger than her brother, Charley, and eight years younger than her sister, Kate. No real brother-sister relationship existed among the children, for Alicia was only four years old when her brother left Kalispell to attend school and only six when Kate departed. So both were absent during Alicia's childhood.

Alicia's childhood was extremely lonely. She said that her mother was afraid the two grandmothers would be disturbed by noisy children. Instead of human playmates, Alicia had cats, 13 of them, and they all lived in the house. She recalled the situation.

> I'd put them in the tub in the morning. They didn't scratch or object but seemed to enjoy the water. Then I'd lift them out and use big sheets and bath towels to dry them. I can remember Dr. Alexander McDonald looking

in one day, when someone was sick. He saw all the cats in the tub and asked, "What are their names?" I said, "Well, I have Adam and Eve." He said, "From the number of cats, there must be one named Philander." I know I wouldn't have been allowed to have so many, except I had been a lonely child, and they were my playmates.

School was a joy for Alicia. She loved to learn and was anxious to leave each morning to be taught some new thing. Nor was homework a burden to her. She found it a challenging way to occupy her mind and to spend time that otherwise might be filled with loneliness. Summer vacation created a void that she tried to fill with outdoor activities. She was an excellent horsewoman. Her favorite horse was a stallion named "Black Beauty." Other family members and the stablemen considered him mean and dangerous, but Alicia had tamed him fully. Many years later, people remembered tiny Alicia, on her big black horse, racing around the streets of Kalispell, with the spirited horse under the complete control of the diminutive rider.

When she was older, Alicia rode one of the first motorcycles in town. She loved the freedom it gave her, but the machine never replaced the horse in her affection. In season, she also canoed frequently on the stream that flowed near the stables. Yet, she spent much of her time alone. For Alicia was too young to share as an equal in the activities of her mother but also too shy and involved in those activities to make any lasting friendships of her own. When Alicia was small, she longed to ride with her parents. For these outings, the horses would be saddled, including Alicia's pony. The three riders would leave the stable area together, but soon the parents' horses would outdistance Alicia's pony. She tried valiantly to catch them, but always fell further behind. At last she would give up and return alone to the stables, forlorn and frustrated, but determined to own a horse that could maintain any pace.

Alicia was 10 years old when her father died. She missed him sorely, even though he had been away from the Mansion much of the time. She had grown to crave the love and attention that he lavished upon her when he was home. She loved the pet names that he called her and the time that he spent with her. When with her father, she felt a real importance — one which decreased when he left on his frequent trips and one which ended entirely with his death.

In Charles' last years, Lettie accompanied her husband on many of his travels. Alicia usually went with them, for the other children were not at home, and they did not want to leave Alicia alone. Before departing on such a trip, Lettie received Alicia's lesson assignments from her school. Either she coached Alicia in her lessons, or, if they were in one location for a time, a tutor was hired. Thus Alicia absorbed knowledge from many, varied souces. By the time she was 18 years old, she probably was better educated than most of the graduates of those institutions of learning which she had been unable to attend.

Charles' death also created a great void in the life of Lettie Conrad. She attempted to fill this void with Alicia. Upon graduation from the eighth grade, Alicia's formal schooling was practically completed, even though she — alone of the children — had evidenced an appetite for knowledge and a desire for schooling. While she remained in good health, Lettie possessed a restless and unquenchable desire for travel. Alicia accompanied her mother on all of these trips, even during her high-school years. Alicia said, "I kept abreast of the assignments and did every bit of the work. When test time came, I would be examined by an accredited person, to see what I had gotten from the coaching. Very rigid and careful, so I was busy." When asked if the high school had given her a diploma, she said, "I don't think they did. I don't know."

Alicia did not form the friendships that normally result from attendance at high school, nor did she participate in the high-school activities that would have united her with her classmates. To Kate and Charley she always was the little sister whom they considered a nuisance. Both were married by the time Alicia was 16 years old. Thereafter they seemed too grown up to be a satisfactory brother and sister.

When Lettie Conrad's health failed, Alicia became her mother's nurse and companion.

> I was always with Mother. I was never away from her from babyhood up. I became a nurse, I mean because I wanted to, of course. I never left her. For instance, with the series of x-ray treatments which were advocated at that time, I always held her hand and stood beside her and took them myself. They thought that would make it impossible for me to ever have children, if I married, but it didn't work that way for me. It was supposed to be harmful in the huge doses that she took, but I was always with her.

The circumstances of Alicia's life permitted little time or opportunity for beaus. An almost total absence of any normal boy-girl relationships left Alicia with a naiveté that ill-equipped her for making sound judgments concerning men or marriage. In 1913, she was 21 years old, a little beyond marriageable age for that era.

Alicia occasionally expected that a prince charming on a white horse would arrive in the front drive, seeking her hand in the manner described in the books she had read. Instead, he arrived at the back door in a grocery wagon, but he was a charmer. Walter Montgomery McCutcheon sold groceries for the Kalispell Mercantile Company, recognized as the best grocery outlet in Kalispell. He was a man of such charm that both maids and matrons were eager to order from him — not just single cans, but cases or whatever quantities Walter might suggest.

Wally M. McCutcheon, circa 1914
Courtesy University of Montana Library

Alicia and her mother were excellent customers, but they were not alone. Upright ladies, who held in great disdain fruits and vegetables in tin cans, found themselves ordering canned products in unaccustomed quantities. The pantries and larders of Kalispell homes became stocked as never before. At the Conrad home, opportunity was recognized by both sides, and soon Walter began arriving at the front door, a suitor for Alicia's hand.

The courtship was not lengthy. The engagement was announced and the wedding date set for June 10, 1914. The match seemed most appropriate, a lovely young daughter of a wealthy family and a handsome and ambitious young man.

The wedding was held at 1 p.m., at Christ Episcopal Church. The *Kalispell Bee* covered the event.

> One of the most interesting and lovely weddings was that of Miss Alicia Conrad and Walter Montgomery McCutcheon, which took place at Christ Church at 8:00, Wednesday evening, June 10, 1914.

> The church, which lends itself to artistic decoration, was never so beautiful as on this occasion.

> The bride walking beside her brother, Charles D. Conrad, looked beautiful and sweet as she proceeded slowly down the aisle. Her pure white

Alicia Conrad's wedding picture Courtesy Conrad Mansion Directors

gown of brocaded charmeuse, trimmed with pearls and lilies of the valley, was exquisite in its simplicity. A filmy veil covered her head and fell beyond the train of her gown. It was held in place by lilies of the valley with maiden-hair fern intertwined. Her only ornament was a lavalier of simple design, the gift of the groom.

The reception was held at the Conrad home, which was beautifully decorated with flowers both inside and out.

From the summer house (gazebo) of the spacious grounds strains of music came as the guests arrived. The guests were served in the dining room and library under the direction of a number of matrons. The repast was most delicious and consisted of chicken salad, saratoga chips, rolls, apple pickles, jelly Nesselrode pudding, fruitcake, angel food and almond cakes and coffee. Orange ice was served during the evening.

After supper the orchestra was stationed in the drawing room and the guests enjoyed dancing.

Mr. and Mrs. McCutcheon stole a march on their friends, who were watching every avenue for them to leave on their wedding trip. They simply took an automobile ride and remained in Kalispell overnight. They left last night for a wedding trip of several weeks duration.

It was fitting that Alicia should spend her wedding night at home, in her own bedroom, situated next to her mother's room. That choice set the pattern for her marriage.

On July 21, 1914, the *Kalispell Bee* reported: "Mr. and Mrs. Walter McCutcheon will return tonight from their honeymoon. During their absence they have visited Portland, Seattle, Victoria, Calgary, St. Paul, and many other cities." Alicia recalled that her honeymoon, too, had been financed by her mother. McCutcheon brought little but charm to this marriage.

Upon their return, Alicia and her husband moved into the Mansion. They were installed in Alicia's bedroom, which adjoined Lettie's. This would be their home for the duration of the marriage.

At the time of Alicia's wedding, the Conrad fortune remained substantial. C. E.'s estate had experienced no growth, but rather was suffering a steady decline, as it was tapped to supply the expensive lifestyles that had been established by Lettie, Kate, and Charles. Alicia always had lived in the shadow of her mother, who supplied her simple wants. But Alicia's marriage changed all that. McCutcheon's desire for money and extravagant living not only matched, but exceeded that of his in-laws. He learned quickly that the money supply was controlled by Lettie and Charles, so he directed his considerable charm toward them. After quitting his job at the Kalispell Mercantile, McCutcheon's main employment was working to gain control of Alicia's share of the family wealth and then spending it upon himself as fast as he could. He apparently was assisted in this job by Charley, for Alicia said that Charley would give money and property to McCutcheon that he would not give to her. However, any money that Charley gave to Alicia's husband always was charged against her account.

McCutcheon treated Alicia as well as was necessary to remain in the good graces of Lettie. When he found that Alicia did not complain to her mother, and that Lettie apparently was oblivious to his treatment of her daughter, Alicia's life became most unhappy. McCutcheon had developed an undiscriminating taste for a wide variety of women, but formerly his low social position and lack of money prevented him from cutting a very wide swath in those circles. However, his marriage not only provided an elevated social position and an access to money, but also offered no impediment to the realization of his desire for a life of philandering. Alicia subsequently learned that her husband was well-known at the houses of prostitution in Spokane and Butte. Here, to impress the "girls," McCutcheon directed them to line up on their hands and knees on one side of the room, while he stood on the other side with five-dollar gold pieces in his hand. The girls then were commanded to crawl to him and scramble for the coins, to amuse McCutcheon and his friends. Alicia remarked, "How I could have used those gold pieces a few years later."

Walter McCutcheon and Alicia's brother were kindred souls. Charles willingly gave Alicia's money to her husband, although he knew the manner in which it was being used. This willingness corroborates Alicia's belief that Charles hated her. She said that her brother was consistently cruel to her. He loved to cause her embarrassment in public, especially at the dinner table, with guests present. When asked if her mother recognized this trait, Alicia replied,

> Yes she would be there, but she never rebuked him. He never liked me, never. He was never kind to me or gentle in any way. He and Kate were close, but with me, well, there was cruelty, coldness, and rejection. After Kate's death we walked back. She was brought back to her home before she was moved to the big house for the funeral. I took two or three quick steps to catch up with him and took his hand. He was going home and I was going back, too, and he flung it as if he could have torn it off my body and thrown it. It almost took it off at the shoulder.

Apparently neither Charles, nor Lettie, nor Attorney Grubb ever attempted to restrain McCutcheon from using his wife's money to indulge his profligacy.

Shortly after her marriage Alicia had received from the estate a ranch in the Creston area, a few miles east of Kalispell, which she managed with some success. Here she spent many hours escaping the unhappiness of her home. Her main crop was potatoes, most of which she sold to the Great Northern Railway. These potatoes were served in the passenger trains' dining cars and were considered "choice grade." When money from the family estate became inadequate for McCutcheon's needs, he persuaded Alicia to mortgage the ranch. When the debt fell due, McCutcheon could produce no money, and the ranch was lost.

In January, 1921, a child was born to Alicia, a little girl named Alicia Ann — thereby continuing that name unbroken in the maternal family line. At last Alicia had someone of her very own to love and to care for, much better than 13 cats, or any number of other pets, or even her mother. Yet any forlorn hope that little Alicia, called "Timmie," might cement the marriage soon was dashed. McCutcheon held no more interest in the baby than he did in its mother. But Alicia's life finally gained a satisfaction and a completeness that she had never known. She focused on the child the great love and compassion that she had tried to shower on her fellow beings, only to be rejected. Timmie made Alicia as happy as she had ever been and gave her life its first real purpose.

Alicia's life during her marriage to McCutcheon is well described in her action for divorce, which was filed in May, 1924. The allegations of the complaint, sworn by Alicia, were several.

That, during the spring of 1915, at the home of plaintiff's mother, and again in 1918, the defendant struck the plaintiff with his fist, knocked her down and inflicted grievous bodily injury.

That, in the fall of 1918, at plaintiff's ranch, in the presence of a number of people, the defendant struck the plaintiff with his fists and knocked her to the floor.

Alicia subsequently said that this incident happened at harvest time, when she was cooking for the ranch crew. McCutcheon had appeared at the ranch at noon and demanded the proceeds from the sale of the potato crop. When Alicia could produce no money, he knocked her down and told the crew, "That's the way I treat a banker's daughter." He then fled town.

The court complaint continued:

That the defendant, at various times and places, in the presence of the plaintiff's mother and others, made remarks such as, "You look like hell. Your clothes look awful. You don't expect me to take you any place looking as you do!" And, "Nobody likes you. Nobody will have anything to do with you. You haven't a friend in the world except your mother. People wouldn't come to see you even if you asked them."

That the defendant, during the marriage, was a habitual drunkard and gambler; that he associated with women of bad repute and used the plaintiff's money for these purposes, leaving the plaintiff nothing for herself.

That the defendant, during the marriage, took the plaintiff's money and property and squandered the same, and gambled and used the plaintiff's money and property in giving drinking parties for men and women of bad repute; that he consorted with other women and that the plaintiff had no knowledge of the defendant's association with other women, until after the defendant abandoned her in June of 1923.

That the plaintiff alleges that, in January, 1921, a few days before plaintiff's child was born, the plaintiff, who was not well, asked the defendant to give her some medicine that had been prescribed by her physician. The defendant, instead of giving her the medicine so prescribed, gave her a spoonful of lysol, whether intentionally or not the plaintiff does not know. Said lysol was a dangerous poison and she immediately asked the defendant to see her physician. When he returned, the plaintiff inquired of the defendant what the doctor had said, to which the defendant replied, "The doctor said that, in case anything happened to you, the baby could be saved, and that is all I care about." Which statement was made in the presence of the plaintiff's mother, and which said statement deeply humiliated and wounded the plaintiff's feelings and caused her great mental anguish and suffering.

That the defendant did, during the years 1921 and 1922, at Kalispell and diverse times and places, commit adultery with one Ruth Hill and other women whose names are unknown to the plaintiff.

When all of the money and property finally were depleted, McCutcheon told Alicia, "I've sucked the orange dry, and I'm leaving for California and a career in the movies." He did leave in June, 1923, and Alicia never saw or heard from him again.

When asked why she had continued to live with McCutcheon and had endured such treatment, Alicia answered:

I stood at that altar and took all those marriage vows about richer, poorer, better or worse, until death do us part. I thought that only adultery would free me, and, Lord, that was going on all the time and everybody knew it, but wouldn't tell me. Mother didn't say anything; she was always looking for the best in him. And Charley and Kate didn't care, as long as they were getting what they wanted.

Alicia and her daughter continued to live with Lettie Conrad until her death in June, 1923. Following Lettie's death, Alicia was destitute. She was unable to work, and her only income was what money she could obtain from Charley and from Attorney Grubb. This income was negligible, for she was told that all of her money and property were depleted. She was allowed to live in the Mansion, but could not afford to buy fuel to heat it.

The years from 1924 to 1928 were terrible ones for Alicia and her small daughter. They continued to use the Mansion as a place of shelter, but were unable to maintain it or to gain much help from Charley or Kate. Alicia described the situation:

Mother died in 1923, and I was permitted by Kate and Charley to be caretaker of the house and live in the house. I couldn't afford to heat it, so I put stoves in the two rooms that had been my grandmothers' and had the door cut from the kitchen into the head of the business study. I kept a fire in the stoves to protect the water, and Charley never came near or was interested in any way, but he did store his booze there. Uncle Hal Stanford told me, "Slats, you're going to wake up some morning with your throat cut. Clear up and down the railroad line, from Havre to Spokane, word goes out that there are some fine old liquors and whiskeys in barrels in the basement. You're going to wake up with somebody that comes after it. I'll leave my revolver. Put it under the mattress and don't you be late in using it."

Although responsible for Timmie, Alicia had no laundry facilities.

I asked Kate if I could do the washing in her laundry and do mine after I did hers. She said, "Well, you can try it." So I did her laundry, and for that she permitted me to use her washroom. By this time Timmie was five years old, and we didn't have enough to eat. (Timmie did not remember a scarcity of food, but rather that it was quite eccentric.) I went over to the south orchard. I had bought Charley's and Kate's shares of the fruit and we'd climb the fence and pick the fruit. We didn't have any fuel. Timmie would go with me to the orchard. We'd use a cross-cut saw, and that dear little girl would help. I did the pushing and pulling, but she held the other handle. We carried anything I could get to burn, up the hill, and pushed it over the fence, and hauled it to the kitchen on a sled. Charley lived across the street and knew I didn't have any fuel, but, even in the blizzards, he never sent me anything.

This style of life continued for Alicia, but she felt that better days must lie ahead.

II. Dream Accomplished

Alicia had dismissed from her mind all thoughts of marriage. The relationship of her father and mother was to Alicia the exemplification of what marriage should be. Her experience had fallen so far short that even to think of marriage was distressing. Then, all changed when sometime in the fall of 1926, Alicia was visiting her aunt, Alice Adams, in Great Falls. At a small function, she renewed her acquaintance with George Campbell, whom she had known prior to World War I. George told her that he was driving to Helena and suggested that she accompany him. Her aunt encouraged the arrangement and, on the trip, the two decided to be married. The wedding occurred on February 1, 1928. For the first time, Alicia believed that she might have secured a protector and a measure of security.

Alicia became even happier when a son was born, for it provided her the opportunity to continue her father's name. The infant was christened Charles Conrad Campbell. Charles eventually chose a career in the U.S. Army Air Force, from which he retired as a Lieutenant Colonel. In this choice, he was influenced by the record of his father, for George Campbell had become an officer in the Army Air Force during World War I and had fashioned a distinguished flying career in the Air Force's infancy.

Alicia and George lived in Great Falls for a time, but Alicia remained concerned about the empty Mansion in Kalispell. It contained many objects of value and was sentimentally dear to her. George was engaged in managing Great Falls-area ranches, whose owners resided in the East. He decided that he could manage from Kalispell as well as from Great Falls, so the Campbells moved into the Mansion.

At this time, the title to the Mansion was held by the family corporation, C. E. Conrad Estates, Inc. But Charley had mortgaged it to the Conrad National Bank, and little prospect existed that the mortgage could be paid. Further, George did not believe it wise to spend any time or money on the repair and maintenance of a property that might be lost. So the Mansion remained more shelter than home to the Campbells.

In 1935 Alicia learned of Charley's scheme to sell the family home and to convert it into a saloon, restaurant, casino, and perhaps worse. This prospect caused Alicia great dismay, for — impossible as it seemed — she dreamed of restoring the structure to its former grandeur. She pleaded with George to help her save the home that meant so much to her. George told her: "I will help you buy the home, but will not spend one cent on it. We will treat it as a warehouse, in which to preserve the contents, and live in it as long as we can. But I will spend nothing to keep it up." Alicia was so anxious to save the Mansion that she would agree to any conditions. In 1935 the Campbells were able to acquire the home, with the help of J. G. Edmiston, director of the Conrad National Bank.

The Campbells continued to live in the Mansion, and its condition continued to decline. The once-beautiful grounds became a tangle of weeds, briars, and brambles. Leaks developed in the roof. When plaster fell from the ceiling of a room, it was abandoned as living quarters. Room after room became uninhabitable, until finally, in the whole house no place existed to live. The building became known as "the haunted house," and Kalispell children were thrilled and chilled to peek at it through the fence and the tangle of growth. A mobile home then was moved onto the Mansion grounds, and George and Alicia made it their home, until George died in 1973.

Largely at his insistence, George and Alicia Campbell lived penuriously, denying themselves even the basic comforts. Nothing was discarded and both the Mansion and the trailer became cramped by stacks of boxes, papers, magazines, and cartons. Thus Alicia was particularly surprised when the appraisal of George's estate revealed that he owned property valued at $571,347.94. In his will, George bequeathed one-half of his estate to Alicia, one-fourth to his son, Charles Conrad Campbell, and one-fourth to his step-daughter, Alicia Campbell Vick. For the first time in her life, Alicia possessed money that she alone controlled, that she could use in any manner she chose. She also held enough money to insure that she could live in dignity and comfort.

By the early 1970s, the once-proud Mansion had become a sorry sight. The house barely was visible from the street, because of the undergrowth. The entire roof leaked; the heating and water systems were unusable. Fallen plaster littered every room. Restoration, if not hopeless, seemed at least too expensive to justify. However, Alicia's dream persisted. The grim realities of Alicia's life always had been softened and rendered bearable by her dreams, most of which circumstances had forced her to abandon. But, with this dream, she held a firmer control of her circumstances.

At the time her father died, Alicia was only 10 years old. Yet, even at this young age, she was determined.

I want this home to go on forever, to show what a happy home it had been when Father and Mother lived in it. I had that wish then, but didn't see how it could possibly happen. I had the feeling that something terrible was going to happen to our home. When Charley wanted to make it a saloon, I thought, "This is it." But we avoided that. I have had the most peculiar life. So many times I was in such terrible peril and escaped it. Then I get the feeling that I was meant to survive for something I hadn't done yet. It couldn't be otherwise. Then it occurred to me that maybe it was to preserve our home. Then people would know about Father and Mother, and all the good things they did. And know what a happy family we were while Father and Mother were alive, and before all those terrible things began to happen.

George Campbell died on January 14, 1973. Alicia finally became the sole owner of the Mansion, to handle as she pleased. Restoring the home and converting it into a museum to depict the way of life of the early pioneers exceeded her abilities either, physically or financially. This goal could be accomplished only by a public or a non-profit body. Alicia hoped that the Mansion could be given to the City of Kalispell for restoration and then opened to the public as a museum and a memorial to her parents.

On October 10, 1973, Alicia's grandson, Chris Vick, met with the Kalispell City Council, in closed session, and offered the Mansion to the City as a gift from Alicia. A letter expressing this intent was delivered to the Council by Vick. On the basis of this letter, the City Council committed City funds and City labor to begin Mansion repairs. The Council made no public announcement, but rumors soon circulated in Kalispell that City monies were being expended, although the City did not own the property. Then began a public debate addressing the propriety of the City's initial actions, and it extended to a consideration of whether the city should accept the property at all.

The debate continued in the local newspapers, both in the news columns and in the "letters to the editor." As a result, the City Council sensed that public sentiment opposed the city's acquisition of the property and decided to put the proposition to a vote of the people. That vote was scheduled for March 19, 1974. Citizens of Kalispell were invited to express their preferences at two polling places, between 8 a.m. and 8 p.m. The result of the vote would not be binding upon the Council; it would be considered only advisory in nature. The result showed 860 in favor of the city's acquisition and 1325 against it. This poll cooled considerably the Council's ardor for accepting the Mansion. On March 26, 1974, the City Council rejected Alicia's offer by a vote of 6 to 2. Only Council President Norma Happ and Councilman E. L. Sliter voted favorably.

312

The Mansion issue then hung suspended, while the debate continued. On October 23, 1974, a suit was filed against the Kalispell City Council, to require the Council members to repay to the City treasury the amount of $15,744.22, which already had been spent on the Mansion from public funds. The *Daily Inter Lake* reviewed the history of the controversy. It noted that no appraisal of the property had been made and that estimates of its value ranged from $150,000 to nothing. Some critics believed that, even if restored, the Mansion would not depict how most of the people in Kalispell lived during that period of history. Others thought that, if supporters wanted the Mansion restored, they were the ones who should pay for it.

On November 13, 1974, wearied by the controversy, Alicia offered the Mansion as a gift to Flathead County. This proposal shifted the arena from the city to the county level. The Commissioners of Flathead County had watched, with detached interest, as the city struggled with problems involved in an acceptance of the gift. Suddenly the Commissioners were faced with the issue, and they did not like the situation. No one knew either what the issue's political implications were or which side would emerge as the more popular. In any event, the County Commissioners rejected Alicia's offer.

Gradually more people in Kalispell recognized the uniqueness of Alicia's offer and its potential value to the community. Simultaneously, a group of interested persons formed a group to design an agreement that would meet the critics' objections to the city's acquisition of the Mansion. The Council members then regained courage, and negotiations intensified. On December 27, 1974, an agreement was signed by Alicia and the City of Kalispell. By this arrangement, the City accepted the Conrad home for preservation as a museum.

The agreement provided that the property would be used only as a public museum and that the repair, restoration, maintenance, and operation would be supervised and governed by a board known as the "Conrad Mansion Directors." To meet the objection that the Mansion might become a drain on public funds, the agreement provided that the City would commit a maximum of $35,000, which would be used for restoration — but only if matching funds, dollar for dollar, were raised by the Board. After the expenditure of the City's $35,000, the City would carry no further obligation for the capital repair, improvement, maintenance, or operation of the property as a museum. These responsibilities would become the obligations of the Board.

The agreement between Alicia and the City further provided:

That, if the mansion is destroyed by fire or other natural catastrophe, or if future events render it unfeasible to continue the museum, or if Alicia failed to give certain furniture, then the Board and the City would agree upon another public use or, failing to agree, the property would be sold at public auction, and the proceeds used for the beneft of the children of Kalispell, by the construction of some permanent recreational facility, dedicated to the memory of Alicia's parents.

That the basic design of the Mansion would not be changed, nor would the rock wall surrounding the Mansion be removed, altered or destroyed.

Alicia reserved the rooms in the northwest corner of the Mansion, formerly occupied by the grandmothers, as an apartment for her personal use during her lifetime. The rooms were restored by Alicia, but she never was able to occupy them.

On December 31, 1974, the deed was filed to transfer the property title to the City, and it was assumed that the matter finally was settled. However, the rumblings and grumblings continued. Some critics believed that opposition to the Mansion remained a useful political issue. A committee called "Concerned Citizens for Voting Rights" (CCVR) was formed to overturn the property transaction by referendum. On March 28, 1975, this group filed suit to require the City to verify its referendum petitions and to submit the matter of overturning the City's actions to a vote of the people. On May 19, 1975, however, this action was abandoned by CCVR. Its stated reason for the decision was that Dale Williams, Robert Allen, and William Bergstrom had been elected to the Kalispell City Council after the filing of the suit. Since all three men had been members of CCVR, the group believed that a potential conflict of interest had been created.

The suit filed October 23, 1974, was dismissed as moot, since the City had acquired the property. The *Daily Inter Lake* selected the Conrad Mansion as the top local news story of 1974. Yet, the controversy dissolved with the election and with the dismissal of the law suits and, on June 8, 1975, restoration work was commenced on the Conrad Mansion. Restorative activities continued for the next year. They were completed in time for the Mansion to be unveiled to the public on June 1, 1976, as a part of Kalispell's celebration of the nation's Bicentennial.

The opening ceremony was held on the east lawn of the Mansion, and Alicia attended. The weather was a little cold, but she sat in her wheelchair through the entire program — and somehow made her seat seem more a throne than a wheelchair. After the ceremony, Alicia was moved into the Great Hall. Here she greeted the visitors, exactly as Lettie welcomed her guests during those years when social life at the Mansion was at its peak. At the end of the exhausting day, Alicia remained exhilarated, and dreams shined from her eyes. Over and over, throughout the day, Alicia declared, "I am so thankful that God let me live to see it."

At the time of the Mansion's opening, Alicia was living at the Im-

314

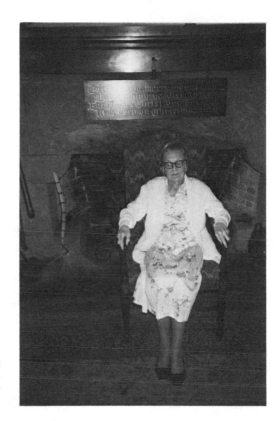

Alicia Conrad Campbell in Great Hall on Valley Days in 1980 Courtesy the author

manuel Lutheran Home in Kalispell. Here she maintained her own room, where she entertained friends of long standing. In the autumn of 1978, Alicia traveled to spend the winter with her son, Charles Campbell, and his family, who lived near Annapolis, Maryland. She had planned to return to the Immanuel Home in the spring of 1979, and her room there was readied. Instead she decided to live with her grandson, Chris Vick, in Helena, Montana. She subsequently moved into a house in Helena, where she was cared for by a housekeeper.

On September 23, 24, and 25, 1980, "Valley Days" were held at the Mansion, and Alicia was invited as the guest of honor. She accepted and planned to attend for all three days. On September 23, Alicia spent the entire day at the Mansion. Hundreds of friends came to greet her. Again the eerie feeling existed that, somehow, both Alicia and her mother were present in the person of Alicia. At the end of the day she returned to her motel room to rest for the next day. Then, during the night, she fell and broke her arm and was hospitalized. When released, Alicia was taken by her housekeeper to Helena. A few days later she was placed in a rest home in Missoula. Here she died on February 4, 1981, at the age of 88.

Alicia lived far longer than any of her family. Charles E. died at 52, Lettie at 62, Kate at 50, Charley at 52, and Edward at 28. Because of

Alicia Conrad Campbell and granddaughter — the most
recent Alicia Courtesy *Daily Interlake*

Alicia's closeness to her parents, people assumed that she would be buried in the Conrad mausoleum, with the rest of the family. However, this was not her desire. She requested that her body be placed by the side of her husband, George Campbell, who was buried outside, and to the west, of the mausoleum.

Services were held for Alicia at Christ Church Episcopal, which had been the church of her family for decades. A blustery day, with slick pavements and sidewalks, kept many of her older friends from the church. The service there was simple, as Alicia had requested. The eulogy, though apt for Alicia, would have embarrassed her.

God gave Alicia eyes that saw beautiful things and reflected a gentle soul.

Given no shield from adversity, she was pelted and buffeted with it through her life. But God gave her the means to screen and purify adversity and use it to mulch and to nurture the growth of her soul.

God made of Alicia a crucible to distill beauty from all things and project it to those who would see or hear.

She was created with a generous heart, by which she shared herself and all she had, but in such an innocent and self-effacing manner that few knew the depths of her generosity.

Alicia was given an active mind, set on a quest for all things good, beautiful, and enlightening to which she clung, held, and shared.

God gave Alicia an ability to love without demanding, to give without expectation of return, to share without diminishing, and to live content with what she had.

Alicia has left so many things to bring remembrance of her and keep clear the image in our minds of the blithe spirit that dwelt among us and enriched the scene she now has left. Alicia's life is now a completed circle. Reunited with those she loved and knew, her greatest joy, so who now can speak of sorrow.

Let our goodby to Alicia be an expression of thankfulness that our lives touched and left with us an ineffable essence defiant of words but so surely felt and known.

These are the words of our parting. Goodbye, Alicia. May God give rest to your gentle soul.

As the service ended, the bluster of the day abated. Alicia was laid to rest with the sun shining, amid the beauty of the cemetery her mother had created in memory of her father.

Alicia believed that she had been granted a long life to accomplish a specific task: the preservation of the family home as a memorial to her parents. That purpose had been fulfilled, so she was not loath to die. Her death brought an end to the family she had loved. Yet, so long as the Mansion stands, it will keep bright the memory of her father and mother, which was Alicia's plan, her dream. That will keep bright, too, the memory of Alicia, who made it all possible.

Timmie Campbell Vick, Alicia's daughter, read the chapter about her mother. She wrote:

I think you caught the spirit inhabiting my mother and caught it well. I think, perhaps, the details of mother's divorce action against my father might be reduced to a briefer account, as, although he is dead, I am still alive and kicking. However, if you think such detail is necessary, I guess it adds to the unreality of Mother's life, as she perceived it. I'm sure there were things to be said on both sides, although I never knew my Father.

Mother's "grand obsession" with the house and the life of her parents had a profound effect on our lives, too. She was a very complex person, one of great charm and ability in many areas — all sacrificed to her total involvement in the life of the house in early times and near the end. A day before she died, she said to me, "We're on a train or ship going somewhere far away, aren't we?" I said that yes, I thought we were and asked her if she were afraid. She said, "No, everything is all right and I'm ready to travel." So, at the end, the obsession faded as her dream was realized.

INDEX

Adams, Alice Conrad (Charles E. & William G.'s sister) 187, 192
Allard, Charley (Charles A.) 139, 144, 195
American Bison Society 197-198
American Fur Company 13, 15
Anaconda Standard 39, 40
Anderson, Leroy 53
Ashley, Montana 141

Bachelor 12, 60-61, 128
Baker, I.G.
    person 22, 24, 9, 45, 115, 133, 212
    steamboat line 9
    store 17, 121, 29
    trading company 24, 26-27, 28, 36-37, 45, 100, 111, 115, 121, 131-132
Baldwin, Kokoa — see Conrad, Kokoa Baldwin
Banking 108, 130, 152, 201, 209, 240, 266-267, 278-279, 288, 297
Benton, Sen. Thomas Hart 14, 15, 16
Benton 57, 58
Bookwalter, J. 204-205
Bradley, Lieutenant James) 29
Buck, W.H. 64-68, 81, 82, 107
Buffalo 45, 194-200
    buffalo crates 196-197
    hides 27

Calgary Record 126
Campbell, Charles Conrad (Alicia's son) 310, 315
Campbell, George (Alicia's 2nd husband) 298, 310
Canada 24, 26-27, 38, 100, 132
Canadian Government 27, 37, 69-70, 71, 104, 132, 213
Canadian Pacific Railroad 32, 111-112, 117, 121
Canadian Parliament 35
Cattle industry 62-63, 69-72, 109, 203, 211-212, 213, 217, 218-219
C.E. Conrad Memorial Cemetery Association 231-232
Chief Joseph 55-56
Chinese 109
Christian activity 30, 146
Christian marriage 43, 253-255

Civil War 6-7, 13, 218
Clark William A. 215-216
Cleveland, President Grover 208-209
Collins, Elizabeth (Mrs. Nat) 211-212
Colonel Macleod 58, 60
Conley Michael C. 153, 155
Conrad brothers 26, 28, 36-37, 45, 69-70, 108, 125, 134, 239, 240, 288
Conrad, Agnes (Charles D.'s 2nd wife) 211, 278, 298-299
Conrad, Alicia Stanford (Lettie) (Charles E.'s wife) 97-98, 136, 139, 152, 156-159, 161-162, 171, 172, 195-196, 200, 211, 226-228, 230-239, 242-248, 258, 266, 270, 284, 285, 288-291, 292-296
Conrad, Alicia (Charles E.'s youngest daughter) 40, 157, 158, 162-165, 179, 182, 197-198, 212, 222, 226, 227, 236-237, 278, 285, 286, 292-294, 296, 298, 300-318
Conrad, Billy (Charles D.'s son) 270-271, 274-275
Conrad, Catherine (Charles E.'s daughter) 99, 157, 158, 172, 179, 235, 239, 242, 280-287, 296-298, 300
Conrad, Catherine (Kokoa) (Charles D.'s daughter) 270, 272, 274-275
Conrad, Charles D. (Charles E.'s son) 98, 205, 206, 209, 214, 239, 262-269, 270-279, 296-300, 306
Conrad, Charles E. 1, 4, 6, 7, 20, 22-24, 38, 39, 43, 45, 73, 92-96, 106, 113-114, 136, 139, 142-144, 152, 156-157, 163, 172, 173, 177, 181, 183, 195, 201-203, 206-211, 214, 216-229, 262-265, 288
Conrad, Charles Edward, Jr. (Charles E.'s Indian son) 44, 94, 212, 241, 253-261, 280-289
Conrad, Fannie Bowen (William G.'s wife) 108
Conrad, James W. (Charles E. & William G.'s father) 5, 6, 99, 187-188
Conrad, Joseph (Charles E. & William G.'s grandfather) 5
Conrad, Kokoa Baldwin (Charles D.'s 1st wife) 267-277
Conrad mansion 153-159, 222-223, 246-250, 297, 298, 308-309, 310-315, 317-318
Conrad mansion garden 167-169
Conrad mansion grounds 165-168

Conrad mansion restoration 311-315
Conrad, Maria Ashby (Charles E. & William G.'s
    mother) 5-7, 99, 155, 158, 184-185, 187-191,
    193, 225
Conrad mausoleum 225, 229-232, 317
Conrad, William G. 1, 4, 20, 97, 107-108, 160, 224,
    239, 240, 259, 266, 267
    articles by 26, 27, 131, 135
    letter from 24, 134
    political career 1, 2, 3, 23, 215-217
Constitutional Convention of 1889 125
Cord wood 10-11, 51, 109
Cow Island 52-56, 109
Culbertson, Alexander 13, 14, 15, 16, 43
Currency 102-103, 104
Cutler, Kirkland K. 153, 154, 155, 156, 163
Cypress Hills Massacre 34-35

Daly, Marcus 216
Demers, Jake 141
Demersville 139, 141, 149
Democratic National Convention 1908 3

Edmiston, J.G. 297, 298, 311
Electricity 112, 119-120, 137, 155, 289
Erickson, Father Carl 97

Farwell, Abe 35
Federal Reconstruction Finance Corporation 297
Flanagan, May 12
Foley, Michael 53, 55
Flathead Lake 139-140
Fort Benton, Montana 1, 5, 9, 13, 17, 19, 21, 80, 82,
    86, 88, 107, 118, 128, 136, 137-138
    naming of 14-15
Fort Benton Record 14-15, 23, 27, 31-32, 62,
    64-68, 80-86, 88, 92, 100-101, 107, 114, 115,
    121, 137
Fort Benton Review 129
Fort Benton River Press 5, 13, 18, 41, 50, 80, 86,
    88-93, 96, 100, 102, 107, 109-111, 121, 123,
    126, 127, 129, 130, 138
Fort Macleod 37, 38
Fort Macleod Gazette 71, 72, 104, 132-133
Fort Whoop-up 37
Foy's Lake 179, 242, 264
freight business 26, 27, 32, 49-51, 100
Freighting:
    by bull train 21, 101-102, 118
    by rail 123-124, 126
    by river 18, 20, 49-51, 58, 60-61
Freight transport 24, 00, 103, 115-116
Freight, types of 12, 18, 20, 103
Frémont, Jessie Benton (Sen. Benton's daughter)
    16
Frémont, John C. 16
French, Lieutenant Colonel George Arthur 35, 36
Fur trade 15, 24, 26-27, 100-101
    hides 76, 100-101, 132, 194
    wolfers 34

Galt, Sir Alexander 117, 121, 123
Gibson, Paris 119, 120, 137
Glacier Park 180, 206, 207

Gold
    as medium of exchange 31, 102-103
    depository 31
    discovery at Grasshopper Creek 17, 18
    placer gold 30, 67, 205
    production 31
Goodnight, Charles 62-63
Grand Union Hotel 109, 111-113, 119
Great Falls, Montana 17, 119, 137
Great Falls Tribune 26, 7, 69, 131, 193, 210-211,
    228-230, 294
Great Northern Railway — see Manitoba Railway
Grubb, George 225, 229-231, 290, 291, 296, 306

Harber, Nora E. 9
Helena Independent Record 108, 109
Helena, Montana 20, 215-217
Hill, James J. 117, 119-120, 123, 143-144, 148-151,
    208, 209, 218-219
Hori 160-162
Hornaday, Dr. William T. 180, 196, 197
Hudson's Bay Company 33, 38, 131-132
Hunter, Mary 8

Indians 43, 126-127, 144, 182, 194-195, 205-207,
    241, 253
    Blackfeet 13, 37, 43, 205, 241, 253
    Blood 13, 43
    encounter with 11, 13, 34-35, 37, 39-40, 53,
        55, 114
    Flathead 144, 195
    Kalispel 144
    Nez Perce 55
    Pend d'Oreille 194
    Piegan 13, 114, 127, 195
    North Assiniboine 35
    Salish 197
    Sioux 11, 109
    trade with 15, 45, 69-70, 104-106, 126-127
    Treaty No. 7 45-48
Ingalls, Emma A. 147-149, 151
Inter Lake 147-149, 269, 277, 283-284, 294, 298,
    313, 314
International Workers of the World 167

Japan 160-162, 244-245
Johns, Sam The Pioneers 142, 147

Kalispell 141-152
    naming of 144
Kalispell Bee 151, 193, 303, 305
Kalispell Fire Department 246-247
Kalispell Townsite Company 145-148, 154, 201,
    231, 300
Kipp, Joseph 205
Kipp, Montana 205

Leeson, M.A History of Montana 29, 108
Lepley, John 131
Lewis & Clark 13, 144
Lewis, Meriwether 16-17
Lintner, Scott 282
Liquor, as trade item 15, 16, 8, 33-34, 49, 52-53
Liquor 278

Louisiana Purchase Exposition 220
Lumber 87

McCarthy, Jack 181
McCutcheon, Alicia Ann (Timmie) (Alicia's
    daughter) — see Vick, Alicia Campbell
McCutcheon, Walter M. (Alicia's 1st husband)
    296, 302-308
MacDonald, Sir John 34, 35
McGarry, Captain James 10, 12
McGinnis, D.R. 143-144
McKenzie, Kenneth 15
Macleod, Major 36, 7, 69

Mackinaw boats 31
Manitoba (Great Northern) Railway 121, 123-124,
    139, 142, 145, 148-151, 219, 306
Miners 29, 31
Mining 125, 206, 208, 220-221
Marconi, Guglielmo 75
Massie, William 57, 58
Merrifield, A.W. 180-181, 209
Missouri River 9-11, 16-17, 119, 128, 137-138
Montana Historical Society 131, 272
Montana Magazine 31
Montana Press (Helena) 106
Montana Railway Commission 151
Mosby's Partisan Raiders 6

Northern Pacific Railroad 32, 51, 117, 139, 142
Northwest Mounted Police 24, 33, 34, 35, 36, 37,
    69, 111

Osler, Dr. William 202
Overfield, George 104
Overholser, Joel 13, 18, 41, 102, 111, 138
Our Fort Benton 9

Pablo, Michael 195
Parmain, Arthur E. 154
Pollock, Francis Baker (I.G. Baker's daughter) 31
Potts, Jerry 37
Power, Thomas C.
    person 12, 19, 129
    store 35, 129
Prostitution 80-81, 118

Railroads 26, 117, 123-124, 139, 148-151
Ravalli, Montana 139
Red Cloud 9-12, 57-60
Red Crow 45, 47
Renner, Frederick G. 211
Roosevelt, Teddy 180-181
Rosebud steamboat 112, 123

Russell, Charles 21-22, 71, 207, 211, 222

St. Louis, Missouri 9, 29
Scheitlin, M.G. 2, 4
Schools 88, 92, 265-266, 280-282, 301-302
Sherman, Gen. William Tecumseh 7
Smith, John 17
Social activities 92-93, 97, 118, 170-173, 174-178,
    179-182, 233-238, 248-252
Spokane, Washington 136, 152-153
Spokesman Review 2
Squatter's rights 19
Stanford, Alicia (daughter) (later Lettie Conrad)
    44, 76-78, 86, 92-96
Stanford, Catherine Elizabeth Alicia Coggin (the
    mother) 72, 78, 155, 158, 172, 174, 185-187,
    191-192, 193
Stanford, Hal (Harry) (son) 77, 222, 266, 293
Stanford, James (father) 75
Stanford, James Jr. (son) 73, 192, 224
Stannard, George F. 142
Steamboat
    travel 9-12, 49-53, 57-61, 118, 123, 39
    freight 20-21, 32, 49-53, 118, 123
Stewart, Lou Stocking 9

Tatten, John W. 19
Three Forks, Montana 16
Todd, William H. 111, 129
Trading posts 26-27
Trainer, Ed 22
Treaty No. 7 47-48
Tyler, J. Hoge 2

Union Pacific Railroad 30
United States Government 27, 51, 104, 207, 241
University of Montana 131, 225

Van Duzer, Egbert James 283-284, 285, 298
Vick, Alicia Campbell — (Timmie) (Alicia's
    daughter) 307, 309, 310
Virginia 5, 135
    state militia 6

Walking Coyote 194-195, 200
Waitman, Alice 158
Wapping Plantation (Conrad home in Virginia) 5,
    188-189
West Hotel 155, 156
Wetzel, W.C. 118
Whoop-up Trail 37
Winter, Captain A.O. 233-235
Wong 160
Wool 123, 219